NEITHER HERE NOR THERE

A First Generation Immigrant in Search of American Exceptionalism

Frans H. Jager

Cover design by Andrea Jager

ISBN: 0692209778
ISBN 13: 9780692209776
Library of Congress Control Number: 2014939633
Castnet Corp., North Ridgeville OH

To Kaelie, Abby, Payton, Emma, Molly, Liam, Reagan, and McKenzie:
The future looks good with you in charge.

CONTENTS

Section II. ON BALANCE 25

What have I done with my time in America? How has it turned out? Looking at the outcome from a personal-, business-, and socio-political perspective.

Section III. CREATIVE DESTRUCTION 97

What can and should change in America if it wants to stay on top of the world in the twenty-first century? Suggestions from a first generation immigrant.

Section IV. THE FINAL ANALYSIS   **213**

How do we get from There to Here? Will America resolve to be truly exceptional again? Will the people in America come back together and retake control of governance, so that America will live up again to its old motto E Pluribus Unum?

INTRODUCTION

It's impossible not to look back and wonder what would have happened if you had had the wit, or guts, or luck to go in some other direction". (Terry Tempest Williams)

The topic of immigration has, rightfully, moved front and center in the political debate about the future of the nation and its prospects to maintain a measure of global leadership in the twenty-first century. As a first generation immigrant I feel very much a party to this discussion.

The writing of this book gives me an opportunity to reflect on the considerations that went into my decision to opt for a future in America rather than the Netherlands, my country of origin. It also allows me to compare the expectations I had at the time—in the early 1980s—of life in America and the prospects for the future of the USA with the way things have turned out. Finally, it offers me a new platform for providing a socio-political commentary on the strengths and weaknesses, the merits and the flaws, of the American system. Commentary as I see it, with the eyes of someone who has deliberately chosen for a future in America and yet not fully relinquished his ties with the country of origin by maintaining Dutch citizenship. Hence the title of the book: *"Neither Here nor There"*.

This title quietly acknowledges the fact that, as a first generation immigrant, I have not been able to completely master the apparent contradiction between my thoroughly European intellectual and normative formation with the determination to make a future for my family in the very different social environment of the USA.

People born in this country have a tendency to take the "American way" for granted as if it is the natural state of affairs. While a small elite of American society is very cosmopolitan and world-wise, it is undeniable that most Americans are not very well traveled (only about a third of the population has a passport) and have nothing with which to compare the American way of life. They have little exposure to different ways of living and cultures. As a result, it is a typical American attitude to measure anything seen or heard about different countries and cultures against the norm established by their American standard. Or, rather, to take it at face value that the American way is the standard against which all other systems should be measured. Immigrants have a different frame of reference. They have lived in other societies and systems and they have an expectation that they can better themselves by coming to America. They typically come with a set of high expectations and are less inclined to accept the status quo as the norm.

Reading this book will have you travel in time as much as across the Atlantic. It will reach back into the lifetime of my parents and look to the future as I see it developing or, more relevant, wish to see it developing. It will pick you up and invite you to virtually travel with me by painting a picture of the places I have been and the people and conditions found there and the lessons I have learned. And it will invite you to travel with me intellectually by following my observations, experiences, thought processes, and opinions developed along the way.

As much as this book wants to be forward looking, I cannot get away from giving you first a feel for where I'm coming from. Where I'm coming from not only physically but, most importantly, spiritually and intellectually, as a commentator on the American way. If there is any uniqueness in this book, it is that it is written by an immigrant. An immigrant who had half a lifetime behind him when he opted for a future for his family and himself in America. Who chose for this country with his eyes wide open and got nevertheless blindsided by the way America changed before his eyes, as time went by.

My dealing with the past will be brief. It is included to make the reader familiar with my path through life before I landed on America's shore. In the first Section of this book, I provide just enough background to give you a view on where I'm coming from, with an emphasis on what I learned along the way and on things that shaped my perspective on the positives and negatives of living in America. Then, in order not to lose you as a reader, I quickly get into the heart of the matter, my evaluation of what's ailing America and what to do about it, leaving a more detailed description of what was left behind in the Old World to a Reference section at the end of this book. This book is emphatically not a comparison between the American way and the Dutch (or European) way. I have not lived in the Netherlands in more than thirty years and I do not know how life has changed there. Anecdotally, from what I read and hear from friends and relatives who stayed behind, I derive that most of the challenges faced by the United States are also faced by the European Union and that solutions may be harder to come by over there than here, mostly because of the lesser integration and unity of Europe. My comparison—for the purpose of this book— is between the vision, the expectation, I had of America thirty years ago, when I had to decide if I was an expatriate or an immigrant, with the reality of what America offers and has to deal with today.

This book is—at its core—a commentary on the notion of American Exceptionalism: The belief that America, and anything American, is "a cut above" all other nations, be it by divine determination, its origin as the first democracy of the modern age, its geographic location, its natural resources, or the spirit of its population of mostly immigrants. It is also very much an evaluation of the relevance, the deservedness of

American Exceptionalism in the twenty-first century. It is the notion of American Exceptionalism that drives people from all over the world to leave their roots behind and look for a (better) future in America. This lure has survived the passage of time and changing global sentiments about the role and the promise of America.

But the notion of American Exceptionalism has to be validated from time to time. The factors that allow America to be exceptional are not immutable. And should never be taken for granted. For those reasons, this book implores the readership, the voting public in particular, to regain control of the political process and get engaged in the process of addressing the challenges America is facing.

At the same time this book is a "Cri de Coeur" to appeal with the American readership for a less partisan, dogmatic, parochial, and preconceived view of what should or could be done to enhance the chance that America will deliver in the twenty-first century on all of its promises and potential. In that context, this book will plead for a return to tolerance, which has been a hallmark of the right kind of true American Exceptionalism but is now largely absent from opinion making, especially in the realm of politics.

On paper, the merge of Dutch and American belief systems around tolerance creates the best of all possible worlds. Few nations have a better reputation for tolerance than the Netherlands with a tradition that goes back to the seventeenth century, the golden age for the Dutch, in commerce and exploration, in science and arts and freedom of religion. The Dutch benefitted greatly in these days from offering refuge to the best thinkers of their time who were getting prosecuted in their own countries when their observations ran counter to the established wisdom of the church. Largely Protestant, the Republic of the United Netherlands, provided a safe haven for the victims of the inquisition and religious intolerance which was pervasive in Europe in the fifteenth and sixteenth centuries. French Huguenots settled in droves in the Netherlands. It was in the golden age that the Netherlands experienced an influx of Jews who, in their homelands, were targets of anti-Semitism that was widespread all over Europe. The famous Baruch d'Espinoza was just one of many Jewish intellectuals who sought and found refuge in the Netherlands and published his works there.

Note that the Netherlands was a Republic at that time, which was an exception in Europe where the Church and the Monarchs represented absolute power. The Netherlands did not become a (parliamentary) monarchy until 1815 by decisions made at the Congress of Vienna that dealt with the aftermath of Napoleon Bonaparte's exploits in Europe.

The American Revolution with its Declaration of Independence and its Constitution became the standard bearer for the principles of freedom and tolerance when the Netherlands could no longer lead the world in these respects. Freedom of immigration is a symbol of tolerance. It is intriguing, and distressing at the same time, that politicians on both sides of the Atlantic are now questioning the desirability of immigration and that, in the debate about this, the principle of tolerance is getting lost.

Tolerance welcomes different opinions and perspectives while the discourse in this country has become increasingly dismissive of other points of view. Reasoning is getting replaced by proselytizing in public discourse like in Congress and other forums of democracy. The two party system in America cultivates an either/or, black/white opiniating that gets more and more entrenched by two popular cable TV channels, Fox News and MSNBC, fanning the flames of reactionary and liberal bias.

In addition to the themes of American Exceptionalism and Tolerance, this book deals with the notion of "Creative Destruction", the courage to start anew even if what you have is not exactly defunct. The courage to say: "If it ain't broke, you still may have to fix it" instead of the conventional "If it ain't broke, don't fix it". This theme is intensely personal, because my life in the Netherlands was far from broke, and yet I chose to start anew in a new country. Creative destruction has helped American business to succeed on a global scale. It is therefore somewhat surprising and disappointing that the same principle has not been put to good use in the public arena. That may have to change.

Just recently, in a column he posted in the February 15, 2014 edition of the *New York Times*, Thomas Friedman made that argument. He titled his column: *"Start-Up America: Our Best Hope"*. In it he puts in contrast the creative ideas coming out of Silicon Valley with the inaction that pervades Washington, D.C. Friedman writes: *"What a contrast. Silicon Valley: where ideas come to launch. Washington, D.C., where ideas go to die."* In his column, Friedman quotes Curt Carlson, the CEO of SRI who states: *"When your mind-set isn't about creating abundance, you go into extractive mode, which is a death spiral."* I'm afraid that is exactly where Washington D.C. drives us.

Ultimately, this book is a very personal account of life on two sides of the Atlantic, with its pros and cons, its ups and downs, and the realization that, whatever decision you make, you have an obligation to make it work and make the most of it. It acknowledges the powerful, maybe overwhelming, influence of Serendipity (the fourth main theme of this book) over the way our lives take shape. Yes, we are making decisions that determine the course and the outcomes of our lives, but we are always dealing with a sleight of hand that we were dealt by a set of circumstances over which we had no influence at all. These are the "Black Swans" that Nassim Nicholas Taleb is writing about in his great book: *The Black Swan: The Impact of the Highly Improbable.*

Note that, in this book, I will typically identify with a person who thinks, acts and believes like an American citizen. Over the more than thirty-five years that I have lived and worked in the United States, I may not have entirely lost my Dutch accent, but I belong nowhere else than in America. That is why in this book you (the reader) will read about "our" president, "our" economy, "our" nation and "our" future and, when I write these words, I mean they belong to me as much as they belong to you even though, technically, I am a resident but (for reasons that I will explain elsewhere in this book) not an American citizen. Some may see this choice of words presumptuous for an immigrant, but living in this country as long as I have with no intention to ever leave again, I feel entitled to it. America is my home, for better and for worse. I am an immigrant, no longer an expatriate. If, in some chapters of this book, I am harsh in my criticism of what I see happening—or not happening—here, it is only because I so desperately want to see America live up to its best potential for the benefit of future generations, including my children and grandchildren. I have placed a bet on America, in a big way and irrevocably. I don't want to lose my bet because someone else is cheating.

This is an optimistic book. I do not share the opinion of those who proclaim that America's best days are over. It is way too easy and popular these days to draw parallels with the decline of the British Empire (or the fall from power of the Netherlands after the Golden Age). You will find me arguing in the following pages that no nation is better positioned and resourced for the future than America. I am in good company there, because Warren Buffett writes in his 2014 Annual Report to shareholders of Berkshire Hathaway that *"America's best days lie ahead"* and he is putting his money where his mouth is! However, success is not a given. It will have to be earned and this book attempts to show the way in which the future that Warren Buffett sees ahead can be secured.

I sub-titled this book "A First Generation Immigrant in Search for American Exceptionalism" for a reason. The world needs American Exceptionalism to be a living reality. The world needs American leadership and the American people need to fend off the specter of complacency after more than half a century of world domination and unmatched prosperity. If Americans cannot wake up to the reality that, for the first time in many generations, there is a better than even chance that their grandchildren, if not their children, will be materially worse off than their (grand) parents—and do something about it—I might come to the conclusion that I made the wrong choice when I immigrated to the United States. That's not where I want to go and that's why this book is meant to deliver a wake-up call. And that's why this book is as much a guide-book—with a map showing both the obstacles in America's path as well as some possible routes to overcome or bypass these obstacles—as it is a personal account of the experiences of a first generation immigrant to the U.S.

———

PROLOGUE

My family is already living in America, on a business visa, and it is time to decide if we want to stay or go back home and give up on our American dream.

Sometime in 1981 it dawned on us (my wife Christie and me) that we had a decision to make. Were we immigrants to the USA or European expatriates? We had equivocated long enough and crossed the Atlantic a couple of times. We had chosen to go where there was a job opportunity and this had set us on a course that kept us criss-crossing between the Netherlands and America. It took us a while, but after a couple of years we realized that we had a decision to make. Let me take you back in time to the period in which we had to decide where we belonged:

It is 1981 and it is time to fish or cut bait. Here we are. A thoroughly Dutch family on Pepperell Drive in the Carrollwood Village section of Tampa, FL, a far cry from the Low Countries with their near permanently grey skies, prevailing Western winds carrying fog and drizzle from across the North Sea and tempera-tures that are mostly a few degrees lower than you would need to feel comfortable.

We are far away from home and all the family and everyone we grew up with, but enjoying the sunshine and the outdoor living, with a pool, a lanai and proximity to Busch Gardens, Cypress Gardens and that brand new attraction, Disney World. We love the restaurant scene in Tampa with the original Outback Steakhouse on Henderson Boulevard, with the Columbia restaurant in Ybor City and Bern's Steakhouse with its fabulous wine list.

My wife Christie and I just had our third child, Thomas, after a hiatus of more than nine and a half years. Our two older children, Nienke and Pim, were both born in The Netherlands, but relocated to the USA at six and five years of age, respectively. The inevitable family dog, a golden retriever named Duke (after my favorite ACC basketball team), completes the family (for now).

We have a Dutch Au-Pair, Chantal, to help out with the care and entertainment of the children. She goes for her senior year to the local High School on a student-visa. She has graduated from high school in the Netherlands and is planning to attend college there but wants to take a year off, look around in that magic land across the Atlantic and brush up on her (American) English. At school in the Netherlands it is still the "King's English" that is taught.

Life is good! Carrollwood Village is a transient neighborhood with new homes surrounding a golf course with a nice club-house, where we are tennis and social members (neither one of us is playing golf). IBM has a large regional office in Tampa and provides a constant influx of transients, including our friends, the Schiffmans, who relocated to Tampa from Poughkeepsie NY. Living in Florida means that we are a magnet for friends and family members from the Old Country who want to visit.

I am vice president of Transnitro, Inc. The company is a joint venture between Nederlandsche Stikstof Maatschappij (NSM), a Dutch nitrogen fertilizer producer, and Transammonia, an American Trading Company founded and privately owned by Ronald Stanton. I am legally in the country on an L-1 Visa that is reserved for persons working in the United States for a subsidiary or affiliate of an off-shore company. It allows me only to work for Transnitro and Christie is not allowed to work at all. We moved here a year ago from the Northern suburbs of New York City in Westchester County when Transnitro decided to move out of New York City. Transammonia, our joint venture partner, already had an office in Tampa and the move provided a cost saving opportunity for the company and its key employees. Lower cost of living, no State income tax, more sunshine, and

*an easy commute were powerful arguments for my colleagues and me to support
the move away from NYC.*

*Ronald Reagan has been inaugurated on January 20 as the 40th President of
the United States, two days after I celebrated my 37th birthday. The global environment gives us a lot to think about: Even though the 52 Americans held hostage in
Iran for 444 days have finally been released, the Iranian revolution has signaled
a break in the grip the United States has held over the oil rich countries in the
Middle East. China has thrown out the Dutch Ambassador to Peking in retali-
ation for the sale of a submarine by the Netherlands to Taiwan. The Cold War
continues unabated with the USSR performing not less than 12 nuclear tests in
1981 and the USA responding with seven of their own. France, Great Britain and
India also test their nuclear capabilities.*

*Thirty-six years after Hiroshima the world powers appear locked in a race
towards assured mutual destruction. Paradoxically they manage to keep the peace
by making the price they would have to pay for war too horribly high to con-
template. China conducted its last atmospheric nuclear test in October of 1980
(the last atmospheric test by any country) but continues with underground tests
through 1996.*

*In terms of other geo-political developments, 1981 is the year of Prince Charles'
engagement to Lady Diana Spencer; Socialist Francois Mitterrand's victory over
Conservative Valery Giscard d'Estaing in the French Presidential election; the
incorporation of Microsoft in the State of Washington; Sandra Day O'Connor's
nomination to the Supreme Court; the firing of 11,500 striking air traffic control-
lers by President Reagan; Anwar Sadat's assassination in Egypt; wide-spread
West European demonstrations against the positioning of American cruise missiles on West European territory; and the U.S. National Debt topping $1 trillion
(it is approaching $17 trillion in 2014). Unemployment in the Netherlands hits a
record high of 475,000 out of a 14 million population (3.4 percent).*

Such were the global conditions under which we decided to apply
for permanent residency in the United States. I mention this primarily to remind the reader how much the world has changed from the
time at which we had to decide on the side of the Atlantic Ocean
we wanted to call our own. Looking at the world around us, and

pampered by our ex-patriate lifestyle, we had no desire to go back to the Netherlands, at least not in the foreseeable future. But we were well aware that our legal status in the United States depended entirely on the whim of my employer, since my work-permit was only valid for my job with Transnitro.

As I looked at the world in 1981—eight years before the Berlin wall came down—I saw an ascendant America, awakened and re-energized by a movie-star turned president from the debacles of Vietnam, Watergate and one term presidencies by Gerald Ford and Jimmy Carter.

And I saw, on the other side, a demoralized Western Europe that turned more and more socialist and pacifist as evidenced by the widespread demonstrations against the positioning of cruise missiles in Germany, the Netherlands and England. After living for thirty-two years in post-war Europe, I was convinced that if the Soviet Union ever had the intent to expand its sphere of influence, if not its territory, to the Atlantic, Europe's war weary citizens would not again take up arms to defend their countries and their freedoms. Fortunately, that belief was never tested. I was convinced that only the nuclear umbrella, held up by the USA, was a credible deterrent for the Soviets. But would America indeed engage the USSR in a nuclear conflict just to save the West Europeans from communism and themselves? I was not eager to find out and find my family right in the heart of the contest. Staying safe in the USA seemed to be the smarter option.

I also saw a Europe—and the Netherlands was no exception—that embraced the notion that the government was there to take care of its citizenry from cradle to grave. The seventies and eighties represented the peak of the belief in the welfare state and it was a belief that I did not share. I was right: Western Europe is still in a decades' long struggle to rewind and dismantle the excesses of the welfare state developed at that time. It found out that, much like General Motors and the City of Detroit, it had raised expectations and made promises that were insupportable in the long run under changing demographics and economic realities.

In these days, I traveled regularly back to Europe for business meetings and vacations. And we talked our pending decision many times over with our most trusted friends and family members. The question always came up: "Why we would leave all that we were familiar with, our culture, our heritage, behind for a society and culture that—in the early eighties—was universally seen in Europe as materialistic, superficial, belligerent and uncaring." My answer became more definitive and heartfelt over time: I acknowledged that Europe had the advantage of its history and culture, but felt that America had the future and that—with four children—the future was what counted most. Europe's Renaissance took place in the seventeenth century. The American equivalent, the American Revolution and the creation of a Republic in which the rule of law would govern, took place almost three centuries later. While the European Renaissance had long lost its impetus, America still looked highly inspired by the ideals articulated in its Declaration of Independence and its Constitution. And America seemed to be finally on track to implement these ideals for all of its citizens (which was a feat that the Founding Fathers could never accomplish).

The belief in American Exceptionalism was palpable not just with me, but with everyone around me. It seemed that each time America was seriously challenged it found a way to respond and it had grown stronger in the process. It served America well that, at critical times, it received real leadership from some of its great presidents. What made these presidents great was that, without exception, they captured the spirit of the country and rallied the public behind them in the course they had set out for overcoming the particular threat the nation was facing at their respective times. Abraham Lincoln was keenly aware of the need for public support. He professed that *"With public opinion there's nothing I cannot do, and without public opinion there's nothing I can get done."* Other than Winston Churchill, it is hard to think of any European politician of the stature and impact of America's Founding Fathers, Lincoln, and the Roosevelts. History may not place Ronald Reagan in that same category, but for me he was the antithesis to the lackluster, defeatist, political leaders in continental Western Europe (the U.K. under Margaret Thatcher was the exception that confirmed the rule).

Since we were living at a time that air-travel had made distances, like the 3652 miles between New York and Amsterdam, much less isolating than they had been in the past, we felt that being an ocean apart from our family was not such a big deal. We were particularly excited about the prospect of hosting friends and family on a regular basis in our newly adopted country.

The logical step to take was, therefore, to get our Green Cards, which would give us permanent residency in the USA and the right for Christie and me to work at any position of our choosing that might be offered to us. By maintaining our Dutch citizenship we were keeping our options for the future open. Our status of permanent residents permitted us to work in the USA as well as in any of the member countries of the European Union (EU). Our youngest two children, born in Tampa, FL. were American citizens by birth.

It took us two years and a lot of money, mostly spent on legal fees, before on May 31, 1983, we were issued our prized Green Cards. None too soon as it turned out, because shortly thereafter the parent company of Transnitro insisted that I would have to come back to its headquarters in Brussels, Belgium. Without a Green Card we would have had no choice but to follow orders from headquarters and abandon our dream of a future in America. As it was, we could call our own shots. The company, NSM, did not make it easy on us. In fact they exerted maximum pressure to have me comply with its wishes, by giving me an ultimatum: Come back to Brussels or your employment with NSM will be terminated.

By then we had four children. Michael, the youngest was born in March of 1983. We just did not see ourselves reversing our decision, giving up on our dreams and relocating the whole bunch back to the old country. We had already been back one time, in 1977, for one year in Boskoop in the Netherlands, with two children, and we were not too anxious to try that again, now with four children in tow. In fact, if we had decided for a future in Europe, we would—barring divine intervention—not have had our second set of children. In a country like the Netherlands, or Belgium, there just is no room left for large families.

Time heals most wounds, and I remember not much of the family discussion that must have been had at the time, but NSM's ultimatum must have been agonizing. It was truly testing our determination to stay in America. We had little, if any, money in the bank, as I was only into my career for thirteen years and had not quite made it to the top. On the upside, other than a mortgage on our house, we had no debt. Credit cards were not nearly as much in use at the time as they became later on.

Other than serving in the Royal Dutch Air Force for two years under compulsory military service, I had never worked for anyone else than the executive team at NSM. I liked living in America, but would I like it as much without a job and without income? I had worked for Transnitro for all of seven years, mostly on the supply and distribution side of the business, and did not have an elaborate personal network. The companies we were working with were certainly more beholden to Transnitro than to Frans Jager. We liked living in Florida, but if I had to look for another job we would certainly have to be willing to move. This was stress, before stress was much talked about!

I got fired from Transnitro on February 9, 1984 without any severance or accommodation of any kind. This came as such a shock, and was so brutal, that I felt compelled to sue NSM for wrongful dismissal, which I had to do before a court in Brussels, Belgium. That turned out throwing good money after bad money. A miscalculation on my part: That a Dutch citizen could successfully sue a Belgian company in a Belgian court for a dismissal that had taken place in the USA.

This experience instilled in me a life-long aversion to litigation. That does not fit well in America, which is a much more litigious society than anything I was familiar with on the European continent. One of the things I'm particularly proud of about my professional career is that, in all of my executive positions in American business, I have been able to stay away from litigation. The businesses I have worked for have never been sued for anything that fell under my authority nor were they ever compelled to sue to accomplish what they set out to do. I accept that there are circumstances under which you have no choice, and I realize that there is a risk in being too timid and conservative in the quest for one's legitimate rights. But, particularly in business, I believe that you have to exhaust all other avenues to defend your legitimate interest before you resort to litigation. The outcome of litigation is so uncertain, the cost of litigation, even if you win, is so high and—most importantly—litigation is so distracting and time consuming that the opportunity cost is almost always outweighing the potential award. If a smart rule in business is to never burn any bridges, then avoiding litigation is a good place to start. Suing someone is a pretty sure way of forever alienating yourself from that person. The same holds good for suing a company. I found that out as, later on, I explored the opportunity to come back to the fold. Even though NSM had since been taken over by the Norwegian giant Norsk Hydro, there were always people around who remembered that I had once sued the company and the avenue to resume my career there never re-opened for me.

Suddenly, my belief in the American dream got severely tested. From one day to the next, I found myself without a job and without any source of income in a country that I had picked as my home for the future but was notoriously tough on the disadvantaged. It was the first and only time that I applied for and received unemployment benefits. I can't remember what it was, but I can remember clearly that is was not nearly enough to support a family of six and a good size mortgage to pay. It taught me that I should never put my faith in the United States government to bail me out if I could not make it on my own.

I had heard that message from the day I contemplated the pros and cons of moving to the United States, and I had articulated in writing to my family and friends that the downside of living in America would be that, if you got seriously ill, handicapped, or unemployed, you would be much worse off in the USA than in the Netherlands. So, I could not say that I was not forewarned. Now I found out for myself.

Our friends in Tampa were very supportive. The typical reaction to a setback like the one I suffered was and is: "Things happen for a reason and we're convinced that this will turn out to be to your benefit." That sounds trite at the time it happens to you. Your neighbors and friends have easy talking, disaster has not hit them and they were American citizens who were much more solidly established in the American system. I was finding out—the hard way—how different it was to be unemployed in the USA versus the Netherlands. But, with the benefit of hindsight, we can say that they were right.

Something else, that was ultimately of more lasting impact, got tested in the process of my termination by Transnitro. That is my somewhat naïve faith in my fellow men and in the safety of working for a company that was well-served by my unquestioning loyalty and dedication. I enjoyed what I was doing and I was good at it. I was highly motivated, given my decision to secure a future for our family in the United States. I was not about to fail. And I was completely convinced that, as long as I would perform, and as long as NSM had a need for a sales-office in the USA, my employment with NSM would be secure. I felt deeply wronged and, being a lawyer by training, I was not about to let NSM get away with a capricious act that threatened to shatter my dreams and jeopardize my future. My instinctive and immediate reaction was therefore to seek justice and challenge NSM's decision in court.

Unfortunately, given the circumstances of the case, I had to sue NSM in a Brussels' court and it ended up being a fruitless distraction from my challenge to dust myself off and look for a new beginning in the land of opportunity. It also further depleted our scarce savings. As explained, the painful experience created a lifetime aversion to litigation in me. Isn't it true that we learn best from getting punished for our own mistakes?

———

As it turned out, my agony of doubt and uncertainty did not last long. In May of 1984, two months after I was let go by Transnitro, I was hired by Tip O'Neill (no, not the then acting Speaker of the House), the founder and owner of International Raw Materials LTD (IRM) in Philadelphia as vice president. My starting salary was the same as I was making at Transnitro and the job came with a company car of my choice (I chose a Buick Park Avenue). IRM was founded in 1979 by Tip O'Neill as a fertilizer trading company with emphasis on close and lasting personal connections between the trading partners. Tip had assembled a small team of young and very talented traders in need of some structured management and coaching and I fit the bill. My European connections in the fertilizer industry and my language skills helped my cause. Our initial conversations about my role in the company included the acquisition of some ownership in IRM, but that never came to pass as Tip and I never developed the commonality of vision and approach to make us viable business partners.

The new job with IRM necessitated a move from Tampa to Philadelphia. As would happen many more times, I went ahead and found a small studio within walking distance from the IRM office which was, and is, located in the Bourse Building on the Independence Mall, leaving Christie behind to sell the house in Carrollwood Village and pack up our belongings.

By myself in downtown Philadelphia, I had time to get much closer acquainted with the historic events that had taken place there more than two centuries earlier. The location of our office at Independence Mall, in view of the Liberty Bell, Congress Hall and Independence Hall was inspirational and deepened my conviction that I had made the right choice in opting for a future in America. It was almost like a vindication of my judgment. I had stood up against (a somewhat milder and contemporary) tyranny and triumphed, much like the participants in the Continental Congress had done a few centuries earlier. The Philadelphia experience has instilled in me an interest in and a deep admiration for the time and the spirit of the Founding Fathers. It made me realize that American history was a neglected subject in an otherwise rich and solid secondary education in the Netherlands. From what I remember, American history lessons in school started with America entering the Second World War or, maybe, Woodrow Wilson's creation of the League of Nations.

The break with NSM forced me to accept in full the consequences of our decision to find a future in America. I was now on my own and had the challenge to turn a dream into reality. Had I stayed with Transnitro, I would inevitably have been encapsulated by the huge organization of Norsk Hydro, where, ultimately the Norwegians were calling all the shots. I can gauge that by the trials and tribulations of my colleagues at Transnitro like Ben Geradts and our good friend Ed Cavazuti. Their record shows that they benefitted greatly financially from staying put, but they were never allowed to stay too long in one place and—even though they held executive positions—they were always second guessed, manipulated, and directed from Oslo.

The break with NSM also forced me to accept our future in America as more definitive, irreversible. As long as I stayed part of a European company and network, I would know that there always would be a way back if I were to find that my expectations of life in America could not be met. My dismissal from Transnitro made sure that I would never look back and was fully focused on making a success of whatever I would do in my new country. I wanted to have the last laugh!

The combination of being on my own, an immigrant by choice, and steeped in American history, awakened in me an interest in politics that would stay with me until this day and ultimately drove me to write this book.

Because of the little or no attention American history was getting in the Dutch schools, very few people I knew had any appreciation of the political movements that had grown out of the American Revolution and ultimately resulted in the two party system that has dictated American politics for almost a century. As I looked at the political reality in 1984 with my European eyes, I was glad that America had escaped the pitfalls of trying to create a welfare state, like virtually all of the countries in Western Europe had done. Immersing myself in the polemics between the Founding Fathers during and following the American Revolution, I came out on the side of limited (federal) government and a large degree of State discretion in the government of its people. As a Resident Alien (Green Card holder) in the United States, I had no voting rights and—therefore—I never had to decide for any party affiliation, but given my experience with socialism in Europe and my evaluation of the origins of American democracy, I found myself more at home with the basic credo of the Republican Party than the platform of the Democratic Party. Since then, however, I have developed serious concerns about the direction the Republicans have more recently taken, particularly on social issues—including immigration—and I am quite content that I don't have to choose in American elections. The biggest concern I have is the increased polarization between the parties and the public in general—evidenced and cultivated by cable TV news channels and other free over the air broadcast stations—the resulting gridlock, the absence of tolerance, and the social divisions showing ever more sharply in American society. But that is the subject for another part, Section III in this book.

———

As much as I like to believe that our decision to make America our new homeland was driven by rational calculations about the future of our children, there is little doubt that part of the motivation was that America had the lure of being the land of plenty and the land of opportunity. Christie and I both came from middle class families where wealth and luxury were not part of the equation and were not consciously pursued either. I remember as the day of yesterday how—at the start of our first tour of duty in the USA—we were met at the JFK Airport by my boss, who handed me the keys to a brand new Oldsmobile Cutlass, my new company car. It did not matter that he and I would commute by train to our office on Park Avenue; the car was part of the package. It confirmed my view of America as the land of plenty.

Also, our first house in the USA, although modest by American standards and purchased in 1976 at an unbelievable $65,000 in the greater New York area, was much roomier than anything we were used to in the Netherlands (in good American fashion we immediately proceeded to renovate the house and finish the attic). It did not help our sense of reality that our first experience with America came in the hay days of the fertilizer business in the early-to-mid-seventies when money was no object. The industry was making money hand over fist and was willing to spend it. In June of 1973, Christie and I flew first class KLM to New York and from there to the Greenbrier Resort in West Virginia for the annual meeting of The Fertilizer Institute. First class travel was still the norm then for intercontinental flights (business class had not been invented yet). In those years as the management team of NSM, we were heavily courted by Ronald Stanton, the owner of Transammonia, and his staff. The creation of Transnitro, as a joint venture between Transammonia and NSM, had yet to be consummated. Wining and dining was on the order of the day. We entertained in the most exclusive Manhattan restaurants of the time like Lutece, The Palm, La Grenouille, Le Cygne, The Four Seasons, and Smith & Wolenski. It was all part of the show. So were regular visits to the best shows on Broadway, where between 1973 and 1980 (our move to Tampa) we saw Jesus Christ Superstar, Godspell, Grease, Ain't Misbehavin, Evita, A Chorus Line, Bubbling Brown Sugar, Chicago, Porgy & Bess, West Side Story, The King and I, Annie, The Best Little Whorehouse in Texas, and Sweeney Todd, all at company expense. American Express was king in those days. It did not take us long under those conditions to adjust to the American style consumerism, that, quite frankly we have never been able to shed again. At times this has seriously tested our earnings capacity.

Our first tour of four years in America and in New York was a whirlwind and never gave us a feeling of permanency. It was interrupted after only a year when I was offered the position of deputy general manager and export manager of Centraal Stikstof Verkoopkantoor (CSV), the export cartel of the Dutch nitrogen fertilizer industry. It was too good an opportunity to refuse for a young man in only the seventh year of his professional career. We sold our newly renovated home in Eastchester, NY, packed up our two children and our belongings and headed back to the Old Country. Not knowing that it would only be a year before we would come back! We landed in Boskoop, a village not far from The Hague where CSV was located. There we had to settle for a small row house at double the cost of what we had sold our house in Eastchester for and we had to swallow hard to accept what we perceived as a step back in lifestyle. But we were back home and amongst friends and family and I had made an important step forward in my business career. The position at CSV made me responsible for all exports of Dutch nitrogen fertilizer—except the Exxon production—outside of the EU and the USA, where anti-trust laws prohibited the Dutch competitors to pool their export interests. It did not last a year. In 1977 the European Commission sued CSV and its partners for infringing upon the anti-trust provisions of the Treaty of Rome that had created the European Union and the shareholders in CSV were not prepared to fight the allegation. They decided instead to liquidate CSV and handle exports individually. I had been in the job less than a year, but I had never been replaced at Transnitro and was hired right back by Ben Geradts, my former boss at NSM, who was Transnitro's executive vice president. I made a promotion. My new title was vice president supply and distribution. The transfer and move were arranged quickly and expeditiously. NSM undertook to sell the house we had bought in Boskoop and we moved to Scarsdale, NY, in time for the two kids to start school there after Labor Day of 1978. We did not have any time to go house hunting and we rented a house, on Elm Street, within walking distance of Scarsdale's commuter railroad station.

This time it felt more permanent. My job no longer had the flavor of an internship it had the first time I came to New York. I had gained valuable management and international experience in my one year with CSV and I was groomed to take over from Ben Geradts, who was destined to go back to Brussels in a couple of years. We took advantage of everything the Big Apple had to offer, even though it was not the best of times for the city. Ed Koch had just come in as mayor and he had a lot of clean-up to do after two failed city administrations by John Lindsay and Abraham Beame. NYC was in a severe budget crisis, crime was rampant, garbage collectors were on strike with regularity and panhandlers were everywhere. It was also a time when homeless people started to camp out in the parks and the streets of Manhattan for lack of homeless' shelters. Living in the affluent Westchester County suburbs we felt little impact of the hard times NYC was going through, but we paid a price in our pay-check by the large cut that NYC tax took out of our salary for the privilege of commuting to and working in the city. My office was at 400 Park Avenue, a seven block walk from Grand Central Station and my commute was normally not much more than an hour door-to-door. Our adjustment to living in a new country was considerably aided by the presence of numerous other Dutch expatriates in New York City. At the time, the greater New York City area counted more than 10,000 Dutch residents among its population. The Big Apple had—and has—a vibrant Dutch-American club, The Netherland Club of New York, which, in the late seventies, had thousands of members.

———

Thinking back upon the time that we had to decide between the Netherlands and America as a place to establish domicile, I get hurled back to an age and spirit of unbridled optimism. At the personal level our optimism was expressed in the expansion of our family. If I was to create a Jager foothold in the USA, I might as well populate it sufficiently to give it a chance to take root!

Life was good, we enjoyed discovering our new environment and we appeared to be capable of overcoming the few challenges that were thrown our way. As a nation America had overcome a protracted period of doubt and confusion, if not chaos, that followed the Kennedy assassination. It had found a way to fully acknowledge that "all men are born equal", resulting in rapidly increasing engagement of minorities and women in the workplace and in the political process. It had overcome the civil unrest of 1968, Vietnam, and Watergate and it was well on its way to winning the Cold War. It had put, as the first and only nation, men on the moon. And it was making great strides in applying computer science to the process of growing the economy and improving peoples' lives. Under those circumstances it was almost inevitable that our choice would be for a future in America. We felt we had a lot to gain and little to lose.

———

SECTION I

WHERE I'M COMING FROM

A look at the family background; my life growing up in the Netherlands; the socio-political environment in Western Europe in the 1970s and early 1980s; my first business experiences.

"Your comfort zone is a beautiful place to be, but nothing ever grows there." (Unknown)

CHAPTER 1

THE COUNTRY OF ORIGIN

"Do you know where the Netherlands are?" That is a question I frequently ask, particularly when I'm being asked "where are you from, originally?" My readership is certain to do better than average, but I find that current generation Americans typically do not know that the country is only about 70 miles (as the crow flies) away from England, separated by the English Channel, which is part of the North Sea. We cannot quite see the white cliffs of Dover from the beach in Scheveningen, but the British coast is close.

No, the Netherlands is not a Scandinavian country and it is not part of Germany. It would have been if America had not intervened with Hitler's plans for hegemony in Europe. For most of my life, the American participation in the Second World War, and the implementation of the Marshall Plan afterwards, have defined the relationship between the two countries. Gratitude and respect towards the USA and the American people were the near universal feelings in the Netherlands of my time. And when the Netherlands experienced a wave of emigration after the war, America and Canada were the preferred destinations. I also remember being in awe as a child of the richness at display in America in the form of its automobiles, airplanes, household appliances, televisions, movies, homes, and skyscrapers. It was not until the later stages of the Vietnam War that public opinion in the Netherlands began to become more critical of America and its foreign policies.

If you are confused about the difference between "the Netherlands" and "Holland" you have good reasons to be. The Dutch use these names for their country as synonyms. That is incorrect and it causes the confusion. Holland is technically the territory of two of the twelve Dutch Provinces, Noord-Holland and Zuid-Holland (North and South Holland). These two Provinces border the North Sea and are home to the three largest cities: Amsterdam (the capital), Rotterdam (the sea port) and The Hague (the seat of the government and parliament). The twelve provinces together are properly called the Kingdom of the Netherlands.

The language spoken in the Netherlands is Dutch. Not the "Pennsylvania Dutch", which is a bastardization of the word "Deutsch", which means German. Dutch is a Germanic language, like German and English. It is spoken in the Netherlands, in the Northern part of Belgium (the Southern part speaks French) and in the former Dutch Antilles. It is at the root of the Afrikaans language developed from the language spoken by the Dutch settlers of South Africa.

With about 16,000 square miles of territory, the Netherlands is about the size of the State of Maryland. The Dutch word Nederland (Netherlands) stands for "Low Country" for a good reason. About twenty percent of the territory is situated below sea-level and a full fifty percent of its territory is no more than three feet above sea-level. It is one of the countries that will be in serious trouble if the worst predictions about the rise in sea-level as a result of global warming come to pass and nothing is done about it. The Netherlands is not waiting it out and is pro-actively addressing the threat of rising water levels by strengthening and heightening their dikes and by creating capacity to store overflow water. The Dutch are very determined to keep their feet dry!

If you want to know more about my country of origin than you will read in this chapter, the Internet gives you a wealth of information. One that I found of particular interest is from IFITWEREMYHOME.COM. It will tell you that if the Netherlands were your home instead of the United States you would:

- Have 46.24 percent more chance of being employed
- Use 40.77 percent less electricity
- Experience 31.33 percent less of a class divide
- Have 27.6 percent more free time
- Have 25.52 percent fewer babies
- Have 24.1 percent less chance of dying in infancy
- Spend 48.19 percent less money on health care
- Make 15.52 percent less money
- Consume 8.72 percent less oil
- Live 1.31 years longer
- Be 66.67 percent less likely to have HIV/AIDS

If you read this you would think: Why would anybody want to leave the Netherlands for the USA. We will deal with these differences in some detail in Sections II and III of this book. Unfortunately, the Internet did not exist in 1984 when we had to decide where we wanted to seek our future. There was no IFITWEREMYHOME.COM and, if that information had been available in the early eighties, it probably would have looked quite different.

There are intriguing parallels between the histories of the creation of the Dutch nation and the creation of the American Republic. Even though the Netherlands is a monarchy today, it started out as a republic; in fact, one of the first republics in world history. It happened in 1579 when seven provinces, governed by Spain, banded together in the "Unie van Utrecht" and created the "Republic of the Seven Provinces". This feat was followed in 1581 by the Dutch equivalent of the Declaration of Independence, when the Staten Generaal, the governing body of the young republic, passed the "Acte van Verlatinghe" (Act of Abandonment) by which the Republic formally severed its ties with the Spanish monarchy. The creation of the Republic of the Seven Provinces heralded in the "Golden Century" during which the Dutch nation rose to world eminence in trade and commerce, exploration, arts and science, and tolerance. The Republic ended in 1810 with the annexation by Napoleon's France. The Netherlands became a monarchy, under the French constitutional model, with the adoption of a new constitution in 1813, even before Napoleon Bonaparte was ultimately defeated in 1815 in the historic battle of Waterloo.

The Netherlands represents a case study in the rise and fall of nations: A republic that shaped history in the age of the Renaissance succumbs to the pressures of the European power brokers and becomes a sleepy, tired monarchy at a time that across the Atlantic a new republic emerges and quickly establishes a dominant position on the world stage. Over time, led by the British refinement of the construction of a constitutional parliamentary monarchy, the sharpness of distinction between a republican and a monarchial form of government has gradually dissipated; but, two centuries ago it had meaningful implications for social and economic development and for personal freedoms and the pursuit of happiness.

In the "Golden Age" of Dutch history, the seventeenth century, the Dutch Navy and Merchant Marines dominated the sea-lanes, resulting in Dutch colonization of parts of the West Indies and most of the Indonesian archipelago. The Dutch flag also flew in China and South Africa. New Zealand was discovered and given its name, but not settled, by the Dutch in an exploratory mission captained by the Dutch explorer Abel Tasman. In much the same vein that the Lebanese are called the merchants of the Middle East, the Dutch were—and are to a large degree—the merchants of Western Europe. But less than a century later that prominent place on the world scene had been lost, never to return.

In the first decade and a half after the end of the Second World War, legions of Dutch citizens emigrated to escape from the drudgery and misery of the post war economy. Many of them were farmers or farm-workers, for whom there was no room for expansion in the Netherlands. Popular destinations were the USA, Canada, South Africa, Australia, and New Zealand. The idea of looking for opportunity outside of the borders was therefore not alien to any Dutch citizen of my generation. The country is simply too small to contain all the population growth and all the ambition of more than sixteen million inhabitants. The State of Maryland is fairly densely populated by US standards, but it has less than six million people on its territory, which is the same size as the Netherlands. It feels cramped living in the Netherlands, particularly in the "Holland" part of the country, where seventy percent of the Dutch population lives.

There are multiple historical, cultural, economic, and social connections between the United States of America and the Netherlands. The Dutch Embassy in the USA publishes a great brochure titled *"Hello Holland"* for the purpose of informing Americans about these relationships. It rightly emphasizes shared history and shared values. The Dutch ambassador writes in the introduction: *"The Netherlands and the U.S. share four hundred years of history, subscribe to the values of tolerance and openness and are committed to sustainability. We work closely together on security issues such as terrorism and international drug trafficking. As economic partners we are important to each other: the Netherlands is the third largest investor in the United States and our ties with the U.S. account for 700,000 American jobs. The U.S. and the Netherlands work together to foster sustainable growth in the global economy."*

All true. And it explains why so many people of Dutch origin feel at home in the U.S. There are nearly five million people of Dutch origin living in the United States. The Dutch began emigrating to North America in the seventeenth century. The largest Dutch communities are in California, Iowa, Pennsylvania, Michigan and New York. The Dutch first arrived on the American shores in 1609, when the flagship of the Dutch East India Company landed at the island of Manhattan. The ship, the Halve Maen (Half Moon), was captained by the Englishman Henry

Hudson, who had orders to seek a Northeastern route from Holland to the East Indies but chose instead to look for a Northwestern passage, somewhere through the American continent.

Russell Shorto[1] has written a magnificent book about this part of the Dutch-American history, aptly titled "*The Island at the Center of the World.*" This episode resulted in a Dutch settlement, called New Amsterdam, which remained under the rule of the Dutch East India Company until it was wrested away by the British in 1664. It was officially ceded to the British in the Treaty of Breda of 1667, which ended the second Anglo-Dutch war.

The connection between the United States and the Netherlands is a two way street. More than 1,750 American companies have a head-quarters in the Netherlands and the country is home to many American expatriates. A symbol of this two-way street is the Holland America Line, founded in 1873 as the Netherlands-American Steamship Company, which maintained for over a century a regular passenger and cargo service between Rotterdam and New York. The shipping lanes, while still extremely important in the movement of goods, have, for passenger service, been eclipsed by air traffic where the Dutch company KLM competes with the large American carriers Delta, United and US Airways for passenger flights between Amsterdam and the major U.S. cities.

CHAPTER 2

EUROPE (THE EARLY 1980S)

What we left behind when we opted for a future in America was an orderly, predictable, life in a Europe that looked significantly different from what it is now. If we pick our decision point as the time, in early 1984, that we decided not to accept NSM's ultimatum to come back to the motherland, then we find a Europe before the fall of the Berlin wall, the break-up of the Soviet Union, and the demise from communism in the rest of Europe. In fact, I can't think of anyone who seriously predicted all of this happening before the decade would be over. Maybe true believers like Ronald Reagan and Margaret Thatcher, but I doubt that even they were confident that early that their tough stand against the Soviets would so quickly pay dividends.

It was also a Europe before the expansion of the European Union (EU) beyond the original West European member countries: Belgium, France, Germany, Italy, Luxembourg, and the Netherlands, joined by Denmark, Ireland, and the United Kingdom in 1973 and by Greece in 1981. Portugal and Spain would join the EU in 1986.

It was a Europe where the political power was typically divided between socialist parties on the one hand and Christian Democrat parties on the other.

All EU member countries were parliamentary democracies, some monarchies, like the Netherlands, and some republics. Left-leaning parties like the socialists and the communists dominated the scene for most of the years after the Second World War and into the eighties. The Netherlands was no exception, although in my country of origin the socialists would almost always have to share power with some of the other parties. I can't remember the communist party ever being invited into any Dutch government coalition and they never accounted for more than 6 percent of the popular vote. There was an abundance of political parties in the Netherlands for all of the 33 years I lived there, most of them affiliated with religious denominations. Conservatives were found both in these Christian Democrat parties and in the Volkspartij voor Vrijdom and Demokratie (Peoples Party for Freedom and Democracy) the largest secular, conservative party in the Dutch Parliament. Coalition governments were a political necessity. If the socialists won an election, they would typically form a coalition with some of the Christian Democrats and if the conservatives won the election, it would be their turn to form a coalition government with the Christian Democrats. Governing in the Netherlands always required the art of compromise, an essential ingredient missing in American bi-polar politics.

Western Europe in the early eighties was very internally focused. From the beginnings of the 1951 Treaty of Paris between the Netherlands, West Germany, France, Belgium, Luxembourg, and Italy, which established the European Coal and Steel Community, Europe's focus was on avoiding another war between its nations. French/German cooperation in the field of coal mining and steel production, that started right after the Second World War, was a political move aimed at reconciling the two long time European adversaries.

The European Steel and Coal Community morphed into the European Common Market and the member nations were busy making it an economic reality. Gradually, the borders between the member nations were opened up for the movement of people and goods and a European Interstate Highway system was created to further enhance traffic and commerce.

Even though member nations of the European Common Market (later EU) were also North Atlantic Treaty Organization (NATO) members, attention to military matters took a back seat to economic development and political and social integration between them. Western Europe, which had been torn apart and devastated by two World Wars in the twentieth century, had become averse to ever again reaching for war as a means of conflict resolution. It supported NATO primarily so that it obtained the protection of the American nuclear umbrella against the threat of the Soviet Union. Western Europe, in the early eighties, was in a pacifist mood and the public at large was opposed to the placement of nuclear missile capability on their soil. This sentiment was widespread and made me wonder if the will would be there to defend against a Soviet invasion, if it ever came to that.

CHAPTER 3

COMING OF AGE

"Wherever your talents and the needs of the world intersect, there lies your purpose." (Aristotle)

Having been born in the middle of World War II, I have come of age in the post war years that were harsh, with the harshness only mitigated by the fact that we were free after five years of occupation. After the War of 1812, America has never again had to fight a war on its own territory in order to defend the freedom of its people against foreign intervention. The only major war fought on its own territory was the Civil War, which, brutal and traumatizing as it was, was not a war against a foreign invader. What sets Europe apart from America, with a lasting impact on the public opinion about war and peace, is indeed the horrific history of territorial wars, with all their devastation and cruelty, which were a regular occurrence throughout its history.

It took the Netherlands, in spite of the Marshall Plan, a long time to recover from the devastation of the war and the German occupation and many Dutch people chose to emigrate and find better opportunity and more space oceans away, but, by the time I was looking for my first employment, the tide had turned and there was ample opportunity.

Only Serendipity explains how and why I found myself in the early eighties having to make a choice between a future in America or staying put on the other side of the Atlantic. If I had not found my first employment in the fertilizer industry with NSM, if natural gas had not been present on Dutch territory and been promoted for industrial development by the Dutch government, if NSM had not scaled up its production of nitrogen fertilizer far beyond the volume of domestic and regional demand, if NSM had not looked towards the USA for an outlet for this surplus production, I doubt that I would have ever considered to look to America for work and a new home. But once I had been given the opportunity to evaluate the work and life environment on both sides of the Atlantic, the necessity to make a choice became inescapable.

Many immigrants to the United States leave their country of origin either because of political or religious discrimination or because of economic despair. None of this applied to us. There was a lot to be pleased with in the Netherlands at the time that we first left for the United States; and also, half a decade later, at the time that we were seriously contemplating where home was going to be for our family.

I had a good job with a good company and the Netherlands was relatively prosperous economically, because of its natural gas and because of its geography, located as it is at the gateway to central Europe at the mouth of the river Rhine. It was also prosperous because of a population with a healthy work ethic and an international orientation. Since the Dutch language does not get you very far in the world, the Dutch are educated from early childhood in several of the modern languages, English, German, and French in particular. Their language skills and a long history of trade and exploration explain why so many Dutch citizens work outside of their country in global operations.

After finishing Law School at the Nederlandsche Economische Hoogeschool (NEH) in Rotterdam, now part of Erasmus University, and serving my obligatory twenty-one months of military service in the Royal

Dutch Airforce, I took my first job with NSM which was located in Zeeuws Vlaanderen. South of the river Scheldt, this outpost of the Netherlands was far away from the hustle and bustle of the "Randstad Holland", the most densely populated triangle between Amsterdam, Rotterdam, and The Hague. We were living in an idyllic, pastoral, environment, close to the waters of the river Scheldt and the dunes of the North Sea coast. Because of my education and my executive position in the management of NSM, young as we were, we were invited in the top social circles of the area. In Zeeuws Vlaanderen we were just where we wanted to be at that time of our lives. We had two beautiful young children, a girl and a boy, and life was good. We had a terrific social circle from within the company I was working for and from the Round Table.

I did not do much with my law degree, but I enjoyed being in business, which was the result of a fateful decision I made shortly before I finished high school. Secondary education in the Netherlands offered several choices. Some were vocational schools, some were providing general education for entry into the labor market, and some were designed to prepare you for higher education. I took the college preparation route and attended the Caland Lyceum in Rotterdam. My Dad was principal of that school and was a history teacher. I attended his classes for several years. We lost him in 1971, shortly after the arrival of our son Pim and well before we first came to America. That now looks ages ago.

The Dutch lyceum curriculum offers two paths for college preparation: One is math and science oriented and the other is language and humanities oriented. No hard decision for me. Math and calculus were not my strengths, to say the least, and did not feed my intellectual curiosity. The life sciences were more up my alley, but they were largely packaged with math and calculus, with the result that I gave up on that area of exploration for further study. So, I immersed myself early on in the humanities. For the curriculum I had chosen, that meant that I would have to acquire active command of three foreign languages, French, English, and German, and mastery of ancient Greek and Latin.

Long hours in school, typically four class hours in the morning and four more in the afternoon, five days a week, and four hours on Saturday morning, were compounded by significant homework assignments that left little time for leisure. My father being the principal at my school, and the class size of less than ten students in any subject, meant that you could not slough off at any time and you certainly could not get away with sloppy or incomplete homework. Since school was about a half hour by bike away from home, not much time was available before dinner and most of the homework needed to be done after the dinner table had been cleared and the dishes had been washed (by hand).

My education has instilled in me a deep awareness that cultures and empires are subject to the proverbial rise and fall, sometimes leaving a void and a cultural wasteland for long periods of time but ultimately always supplanted by a stronger, more cultivating, and more sustainable successor nation. As I think back about my education in humanities, I find the greatest value derived from it in my appreciation of what ancient and foreign cultures have contributed to the cumulative knowledge and understanding that we have today. And in the aforementioned awareness that much of what was once achieved and understood can be lost if it is not constantly cultivated, built upon, and perfected. That lesson from history is much on my mind as I try to articulate in this book why America simply cannot rest on its laurels and get away with a less than stellar performance.

From a practical perspective, I cannot say that the six years spent at the Caland Lyceum contributed much to my career. But I keep in mind that it was not until my senior year that I suddenly changed course and decided to pursue a career in business. Had I made that choice much earlier, I would have definitely picked another curriculum. As it was, having studied Latin was a prerequisite for attending Law School in the Netherlands, where the code of law is largely based on Roman and Napoleontic principles.

From a formative perspective, I am grateful for the path that was carved out for me. It has instilled in me a deep intellectual curiosity and a belief in the supremacy of the spiritual, the immaterial world over the material world. It also has given me a keen sense of morality and equity, that was reinforced by my law studies and has helped me a great deal in business, where I have become a believer in the creation win-win situations, knowing that a deal is no good and has no lasting power if it is good for only one party in the transaction.

My interest growing up was books and literature, including classical literature in foreign languages, and I relished studying Greek and Latin and the three modern languages. I had a youthful disdain for the material world and looked upon mathematics, algebra, and science as necessary evils. As I advanced in my secondary education, I was convinced that language arts would be my choice of study in higher education. I was particularly enamored with the study of Dutch language and literature, which, if I had persisted, would have given me little choice but to find a job in education. That would have kept the apple right under the tree, because virtually everyone in my family was a teacher or would become a teacher.

As it turned out, the father of my best friend in school, Jan van Stuijvenberg, was a professor in History of Economics at the Nederlandsche Economische Hoogeschool (NEH) in Rotterdam and he quizzed me on the wisdom of trying to make my hobby—literature—my job. He informed me that the NEH was planning to convert from a School of Economics to a full-fledged University by adding faculties for Law, Sociology and Medicine. The Law School would be different from the Faculties of Law in other cities like Leiden, Utrecht, Groningen, and Amsterdam in that it would focus on business-law. After all, Rotterdam was the center of business activity in the Netherlands, much like Amsterdam was the center of arts and The Hague was the center of government. Professor van Stuijvenberg persuaded me to plan on a career in business, with the intent to make enough money that I could continue to cultivate my hobby of literature. Serendipity at work! Without van Stuijvenberg quizzing me hard about my motivations and ambitions, I would have never made a career in business and I would have never immigrated to America.

At the time, in 1962, when I was due to graduate from Lyceum, there was no university level business education in the Netherlands and preparation for a career in business typically meant a degree in engineering, economics, sociology, or law. Engineering clearly was not my bailiwick, and I felt more affinity with the study of law than the study of economics or sociology.

Like any other kid 18 years old, I had a tendency to want to go against the grain and came to the conclusion that I would want to do anything but become a teacher, like my Dad, my siblings, and my aunts. There was no tradition of business in my family. I had an uncle, my father's only brother, who was an accountant and a grandfather who had been a carpenter, but that was it. I would be doing something alien to the family and that suited me just fine. In the back of my mind, I had the idea that business might be a way to a comfortable life-style, and that suited me fine as well. Studying law at the NEH would have the advantage that I could stay in Rotterdam, where I had lived since I was nine years old.

As it turned out, the Faculty of Law at the NEH did not get off the ground until 1963 and I enrolled at the NEH for a first year of study in economics and then transferred to the Faculty of Law the next year. It meant that I had both my secondary education and my college education at an institution that was just coming off the ground. The Caland Lyceum I attended in Rotterdam was a new school that started in 1956, the year that my twin sister Anneke and I finished grade school and had to do our entrance exams for our next level of education. As a result, I graduated in 1962 with a class of seven students, after getting near private education for the six years of the Lyceum curriculum that I had chosen. The same situation repeated itself when I enrolled in 1963 for the first year of the Law Faculty at the NEH. I do not remember the exact number of students in my class, but it was certainly no more than twenty-five. It gave me close and personal contact with—and scrutiny from—my professors and a thorough immersion in the world of corporate and commercial law.

My six years in college were among the best times of my life. My parents supported me completely and gave me every opportunity to make the most out of my last years of studying and growing up. College tuition was negligible in the Netherlands at the time (I guess higher education got funded out of tax revenues) at all of the universities, which were public institutions. But I was allowed to move out of my parents' house and into student housing and join the Rotterdamsch Studenten Corps (RSC), a student club with fraternity-like features that ended up demanding a lot of my time and even more of my parents' money. I never worked in my student years and had no money of my own. My involvement with the RSC peaked in my third year, when I was invited to join the Senaat, the governing body of the RSC, which became a full time diversion for me with all kind of extra-curricular activities and long nights of fraternization at the Societeit, the club-house called Hermes. My involvement with the RSC, while offering me an early brush with social networking and leadership training, ended up costing me a full year of time and money. I could have completed my law study in four years, if I had fully dedicated myself to earning my degree. But by studying economics in my first year and then sacrificing a year to playing around, it took me a full six years to get my law degree. When that was done, while I was 24 years old, I still had to fill my national duty of military service. I graduated on October 5, 1968, got married on October 25, 1968, and enlisted with the Royal Dutch Air-Force on November 2, 1968.

An important takeaway from this reflection is that in the Netherlands, in the 1960s, it was possible for a young adult to finish a higher education at a first class university, with a very active and participative social life and without working part time, without debt and without putting a high financial burden on the parents. Kids growing up in the United States today cannot imagine such luxury and comfort.

———

I guess, I never truly and fully left the Netherlands behind me. There were times that I came close. I came close to abandoning all attachment to the home country at times that I was riding high with professional success, like during the first years of my time in Tampa as general manager of ContiChem, during my middle years as vice president with Lesco, when I was valued there as a key contributor, and during most of my tenure with PrimeraTurf, when I saw what a difference I was making in the business of the members of the co-op.

During those times, I felt in the right place at the right time, was extremely wrapped up in my work, and took little time off. The little time I took, I rather spent with my family at the beach in South Carolina then back in Holland. I looked at the Netherlands as cold, crowded and parochial. During those years, I was also much less concerned than I am now with the direction in which my adopted country was heading. Those were the years of Ronald Reagan, H.W Bush and Bill Clinton, which, with the benefit of hindsight, can now be considered pretty good years for the nation. Those were the years that the USA stood alone as a super power between nations. I felt comfortably at home in America and had little reason to look back. I had left Holland behind.

CHAPTER 4

MY PARENTS

War always has life changing and—inevitably—unintended consequences. Not only for the nations involved, but also for their citizens. The early part of my life was shaped by the timing of my birth, during World War II and under German occupation. Ironically, it may very well be that my twin sister Anneke and I owe our lives to the Germans. We were born in January 1944 when our mother was 41 years old. She already had three boys, one of which was seriously handicapped from birth by Down's syndrome. He was born in 1932 and had to be institutionalized in 1943 when my mother could no longer handle him. He died at 18 years old without ever coming back home. My father was not around very much during the second half of the war. First he was taken away by the Germans, allegedly in reprisal for acts of sabotage by the Dutch resistance, and interned at a Gestapo prison in Amersfoort and, later on, because he had to go underground in order to escape from forced labor in Germany. He apparently was home sometime in April 1943, probably just released from Amersfoort and happily reunited with my mother, because that is when my twin sister and I were conceived. I doubt that this would have happened under peacetime conditions.

Serendipity is present in virtually all aspects of my life, from the very beginning. My parents had their moment of bliss to forget the anxiety and misery! Ahead of them lay a long arduous road of separation and depravation caused by two more years of war and occupation.

My parents had a hard life by our standards, measured only one generation later. They lived through the First World War although the Netherlands was minimally affected, as its declared neutrality was respected by the fighting parties. They lived through the depression of 1929 and then the Second World War and its aftermath. On top of that, they had to deal with a severely handicapped child and were deprived of the many comforts that make our lives so cushioned. Time and again they had to overcome adversity and the cumulative effect of all the setbacks had knocked the wind out of them.

When the time came for them to retire they had reached the end of the rope, especially my father. As far as I know, once the war was behind them, they never lacked in anything of life essentials, but they lived a bare bones life without luxuries. They never traveled first class, by plane or by train.

My father died in October of 1971 at the relatively young age of 65, shortly after he retired from his job as principal of the Caland Lyceum in Rotterdam, less than a month after our son Pim was born, and well before we first moved to America. He died in his sleep of apparent heart failure. The fact of the matter is that he was worn out. He was an old man in his early sixties and so were his friends. I simply cannot get over the fact that life has changed that much in only one generation. There is a reason that, for the longest time, 65 was recognized as retirement age. In my parents' generation, few people lived long beyond that threshold.

In sharp contrast with the life of my parents, other than the first two years of my life, I have never had to cope with war. And the economic downturns that we have experienced have never taken food off our plates. Comparing our generation to the one of my parents makes it abundantly clear how much has changed in the world in just my lifetime.

Even though my mother survived my father for seven years, she too was worn out by the time my father retired and then she had to struggle on without him, without ever being able to fully enjoy life in retirement.

My parents have long been gone from my life. That is one of the unfortunate aspects of being born the youngest in the family: A "na-komertje" (afterthought) as the Dutch say, which I like much better than the American equivalent "accident". As, in preparation for writing this book, I think about my parents, I feel nothing but gratitude. Gratitude for the Serendipity of having been born to such devoted parents. Gratitude for having been born at all. And gratitude for the fact that my parents gave my siblings and me all they had to give. Other than the prevailing sentiment of gratitude, I have the overwhelming sense that the relationship with my parents was mostly a one way street.

My parents did everything for me that I possibly could have wanted. They gave me love, shelter, and guidance. And when it was all said and done they even left me a little money. They instilled in me the importance of a good education and the imperative of being a good human being, son, friend, and family member. They led by example, which was simple, humble and integer.

What I miss now about the relationship with my parents is that I can think of so few times where I felt that I had become important to them in the sense that I was aiding the fulfillment of their lives.

They did so much for me, and I gave them so little in return, other than becoming the person they hoped I might be, but that was always a work in progress and an imperfect one at that. I can think of so few moments where I had the fortitude or courage to reach out to either of them to see how they were doing; what their hopes, aspirations, and anxieties were. Particularly with my father, who was gone when I was 27, and had not been very accessible, mentally, in his last five years. It put me in a position that, at his memorial service (both my parents chose to be cremated), I felt that I had to apologize for the fact that I had dragged my heels and wasted time in getting to know him more intimately. You always figure, wrongly as it turned out, that there will be time later and then suddenly...it is too late.

As I have become a parent—and then grandparent—myself, I look at the equation from the other side and find that, for most of the time, parents and children find it easier and more comfortable to skirt the big topics and chat and communicate mostly about the day to day life and events. Having learned my lesson the hard way, I press very hard (I sense that my wife and children think I'm pressing too hard) to make sure that I have been clear and honest with my family on where I stand in life and what my remaining aspirations for our lives together are. And I am asking them to reciprocate.

I was definitely closer to my father than my mother. My dad was the intellectual type, who, as a historian, had an inquisitive and analytical mind, which I seem to have inherited.

My mother was all heart and worry. I suspect that both my parents were always afraid to drop their guard and get too happy, after all the negative experiences in their lives, for fear that the other shoe—their last—might drop.

My best memories are of the long walks my Dad and I took in Rotterdam after lunch on Sundays or holidays. We never had pets and we were not much for just going around the block. We typically picked a destination, ten to fifteen kilometers out, and then planned on taking public transportation, train, bus, tram, or trolley, back home. I believe we did not talk much, but we thoroughly enjoyed the fresh air and each other's company and we always found a spot where we could take a break and enjoy a refreshment.

There was nothing awkward in our father-son relationship, and yet there was always a distance between us. He was 40 years older than me and these 40 years had not been easy on him.

One source of bottomless pride for my Dad were the career accomplishments of his children and, once he had absorbed the shock that I would not follow in his footsteps, he took great interest in my law studies, my Air Force duty and my start in business with NSM. Of even higher pride and joy were his grandchildren. He got to know eight of them, but our first two kids, Nienke and Pim, only for a brief period in the last two years of his life. I can't ask him anymore, but I'm pretty sure that he would have taken pride and joy in our American adventure. He was forever grateful to the Allies who liberated us from the German occupation and, as a historian, he appreciated the American Revolution and the rise of a new nation on the firmament of civilizations.

My mother was the nurturer and caregiver in our family. She took care of everyone and everything. She was the manager of the household, the bookkeeper, and the financial planner. Only she knew the cash book and she always had a little savings stashed away for emergencies and special needs. At numerous times during my college years she doled out a ten or twenty guilders when I ran low on my allowance and did not want to compromise my lifestyle, which included more extravagances than my parents ever indulged for themselves.

My parents were not deeply religious, but not atheists either. They were brought up Protestant but had little or no time for organized religion. I was never baptized. Mom and Dad believed that children had to find their own religion and make their own choice of belief. They sent us dutifully to Sunday school, but that was it, except for an occasional attendance of Christmas service. We all liked the music and pageantry that belongs to Christmas and still do. Since both of them died in their sleep, they did not have to decide if they had to make peace with their Maker. I'm sure they are in a good spot given the exemplary lives they led.

———

SECTION II

ON BALANCE

What have I done with my time in America? How has it turned out? Looking at the outcome from a personal-, business-, and socio-political perspective.

"If you don't have time to do it right, when will you have time to do it all over again?" (John Wooden)

CHAPTER 1

SERENDIPITY

Immigration is a hot and contentious topic in America today. That is somewhat surprising, if you consider that virtually all American citizens are descendants of immigrants, who arrived in this country less than 500 years ago and if you consider that this country would not be what it is today, if that migration had not taken place. Admittedly, most, but not all, the contentiousness is about illegal immigration. One of the ironies of American immigration policy is, that it has created a situation where illegal immigration is larger and—in many respects—easier than legal immigration. It should not be that way and it demonstrates the urgent need for Congressional action.

As an immigrant myself, it is hardly surprising that I join the chorus that claims that, *"migrants are a force so powerful and so germane to the times in which we live that our culture will suffer from serious atrophy, our economies will become less competitive and relevant, and our security will reveal more vulnerability unless we open our minds to the vertiginous cross-fertilization that a world with massive movements of people across continents entails."*[2] I can hardly believe that there even is a serious discussion about the desirability of immigration in America.

When I hear and read what the opponents of the immigration re-form bill, created in 2013 by the bi-partisan "Gang of Eight[3]" and passed by the Senate, say about immigration, I miss any sense of tolerance and I realize that these people and what they are saying are a large part of the reason why I have not unequivocally embraced contemporary America and why the title of this book is NEITHER HERE NOR THERE.

To be sure, I'm all for curbing illegal immigration. In fact, I have long argued that every sovereign nation has a need and, indeed, an ob-ligation to control its borders and a legitimate need to know at any time who is residing within its borders. But that does not mean that we should indiscriminately punish people who have taken advantage of our lack of effective border controls, who are working here, mostly in jobs for which no true blooded American employee can be found, who are paying tax-es and abiding by our laws, and who want to be here and be part of the fabric of life in contemporary America. Much less should we punish the children of these people.

I will argue that the only legitimate reason to expel undocumented aliens from this country is if they have a criminal record unrelated to their entry into this country, if they pose a significant security risk, or if they have no capability or intent to contribute to the U.S. economy and they have no family members willing to support them.

In Section III of this book, I will present some thoughts on how to achieve open borders and yet enhance safety and security.

———

Christie and I are immigrants of the rare breed that has not taken the final and conclusive step of becoming U.S. citizens. On balance, there are two sets of conditions holding me back from taking the logical next step and becoming a U.S. citizen. One is practical and the other spiri-tual. From a practical point of view, there are two reasons why I *should* make that final step and become a U.S. citizen: 1) to get the right to vote;

and 2) to protect myself from any future discriminatory action against resident aliens.

There is also a practical reason *not* to take that final step: I would have to give up my Dutch citizenship and, therewith, my right to move back to the Netherlands in case of need, and my right to work anywhere in the European Union. For reasons that are not entirely clear to me, the Dutch law does not permit me to have dual citizenship (U.S. and Dutch).

I am at a stage in my life that the entrapments of the welfare state finally have some, limited, positive appeal. Let me explain. There is little doubt that the safety net underneath people who can no longer fend for themselves is a lot wider and stronger in the Netherlands than it is in the United States. The retirement funds that we have built up over a long career provide little protection against major setbacks in physical or mental health that may hit us as we grow older. Long term care insurance only goes so far and the cost of long term care is much higher here, in the United States, than in the Netherlands. Also, the rules managing end of life issues in the Netherlands are much more to my liking than the patchwork that exists in the United States, where the state in which you live and the medical staff responsible for your care, will largely determine how much or little say you have in shaping the transition from life to death. These considerations, all together, give me powerful practical reasons not to give up my Dutch citizenship and trade it for American citizenship. I full well realize that in taking that position I keep myself in limbo, neither here nor there.

In truth, the decision to immigrate to the United States was arrived at with an eye on the opportunities for our children and grandchildren much more than on our own futures. It was a decision made upon my evaluation at the time—in the early eighties—of where Europe and America were heading in a comparative sense. And, at that time, I had a lot more confidence in the direction America appeared to be taking than the (lack of) direction I saw on the other side of the Atlantic. In this Section we will explore in some detail how actuality has deviated from the assessments made at the time.

But it is almost like water under the bridge: Our children and grand-children are all American citizens. They are firmly established in the fabric of American life. Each of our four children has married American spouses (all only second or third generation immigrants) after attending American colleges. Two of the four were born in America. All four are, for all intents and purposes, indistinguishable from American citizens with a longer track record in the United States. Mission accomplished!

Christie and I set out to provide our family a future in America and that is what happened. Their presence here will keep us here, unless dramatically adverse circumstances force us to face the end of our lives in the home country. In other words, I do not think that there is any-thing more to accomplish on our journey from there to here, nor do I think that my nationality has any bearing on my descendants' futures in America.

The emotional condition holding me back from opting for American citizenship is at the heart of this book, as expressed in its title. I am just not sure that I have made the transition from the Netherlands to America in the spiritual sense. There was a time, shortly after obtaining my Green Card, that I thought I had arrived in making the transition both physically and spiritually. But those were the Reagan years prior to the time of the collapse of the Soviet Union and communism in gen-eral. A lot of water has flown under the bridge since that time and the truth is that, as I look around now, I would like to see a lot of things change before I would call myself an "American" in every respect and with all of my heart. In this thought process I know that I am opening myself up to the criticism that, by not applying for American citizenship and thus foregoing the right to vote, I make myself an armchair critic. I'll take that on the chin. After all, I'll be in good company: Less than sixty percent of American citizens exercise their democratic right to vote when they are asked to do so. Most of the other forty plus percent appar-ently believe that their individual vote does not make a difference and who can blame them? Gerrymandering of voting districts and the power of the incumbency together with the money influence in politics have made a mockery of the open and democratic process that elections in the U.S. are supposed to be. Plus, quite honestly, in most of the important electoral races, I can't identify myself with any of the candidates, or the positions that they have to take in order to get elected.

My foot-dragging in the matter of American citizenship finds its origin in the Serendipity of the conditions under which I had to make up my mind on seeking a future in America or in Europe. I can only hope that it will not be interpreted as evidence of a lack of respect for my host country that has provided me a home and aided my career for more than forty years. I have paid my fair share of taxes and still do. I can sing the national anthem with the best of them and without mangling the words. I will take off my hat and cross my heart when the Star Spangled Banner is played at a sporting event and I will defend America against unfounded criticism from abroad that almost always is based on political bias or uninformed judgments. I work very hard on staying informed on what's happening in our economy, our society, and our environment, displaying a level of intellectual curiosity that I do not often find matched in my American network. And I provide feedback, as much as I can, with suggestions and observations towards positive change when I encounter imperfections in the American system. The writing of this book—after a long time of writing socio-political commentary in column form for various publications, including my own blog Castnet Commentary—is part and parcel of my way of contributing to the perpetuation of the American success story. Do I really have to be an American citizen to feel fiercely loyal to the best that America has stood for in the past and still stands for in its best moments? If dual citizenship was permitted in my case, no doubt would I have added the American citizenship to my Dutch nationality. But I would not have renounced my Dutch citizenship. Does that not tell me that I have not truly and completely made the transition? That work is done, naturally, for me by my children and grandchildren.

In the final two Sections of this book I will articulate what needs to change in America for me to feel completely "at home" and no longer somewhere in between, neither here nor there.

———

Alvaro Vargas Llosa has written eloquently and convincingly about im-immigration. He explains in detail why immigration is as important today to America as it ever was in its still relatively short history of modern migration. I subscribe fully to all of his arguments for a smart and lib-eral immigration policy, which is unfortunately missing right now. In his excellent book "Global Crossings", Alvaro Vargas Llosa also convincingly dispels the myth that immigrants come here exclusively for economic reasons[4].

I have asked myself numerous times what my primary motivations were for trading my expatriate status in the USA for permanent resi-dent status. I was well-positioned and secure in my job with NSM. My two bosses were respectively 12 and 24 years older than me, and I had proven myself as a contributor. With the benefit of hindsight I can say that, from a merely financial point of view, I would have been better off had I followed the orders of NSM, stayed in the organization and come back to Europe. This is particularly evident at this stage of my life, where I have retired from active duty and I am relying on my IRA, my 401K, my Social Security and some consulting income to get me to the finish line without running out of funds. Had I retired from Norsk Hydro, which acquired NSM in 1979, I would have no such worries because I would have been a participant in a defined income pension plan that is very generous for former executives of the company (although pension plans in the Netherlands are also upended under the pressure of changing demographics and economic realities).

Whatever my motivations for settling in America may have been, I have come to realize that I would almost certainly not have immigrated to the United States if I had not already lived and worked in the country for several years. Call it therefore Serendipity that brought us here. It was certainly not driven by economic considerations.

The decision to come here the first time, in 1976, on a business visa, was relatively easy: Nothing ventured, nothing gained. Although the truth compels me to admit that it was my wife Christie more than me who felt that I should take advantage of the opportunity Transnitro gave me to experience life and work in the USA. I was comfortably settled in Brussels in my role as export manager for NSM. We had made many good friends in Rotterdam, in Sluiskil, and in Brussels and my career prospects looked good, regardless of what job I would hold. But Ben Geradts wanted me in New York, my wife thought it was a nice adventure, and so we went. It was meant to be a temporary assignment and, as it turned out, it was, because a year later I was back in the Netherlands, working for CSV.

The moment of truth did not arrive until after a few years into my second assignment with Transnitro. By then, we had moved to Tampa and our family had expanded to six. Our one year back in the Netherlands, living in Boskoop with two children, had not been a positive experience in terms of life-style. I knew I would have to make a decision sometime soon about our future and we liked living in the USA. The step to apply for a Green Card was just a logical, practical, decision in that it was required if I wanted to keep my options open. In a way, we had maneuvered ourselves sub-consciously to a point of no return. Who knows if we had ever made up our minds if NSM had not forced a decision by presenting me with the ultimatum of returning to headquarters or losing my job. I rationalized my decision to stay in America by contemplating the threat of communism and the lack of push-back against creeping socialism in Western Europe, but was it not first and foremost my personal pride that ultimately decided the argument? I did not like to be pushed around and being treated like an indentured servant for nothing but self-serving reasons. A lot of things had to fall in place for me to start thinking about immigrating to the USA. And one after another they did. That is Serendipity.

The bottom line is that, while I wanted the Jager family firmly settled in America, I never felt like I had to escape from the Netherlands and that America was my sanctuary. In other words, our decision to immigrate to the USA was a decision for America, not a decision against the Netherlands. We felt like citizens of the world more than citizens of any particular country. In many respects, that is not a bad feeling.

CHAPTER 2

FORMATIVE EXPERIENCES

"We made plenty of mistakes, but we never tripped anybody to gain advantage, or took illegal shortcuts when no judge was around." (Wallace Stegner)

In the Prologue to this book, I outlined the circumstances under which we chose, thirty years ago, to settle our family on America's shores and experience American Exceptionalism for ourselves. The question inevitably arises: "How did it turn out?" The answer to that question is still open, as you will read in "The Final Analysis" at the end of this story. What is no longer an open question is what I have learned in the intervening thirty years and in the following pages I will share with you my most formative experiences, because they are fundamental to the perspective with which I come to the socio-political evaluation, which is the heart of the matter and the core and purpose of this book. I'll be brief, but I ask you—the reader—to stay with me, because it will be hard for you to understand where I'm coming from in my evaluation, my critique, and my recommendations, if I do not first give you some insight on how my belief systems have been influenced and developed by thirty years of active participation in American life.

From the time I parted ways with NSM in 1984, I have held six executive positions in business if I include my current position as Principal of Castnet Corp. In the Prologue to this book I have already elaborated on my time in Philadelphia with International Raw Materials (IRM). It was a God-sent in the sense that it came quickly after I was left in the cold by my first employer. It kept me in the fertilizer business and it brought me in contact with a whole new slew of players, suppliers, and customers. Most importantly, it allowed me to stay in the USA and it connected me with Jerry Crossan and Nick Adamchak, two of the best young traders in the business and two talents I later recruited after I had joined ContiChem.

Within a year though, Tip O'Neill and I had figured out that ours would not be a lasting partnership. Wisely, he never followed through on offering me an equity position in IRM and pretty soon we stopped confiding in each other and no longer saw eye to eye on what to do in the business and how to go about it. Tip encouraged me to start looking around for a more suitable position and it did not take long for me to hook up with John Surless and Al Byrnes, whom I knew from my Transnitro days. Both John and Al worked then for Ronald Stanton at Transammonia and now they had teamed up to bring Continental Grain Company into the fertilizer business.

Continental Grain was, at the time, one of the largest privately held corporations in the USA. It was, with Cargill, Andre, Dreyfus and Bunge, one of the five famed "Merchants of Grain", immortalized by author Dan Morgan in a book carrying the same title[5]. Established in 1813 by Simon Fribourg, it was in 1985 headquartered in New York and still privately owned by Michel Fribourg. Michel Fribourg's son, Paul Fribourg, was the driver behind diversification of Conti's trading operations into cotton, rice, financial instruments, LPG and fertilizer. John Surless had been president of Transammonia and was brought in by Paul Fribourg to bring Continental Grain Company into the gas and fertilizer trading- and distribution-business. John drew heavily on his former Transammonia staff to populate the new business, called ContiChem. The operation was already up and running when I was asked by John Surless and Al Byrnes if I was interested in setting up fertilizer distribution operations for ContiChem in Europe.

That question posed an intriguing dilemma for me. Would I, little more than a year after refusing to go back to Europe for Norsk Hydro, be willing to relocate my family to the old world for ContiChem? My answer, after a lot of soul searching, ended up being "yes". That positive response was conditioned by a number of demands that mainly had to do with preserving my permanent resident status in the USA and describing my stationing in Europe as a temporary assignment. It was well understood that my permanent residence status in the USA was to be preserved under all circumstances and ContiChem accepted the expense of an immigration lawyer getting a Re-Entry Permit for all of us every year of our assignment in Geneva. Maintaining our Green Card also required an annual "home leave" for the whole family to spend in the USA. It was for this purpose that we invested in 1986 in a membership in the Melrose Resort on Daufuskie Island, a barrier island across the Calibogue Sound from Hilton Head Island.

When I was asked to take on this challenge, I already had a job offer from Jim FitzGibbon, the founder and principal owner of Lesco, Inc., then the largest distributor of turf maintenance products in the USA. Jim was looking for a professional buyer for his rapidly growing company, which was located in the suburbs of Cleveland, OH. I knew Jim from selling him fertilizer on behalf of Transnitro and IRM. He was a prototypical entrepreneur and a great person. It would be hard to turn him down.

I went for the money (the ContiChem offer was substantially better than Lesco's) and for the challenge to start something new, from the ground up, and as the leader of the team. Up to that point, I had not been directly responsible for a business unit. Shortly after my hiring, I persuaded John Surless and Al Byrnes to hire Jerry Crossan away from

IRM to set up a ContiChem office in Hong Kong. It was the start of a pattern that I would maintain throughout my career: Surrounding myself with talent that I had come in contact with along the way. Finally, it had a good ring to be working in an executive position for one of the largest privately owned corporations in the USA. A good resume builder if nothing else. Little did I know that, in less than a decade, I would be in Cleveland, working for Jim FitzGibbon anyway. Even as I turned him down, he graciously told me that, if my adventure would not pan out, he would be glad to extend a new job offer to me.

As good as Geneva was from a leisure and financial perspective (the life of an expatriate in a multi-national corporation is hard to beat) I was struggling to make a success out of the plan to build a fertilizer distribution business on top of the grain trading infrastructure offered by Continental Grain. There were several reasons for this. In the first place, I don't think that the plan had the unequivocal commitment from Conti's management team in New York. It may have had the support of Paul Fribourg, but Michel Fribourg and Don Staheli were still calling the shots and controlling the purse strings. Another handicap was the decentralized nature of the Conti organization in Europe. There were separate fiefdoms in Geneva (Finagrain), in Paris, London, Rotterdam, Lisbon, and Athens and they all pretty much did their own thing. None of the leaders of these organizations were made aware of what the ContiChem plan was and how they were supposed to contribute. As a result, they withheld their support or only paid lip service to the new mandate.

It still was not a waste of time, for me or for ContiChem. By being located in Europe I served as the procurement office for the international trading operations that were run by John Surless and Al Byrnes from New York and included Jerry Crossan in Hong Kong and Chris von Kuhn in Singapore. By having me located in Geneva, I was close to our primary supply sources, which were located in Romania, Bulgaria, Russia, Tunisia, and Morocco. The Geneva office of ContiChem never became its own profit center as it was set up to be, but it made significant contributions to the financial success of the parent organization in New York. It gave me the opportunity to hone my procurement- and negotiating skills and it set me on the track of becoming accomplished in general management and in supply chain management, which prepared me well for what would be asked of me later in my career.

In the meantime it became clear that operating from Geneva was extraordinarily expensive for an operation like ours that had no business in Switzerland itself. In large part this was due to the slide of the value of the dollar against the Swiss franc. The decision was made to move the ContiChem office to London in 1987. London turned out to be one of the shortest stops along my career path. It was not long after I had settled into my routine of rail commute and pub lunches that I was asked to come back to the United States to replace Bill Demoss as general manager of the ContiChem operations in the USA, located in Tampa, Florida. This was my ticket back to the country that I had picked as my home for the future and I could hardly believe my good fortune. I did not waste any time getting back to the place where we had come from only three years earlier. Christie still chastises me for not wanting to experience a London Christmas. Instead we loaded our belongings in a container and spent Christmas in a hotel in Tampa.

The U.S. fertilizer operation of ContiChem (ContiChem was also in the gas—LPG, Butane and Propane—business) consisted of a trading and distribution business. It specialized in the importation of nitrogen fertilizers which were then marketed to wholesale distributors in selected markets. The operation, which had floundered under incompetent management, became consistently profitable with my arrival on the scene. That was made possible, in large part, thanks to the presence of a highly talented and productive domestic marketing talent in the person of Ted Schulte. Ted had come to ContiChem from Iowa where he worked for United Suppliers, a large wholesale distribution cooperative. He had no respect for his boss and had just about given up on ContiChem at the time that I came on board. Fortunately, Ted and his wife Rose loved Florida. They had a nice house in Brandon, three young children and Ted was prepared to give Conti and me another chance. The combination clicked. Ted and I worked hand-in-glove and, in the process, became good friends.

We both knew and liked the fertilizer business and we complemented each other perfectly. I was experienced and proficient in the procurement side of the business and Ted was a master on the sales and marketing side of the operation. He had built a strong reputation for himself and had established a network of domestic wholesale and retail accounts that became reliable customers for the cargoes of fertilizer I brought in from overseas.

This is where I developed an appreciation for, and a deeply ingrained belief in, partnerships in business. There was no duplication of effort or competition for honors between Ted Schulte and me. I did not try to do his job or second guess him and he loyally let me run the ship and let me deal with the inevitable corporate reporting that had to be done. Our operation reported to Ed Karam, President of the General Commodities Group of Continental Grain. Ed Karam was an old hand from the glory days of the grain trading business with the Soviets and had no affinity or interest in the fertilizer and gas business of ContiChem, other than to the extent that it delivered to the bottom-line, his reputation, and his bonus. His preoccupation was to control expenses and avoid risk, which is hard to do in any kind of trading operation.

Our business was to buy cargoes of fertilizer from off shore sources at a cost that would give us a good outlook at making a profit by the time the product arrived at the U.S. shores. I was the one traveling to the places of origin, mostly Bulgaria, Rumania and the Soviet Union, to make the deals, based on feedback and projections I got from Ted Schulte and my trading network. This was the time that I was away from home and pretty much incommunicado for extended periods of time.

It was before glasnost and the fall of the Berlin wall and once you were behind the iron curtain you were pretty much on your own. I communicated with my office by telex (do you remember that?), always very aware, that every word I sent or received would be monitored by government watch dogs. To call home I would have to go to the hotel operator who would have to set up the international call for me, which could take hours, leaving me no choice but to wait in my hotel room for the call to come through. Every call I made was listened to by someone from the state security system. As much as I would have announced my visit and its purpose, I could never go in one day behind the iron curtain and out the next with my mission accomplished. Hardly ever did I spend less than ten days to buy one cargo of fertilizer. I stayed with it, because the East Block was the place where, with hard currency in hand, you could make the best deals, if you knew what you were doing and had patience. The days were spent kowtowing to the communist officials who had the authority to sign off on a deal, entertaining them at bars, restaurants, and night clubs that were reserved for foreigners with hard currency. It was frequently painful and exasperating to get a deal accomplished, but once you had arrived at an agreement, it was normally executed without further shenanigans. I could not have asked for a better training in negotiation. It served me well throughout my later career. Dealing with the communist Bulgarians and Rumanians taught me to be well prepared, patient, alert, and, most of all, unintimidated. It also taught me to always go in with a clearly defined and delineated target in mind. When traveling behind the iron curtain, I always knew what I wanted and where I would draw the line, pull back, and try again later if I could not reach my target.

Once we had made the purchase, we were at risk of the market at destination turning against us. Large purchases of fertilizer, mostly 10,000-20,000 tons at one time, were made with only a couple of dollars per ton as projected margin. Market timing was of the essence. For this, Ted Schulte and I designed and implemented a unique tool to mitigate the risk without giving away too much of the upside potential (which was what we were betting on). We had negotiated with a number of large regional fertilizer retail operators a deal that we termed a "strategic alliance", which was in effect a virtual joint venture. In this arrangement, ContiChem and its alliance partner identified the market requirement for product and the price potential. ContiChem then went out, at its expense, to source the required product and arrange for transportation of the cargo(es) to the U.S. destination. At destination, the alliance partner, arranged for storage, insurance, sales and marketing. The profit resulting from the sales (after all out-of-pocket costs incurred by the alliance partners was accounted for) was then paid to the alliance partners in a pre-arranged split, which was typically between 60-70 percent going to ContiChem. These types of deals kept us out of trouble and during my tenure we never experienced a losing year at ContiChem. I would end up using the concept of a strategic alliance many more times in the later stages of my career.

Resorting to this type of business construction is tantamount to acknowledging that, by yourself,—whether you are an individual or a corporation—you can be good at only so much and that many times, by partnering with someone, you can achieve much more than you ever can on your own. My name for that phenomenon is: "One plus one = three". It requires that you combine complementary competencies and establish a high level of trust between the two parties involved in the alliance or partnership. It was in this process that I learned about the concept of 100 percent accountability, which I now firmly believe in. The concept says that a partnership or team works optimally when each of the members of the team are willing to hold themselves 100 percent accountable for the results of the team. This way, weaknesses or failures of one or more of the team members are compensated by other team members stepping in to protect the team's performance and outcome.

It also helps when you actually like the business you are in and you have fun making the most out of the opportunities it provides. We did just that when Ted Schulte and I were managing the ContiChem business in Tampa. It was a good time both from a personal and business perspective. I felt right at home in America.

But the handwriting was on the wall that Conti's heart was not in it. Ted saw this before I was willing to acknowledge the fact, and he resigned in 1990 to take an executive position with Arcadian Corp., a newly formed joint venture of several U.S. fertilizer manufacturers. (From there he went on to make an impressive career with Airgas where he became a group president). Unbeknownst to me, Continental Grain was in negotiations with Cargill to sell its U.S. trading operations and Cargill did not need another fertilizer operation: It had its own. I was asked to liquidate the fertilizer operation of ContiChem, which I did; and was offered a position within the ContiTrade (financial services) organization, but it would have required my family and me to move back to Geneva, Switzerland and, this time, without any certainty or promise that I would be given a path back to the United States.

I seriously considered to start my own business with the pieces that Continental Grain was leaving on the table. I had developed solid relations with the East European suppliers of fertilizers and they were at risk of losing an outlet for their products with ContiChem going out of business. At the other end of the supply chain, ContiChem's distribution partners were concerned about losing their source of supply. I went as far as creating a new company, named Nitrade Inc., and I had convinced the ContiChem staff to stay with me and continue the business under another name. But I could not pull it off. I just could not replace the financing, that Continental Grain had provided to ContiChem, with funds from other sources and it was hard to get firm commitments out of the Bulgarians, Rumanians, and Russians who had come from under the communist regimes but were very unorganized and uncertain of the future. I looked in the direction of Transammonia and ContiTrade for support and perhaps another strategic alliance, but I ran out of time and money to get any of this accomplished. That may have been a blessing in disguise, because the supply of nitrogen fertilizer out of Bulgaria and Rumania dried up quickly once their antiquated, state-owned, operations had to compete in a free market on capitalistic terms.

So, it was time to call on my good old friend Jim FitzGibbon, to see if he would still make good on his offer to give me a job, if I ever needed one. We were now in 1992 and the last time I had spoken with him about a Lesco job was 1985. We had stayed in regular contact and ContiChem had become a primary supplier of urea for Lesco's sulfur coated urea plant in Martins Ferry, Ohio.

The timing could have been better: Jim had suffered a couple of set-backs with his health and he was exploring the possibility to sell the Lesco business, so that he could extract the value of the business he had started, and then retire. In fact he had found an interested buyer and he was negotiating the transaction. This situation cast a spell on my prospects for a career move to Lesco and I had no choice but to cool my heels and accept, in principle, my new assignment with ContiTrade in Geneva. We even went through the charade of bringing Christie over to go "house hunting" in Geneva, but before too long I got word that the sale of Lesco had fallen through and the coast was clear for me to become vice president purchasing for Lesco.

Lesco was the largest national distributor for the supply of grounds maintenance products to the golf industry, the lawn care and landscape industry and similar businesses, collectively called the "Green Industry". Jim FitzGibbon had started the business in 1962 and gone public with it in 1984 for the simple reason that he needed access to working capital to expand the business. Going public also gave him and his loyal team that had helped him get Lesco off the ground, the opportunity to cash in on the shares he had liberally handed out in lieu of cash incentive compensation when cash was scarce in the start-up period of the company. The FitzGibbon family retained a controlling interest in Lesco even after its stock was listed as LSCO on the NASDAQ.

My new assignment kept me in the fertilizer business, since fertilizer was a significant component of the Lesco sales assortment, but it brought me from the commodity trading business into the wholesale distribution business of turf fertilizers, grass seed and pesticides. It brought me into the Green Industry.

Lesco, which later became part of John Deere Landscapes, was not only a distributor but also a manufacturer of turf fertilizers and slow release fertilizer (SCU) and, until the late nineties, a manufacturer of lawn care and golf course equipment.

I had a lot to learn and I had to learn quickly. For good reasons, no one in business is patiently giving a rookie time and a chance to get his/her bearings straight. The rule is baptism by fire. But here again my partnership instincts helped me out. I found Bob Yarborough, who was an old pro in the chemical business, more than willing to take me under his wings and teach me the intricacies of active ingredients used in the pesticide business. Bob was director of marketing at Lesco; and he and I made a good tag team when it came to negotiating supply agreements with the large chemical companies like Bayer, BASF, Dow and Monsanto. Bob provided the product expertise and I provided the purchasing acumen, leaning on my legal training and the schooling I had undergone behind the iron curtain. Again, it was fun to be part of a team and we did great things together for Lesco.

Jim FitzGibbon's health, in the meantime, continued to deteriorate and a year after my arrival at Lesco he relinquished the leadership of the company to Bill Foley, who had been selected by the Lesco Board of Directors to succeed him as president and CEO. Jim stayed on as chairman but passed away within the year. With him the company lost its entrepreneurial spirit and, although Lesco capably grew the top-line, it was a perennial disappointment on Wall Street in spite of its leadership position in the industry and the unique marketing concepts it developed with its drive-through service centers catering to the lawn care and landscape business and its "stores on wheels" catering to the golf course industry.

I stayed with Lesco for eight years. With the benefit of hindsight I can say that I overstayed my welcome. I spent six pleasant, productive, years at Lesco but spun my wheels for the last two years. Increasingly, I found myself out of tune with Bill Foley and his ever-changing staff. The company just never delivered on its potential. And the expectations that Bill Foley, who was a very charismatic and well-spoken CEO, raised year-in and year-out with the Wall Street community were never fulfilled. Under those circumstances I found it difficult not to openly voice my doubts and criticisms and that, in turn, obviously meant that Bill Foley kept me at a distance. The only reason why he did not fire me earlier was the fact that I was too much of a contributor to the bottom line in my purchasing role.

While I overstayed my welcome at Lesco and, for the first time in my career, found myself spinning my wheels, there were some benefits that came out of my reluctance to accept the fact that it was time to move on. Lesco acted first and fired me, on October 25, 2000 (our wedding anniversary), which earned me a year severance and the services of an outplacement office. I would have done without these benefits had I taken the initiative myself and resigned. The outplacement counselors prevailed over my natural impulse to get back into the battle right away and line up the next job. After all, I had not done much of anything for almost two years, other than going through the motions and I was chomping at the bit to get back in the race. But the outplacement office of Right & Associates convinced me to first take inventory of my life and make an assessment of what my strengths and weaknesses were and what I should be looking for in my next job.

I complied and benefitted greatly from checking in every day with the counselors at Right & Associates and completing their course for job seekers. For one thing, it brought me in contact with a number of great people who were in the same boat that I was in. Many of them were experienced business executives who, for one reason or another, had missed the boat and were now forced to look for a career change. I quickly figured out that I was not alone in experiencing a dead end with a company I once joined with so much belief and enthusiasm.

The main take-away from my outplacement time at Right & Associates—I stayed with them for a full three months—was that life is too short to settle in business for a position that is no good match for your competencies and ambitions. I learned that the question to ask yourself, if you are faced with having to make a career change, is: "What do I really like doing and what am I good at doing?" Once you have answered these questions, go out and find the position that satisfies both of these criteria. I firmly believe that, if you want to work in business, and if you are ambitious and want to succeed, you need to get very good at something that you enjoy doing every day. For me, that turned out to be acceptance of a leadership role in a business that drew on my expertise in the Green Industry and my passion for creating cooperation between companies that understood that on your own you can only get so far. I would have never had that opportunity if I had pursued and accepted the first job available after my dismissal from Lesco.

My forced sabbatical in outplacement afforded me the time and peace of mind to make some resolutions for the continuation of my career, the most important one of which was that I vowed that I would never again accept a position where I would be asked to execute orders, given by someone above me, whether or not I agreed with the content of such orders.

My patience, and the lessons I learned in outplacement, paid off in that it allowed me to gain the best job of my career at the end of its path. It put me in a position to exert leadership the way I wanted, without ever having to compromise my values and beliefs. It offered me the opportunity to set and stay my own course and avoid the mistakes of arrogant and disrespectful leadership that I had been subjected to at several stages in my career. Here, too, a great deal of Serendipity was involved.

———

Unbeknownst to me, a small group of independent distributors in the Green Industry—small regional competitors of Lesco—had created a cooperative for the purpose of combining purchase volume to gain better support and better pricing from the manufacturers of Green Industry products like fertilizer, grass seed and plant protection products. The Co-op had been formed and named—PrimeraTurf, Inc. —but the founders discovered that they were too busy running their own businesses to also be able to run the Co-op. Nor did they have the experience to build and manage a cooperative of many small companies operating in all corners of the nation.

PrimeraTurf had been incorporated in January of the year 2000, but was rudderless at the beginning of 2001 when I came out of out-placement. An attempt at outsourced management was failing and the founders were about ready to give up, when, at the Golf Course Show in Dallas in February of 2001, Bob Yarborough told one of the found-ers, Kip Connelly, that he knew just the right person to give them the leadership they needed for the Co-op. Bob Yarborough, who had been my mentor and wingman at Lesco, could have offered himself for that position, but he did not and mentioned my name and credentials to Kip Connelly. I was highly interested and intrigued. To me it looked like just the opportunity for which I had been waiting. However, it looked for a while as too little, too late. The board of directors of PrimeraTurf was ready to throw in the towel.

But the hired hand providing outsourced management services to PrimeraTurf, went ahead and hired me to take over the management of the Co-op, without asking for board approval. Delighted with the opportunity, I set up a meeting with the board of directors (founders) of PrimeraTurf at a rental office in Richmond, Virginia and presented my credentials and a plan for the business of PrimeraTurf. You cannot dream up the stuff that happened next.

The management company, which—unbeknownst to me—had hired me without consulting with the board, had taken out an unauthorized loan from the National Cooperative Bank, and had proceeded to pay itself for the management services provided to PrimeraTurf. The Co-op was deep in the red, had only a handful of members, no significant sup-plier support, and no revenues.

I remember like the day of yesterday that, after the meeting in Richmond, I came to my son Pim's house (he lived in Richmond) not knowing if I had a job or not. I was jubilant about the opportunity, but apprehensive that it might slip away from me. It would require another meeting with the board, this time at Washington's National Airport, to convince PrimeraTurf to take a chance on me and that would not have happened, had not Kip Connelly offered to bankroll me until PrimeraTurf had had a chance to sort out its finances.

We convinced the National Cooperative Bank to forgive PrimeraTurf the $100,000 loan, which had been taken out and approved by the bank without board authorization. And I went to work to recruit more members for the Co-op and arrange for supplier support from some of the prominent manufacturers in the industry. Within half a year, the Co-op had grown from seven member companies to eighteen member companies and our cash-flow was positive. On October 1, 2001, I was named CEO of PrimeraTurf and I had embarked on the last phase and the most rewarding leg of my career in management.

This was the first time in my career that I could call all the shots, as long as I was able to convince the PrimeraTurf board of directors to go along with what I set out to do. My job at PrimeraTurf was twofold: Grow and manage the membership and make them money by negotiating supply contracts and deals with the major suppliers to the Green Industry.

I served exactly ten years as CEO of PrimeraTurf and over that time period PrimeraTurf grew its membership to fifty companies—all independently owned—scattered all over the U.S. And PrimeraTurf grew its distributable income to almost $4 million, representing somewhere between 20-30 percent of the members' net income before taxes.

From day one at PrimeraTurf, my pre-occupation was to build a business that was rules-based and a company that was clearly structured and codified. I believe that corporate durability comes with structure, good staffing, and good process. We also wanted to be transparent in what we set out to achieve for our members (shareholders), our suppliers, and other stakeholders. We embraced the principles of John Carver's "Policy Governance" and wrote an elaborate Corporate Policy Book, including a Members' Code of Conduct. We also started publishing a monthly newsletter that provided commentary on the economic, political, and industry environment in which we were operating. This newsletter was offered by email to any subscriber who was a shareholder, supplier, or stakeholder in PrimeraTurf. Upon my retirement from PrimeraTurf I continued that commentary in my blog "Castnet Commentary".

I worked very hard to get the board of directors to set policy and design the major strategies for the business, but found time and again, that they were looking at me to suggest to them the strategic direction for the cooperative. In this, I found an ally and a lot of inspiration in Aileron, a Dayton, OH, based training institute[6] for small business owners. Explaining what Aileron is all about falls outside the scope of this book, but suffice it to say that I channeled first the board of directors and then as many PrimeraTurf members as I could through Aileron's flagship course: The Course for Presidents. This two-day course taught the owners of PrimeraTurf member companies all they needed to know about "Professional Management" as a tool to grow their business and, as Aileron proclaims, work "on" the business rather than just "in" the business[7]. Professional Management means, by my definition, *"Building and maintaining a purpose-driven organization of people who chase a dream, all aligned behind a clearly articulated mission, who are competent and accountable for their functions within the business and are thriving in the corporate culture established for the business by its owners."*

It was at Aileron that I hooked up with the most articulate and convincing teacher of sound business principles I have ever come in contact with: Dave Sullivan, who, at the time, was the business advisor in residence at Aileron. PrimeraTurf organized several membership functions at Aileron to make sure that the members gained insight in the services that Aileron could provide them, with the thought that you could lead the horse to the well, even if he was not always thirsty for learning.

Aileron puts a lot of credence in developing a vision and articulating the mission for a business and that is part of what we did, early on, in PrimeraTurf. We ended up with a vision for the business that said: *"PrimeraTurf exists so that its Members, Independent Turf & Ornamental Distributors, can compete on a level playing field with National and Regional distributors for access to goods and services at comparable net acquisition cost and thereby enhance the natural strengths they have in common.*

1. *Members are the distributors of choice for end-user customers who consider expertise, quality, service, and fair pricing as the primary factors in selecting a distributor.*

2. *Members are the preferred channel partner for manufacturers who want to be represented by distributors who provide expertise, quality service, and fair pricing to end-user customers.*

3. *All Members know and contribute to collective ownership as their competitive advantage."*

This vision or 'ends' statement combined the purpose for which the Co-op was created with the definition of the desired stage of the business PrimeraTurf would arrive at if it completely fulfilled its mission.

PrimeraTurf, in following my belief system, cared a lot about the way in which it would complete its mission and that meant that it had to be guided by a set of principles or values that were underwritten by any company seeking membership in PrimeraTurf.

The values that were underwritten by and for the Co-op were:

1. *Frugality: PrimeraTurf is committed to running its operation in the most cost effective manner.*

2. *Quality: PrimeraTurf is all about the best. The best distributors, the best suppliers, the best products, and the best service.*

3. *Integrity: PrimeraTurf will rather pass on a good deal than compromise its integrity.*

4. *Member Participation: Member participation is critical for keeping the cost down, for good governance, for assuring alignment between the membership and management, and for creativity and innovation.*

5. *Accountability: Involvement with PrimeraTurf implies being 100 percent accountable for the decisions made. Participation and accountability go hand-in-hand.*

PrimeraTurf also placed a lot of emphasis on the stewardship that was expected from its members. It adopted a code of conduct that stated (in part): *"Members are expected to be good citizens and a positive force in their local communities and good stewards of the natural environment entrusted in their care."*

Not surprisingly, here too, did I reach for those trusted and reliable tools of partnerships and strategic alliances. Many in the business world believe in the "Walmart Model" of squeezing your suppliers until there is nothing more to give and leveraging one against another. I do not subscribe to that belief and I have never applied that procurement model in any of the businesses for which I have been responsible. I love to make a good and a smart deal, but I have quickly found out that there is no durability in a supply relationship that does not evenly benefit both parties in the transaction. PrimeraTurf chose to develop close and durable relationships with those suppliers who were eager to work with the co-op and were willing to get their products to market through our chain of independent distributors.

The board asked me several times along the way how long I was willing to do the job and, in the beginning, I had not given that question much consideration. They first asked me when I was about six years into my tenure and I was having fun. Also, my job was far from done. We were still growing the business, both in terms of member count and in terms of revenue and we were still perfecting the model. But I was fifty-seven years old when I started with PrimeraTurf and I was slowly approaching the sixty-five year milepost. This is when the board and I agreed that I would complete a ten year term as CEO and that the board would start looking for my successor. The retirement date was set for September 30, 2011.

The ten year term was just right, for me and for the organization. At the end of the term I had accomplished everything I set out to do in PrimeraTurf, including a smooth and seamless management transition to John Gertz, who was the unanimous selection of the search committee and the board.

I had also come to the conclusion that the law of diminishing returns was in effect. Not sure if it had to do with my advancing age, but as I got to the end of my term, I no longer had a long list of things to do for PrimeraTurf, that were feasible given the resources we had available, and had not already been accomplished. The company did not need me to preside over a mature organization in a maintenance mode. It needed to find new avenues for growth and prosperity. It certainly had not arrived at its "desired state" as described in its vision statement.

This experience, of running out of steam, was not new for me. As I reflect on all I have done professionally over the years, I find that spending six to ten years on a job is probably as long as anyone should aspire to take on an assignment. Taking on a challenge, like I took on the challenge of turning PrimeraTurf from an empty shell into a pivotal player in the Green Industry, starts with a vision of what can be achieved, a passion to achieve it, and a belief that it can be achieved, sometimes against high odds. It gains momentum early on, because of the opportunity to pick the low hanging fruit first. Then it maintains momentum from building structure, framework, and process. And ultimately, it ramps up, based on results it delivers for stakeholders; and, it becomes somewhat self-propelling. At some point, as the leader of the effort, you have done everything you can think of to promote the cause and then it becomes a matter of either doing more of the same or handing it off to someone who looks at the situation with fresh eyes and comes at it with a different frame of reference. Handing off is, more often than not, the better solution, because doing more of the same is a path to a slow death and requires a different mind-set than building and growing a business.

The last thing I did for PrimeraTurf was a face-to-face visit with the principals of each of the member companies, conducting an exit interview with each of them. Given the geographical spread between members, from Southern Florida to Massachusetts and from Long Island to Oregon (and just about everything in between), that was a significant undertaking in time and travel expense. But it was worth it, because meaningful feedback was hard to come by from the members unless I was prepared to come get it. Some of the things I learned in the process are:

- In communication with small business owners there is no substitute for face to face contact. Emails, newsletters, memoranda and PowerPoint presentations find little penetration.
- It's all about "what have you done for me lately?"
- A co-operative for independent distributors is an oxymoron. Members want their cake and eat it too. They don't want to give up any part of their independence, but still want the benefits of belonging to a larger community.
- Each member is convinced that they have the secret to success and don't want to share it with their peers.
- Many of them are business owners because they could not work in a larger organization in anything but the leadership position.

The exit interviews allowed me to hand over to my successor, John Gertz, a status file on each PrimeraTurf member company with recommendations for action or attention.

———

My replacement was in place in June of 2011 and my retirement date had been set for September 30 of that year. It gave me time to hand over the business in an organized fashion and it also allowed me to make an inventory of what I had learned about doing business in the USA. I made my findings the centerpiece of my farewell presentation at the 2011 annual meeting of the Co-op, much like I had, in previous years, made up the balance on what had been achieved by, and for, PrimeraTurf. I ended up putting it as follows in my farewell address to the PrimeraTurf membership:

"I could write a book—and one day I may just do that—about the things that I have discovered about success in business, but let me try to condense my top critical success factors here for you to the bare essentials:

- *Don't burn any bridges*
- *Control the things you can control and don't waste any time worrying about things you can't control, including your competition*
- *Know what you're in business for (your mission) and make sure everyone around you knows it as well*
- *Make sure your organization runs on all cylinders*
- *Know who your stakeholders are and never deceive them*
- *You can't save your way to prosperity; entrepreneurship is all about putting capital at risk*
- *Know at all times if, when, and where you are making money (or not)*
- *Judge people by what they bring to the table, not by the hours they spend on the job*
- *There is always more than one way to skin the cat*
- *When in doubt say no before you say yes; you can always reverse a decision but you can't renege on a promise*
- *Simplify your life and your business; cut through the clutter and get rid of distractions."*

(Dave Sullivan, who had become somewhat of a mentor to me, would emphasize the last bullet point. He told me that his biggest lesson was that the more he let go, the more he was in control. He taught me to only hold on to the "make or break" issues.)

Following that presentation, PrimeraTurf threw me a fabulous retirement party in Minneapolis in July of 2011 and the board expressed its gratitude for ten years of service by buying for me and my three boys a fishing trip with Classic Alaska Charters[8], Captain Rob Scherer, for five days and four nights on the MS Saltery C, a 40-foot triple decker, out of Ketchikan, Alaska. We took the trip in June of 2012 and it was an unforgettable conclusion of my tenure with PrimeraTurf.

Christie had retired at the end of the school year in the summer of 2011 and now we were both without an immediate mission in life. We deferred dealing with the new reality by, immediately upon my retirement, embarking on a trip we always wanted to make but never had the time to take. The first six weeks of my retirement we traveled to and all over New Zealand, together by car and covering the two main islands of the island nation from top to bottom. We started in the snow, skiing the Southern Alps from a lodge in Methven on the South Island, and ended up on the beaches of the northern tip of the North Island, before flying back home out of Auckland.

We came home shortly before Thanksgiving and the holiday season gave us another reprieve from reality, but early in 2012 the big question could no longer be skirted: What now? For Christie that was not much of a question. She finally had her hands free to spend time with her children and grandchildren. While three of the grandchildren were at some considerable distance in Richmond, VA the other three were living nearby in the Western suburbs of Cleveland and—with both parents working—are always in the picture. And the count grew from six to eight grandchildren (seven girls and one boy) and still counting. Christie also volunteered to substitute at the school from which she had retired so that, when all of that was added to keeping the home, she had no need for more purpose in life.

But I quickly found out that I was not ready for retired life. If I could not be fishing the surf in low country Carolina, or explore the wildernesses of the world, I did not really know what to do with my time. Reading and learning remains a passion, but not for every hour of every day. I set up an S-Corp, which I named Castnet Corp. in reference to my favorite beach activity, in order to be able to do some business consulting, with the PrimeraTurf member companies as primary target clients. My time at the helm at PrimeraTurf had given me ample evidence that many of the PrimeraTurf members had a need for coaching and management support and my exposure to Aileron had given me the right platform from which to offer my services. Dave Sullivan had planted the thought in my mind that I should not be thinking about retiring "from" but retiring "to" and that is what I did.

My overarching motivation was that I wanted to find a way to deploy the depth and scope of my accumulated business savvy for the benefit of business owners who were eager to listen and to learn. Like Aileron and Clay Mathile, its founder, I believe in capitalism and in the value of small, privately held business, as engines of growth for the U.S. economy and for gainful employment. Since small business owners are notoriously frugal, other than when spending money on their toys, calls for my consulting support were coming in few and far between and I chose to dispense my insights and beliefs by putting them in writing—as I had done for many years in the PrimeraTurf monthly newsletter—and publishing them in Green Industry magazines, on my blog "Castnet Commentary"[9] and on the Aileron blog.

The writing of these columns planted the seed for the writing of this book, which is very much about sharing my experiences, in life and in business, as a first generation immigrant to the USA with anyone who can benefit from them. Why would anyone want to reinvent the wheel and why would anyone not want to learn from the mistakes made by the ones who went before you? Dave Sullivan would tell you: "*The future has already been created somewhere – let's go find it and save time and resources.*"

Having arrived at the end of the road of active business participation, I can now say with some certainty that, at least from a business perspective, the decision to make America our home panned out as expected. From the twenty-four years I worked in the USA up to my retirement in 2011 (not counting the three year intermission in Switzerland and England), I worked sixteen years as the leader of a business and eight years as a senior executive for a publicly owned corporation. The time I was given at the end to lead an organization as chief executive has fulfilled my ambitions and expectations of working life in America.

It has also given me the opportunity to—once and for all—vindicate my decision, made at eighteen years of age, to seek a career in business and then have the hutzpah to practice it in a new country. I find business in America generally in good shape, much better than the public sector. Small, privately owned business is indeed a formidable engine of innovation and economic growth. It is also a powerful path to personal wealth creation. To be successful it just has to follow a few simple, basic, rules. The ingredients for success in business are easily identifiable (in no particular order):

- A strong balance sheet
- A lean, knowledgeable, and motivated organization, top to bottom
- A fanatic desire to be in business, combined with a clear sense of direction
- A fanatic dedication to the success and satisfaction of the customer
- A capacity to keep business simple and predictable
- Alignment with the best supply chain partners in the business
- Forward thinking ownership and executive leadership
- The ability to trust yourself, your organization, and your key people

The nation as such could benefit from adopting the same critical success factors in the (political) management of its affairs. It could also benefit from applying some serious creative destruction here and there. We will address this in better detail in the next Section of this book, but I will stipulate here that the nation would be much better off if it were run more like a business conforming to these simple rules. So, unequivocally, I have, from a business perspective, no regrets about coming to America.

———

Life is full of surprises; and who knows what kind of a career I would have made if I had not left the European continent? If I look, though, at the people with whom I worked in the years before I parted ways with NSM, (and who all stayed put to enjoy the job security of a large successful and growing business that Norsk Hydro was), I have to rate chances high that I, too, would have succumbed to the comfort of staying in place. Large corporations are awfully good at handcuffing the people they want to keep with deferred compensation and retirement schemes that, after a certain tenure, make it virtually impossible to leave before retirement eligibility.

I was no more nor less talented than most of my peers, and I would have had to acquiesce in the reality of working in a Norwegian company where the top roles were always reserved for Norwegians. It would have deprived me of the opportunity to lead a business and give shape to a business that was not there before.

CHAPTER 3

THE IMMIGRANT EXPERIENCE

America has been good to us. Like any other family, we have had our ups and downs, but it would be foolish to think that we would have escaped from any downs if we had stayed on the other side of the Atlantic. Most of our downs have been of a financial nature or been a direct result of financial challenges we have encountered along the way. Most of them have been self-inflicted. It is clear that having grown up in and with the welfare state in the Netherlands, I have never fully understood the difference in personal financial management required under the American system and adjusted for it; however, I learned the hard way. The burdens on members of the American middle class, to which we definitely belong, are phenomenal (and they have only increased over time).

For families with four children, who all have the talent and the ambition to go to college, just the burden of tuition, living, and travel expenses is enormous relative to middle class after tax income. For us, like for most people, that burden hit at the same time as the need to save for retirement. If we had a chance to do it all over again, we would live our lives differently and control our expenses much better than we did.

In America, I have worked all of my life for companies who paid a fair salary, but held out the promise of significant incentive compensation at the end of the year. Sometimes these promises were fulfilled, but in many years they were not.

Very confident in my own capacity to perform and achieve my own goals and the expectations for my area of responsibility, I kept falling into the trap of counting my chickens before they had hatched, forgetting that, in most instances, it was overall corporate performance that determined if there was a year-end pay-out or not. The combination of systematic overestimating my earnings capacity and underestimating the demands of our lifestyle and our parental obligations, put us in a bind that ultimately led us to file for Chapter 13 bankruptcy, which has cast a long shadow over our life and our financial future in this country. I can say with a high degree of confidence that this would not have happened to us in Europe. For sure, at the bottom of our problem was the lack of proper financial planning and responsible financial management, but this weakness was exploited by all the banks and other institutions that kept offering us and our college going children credit, mostly in the form of credit cards, without any regard to our capacity to keep these accounts current. We complain—with good reason—about the fact that, since the start of the 2008 recession, credit has been so restricted that it has become hard to operate—much less grow—a business with high working capital requirements. And we rightly complain that this condition has prolonged the agony of the recession and impeded the economic recovery. But we easily forget that this same recession was brought about by indiscriminate credit extension, mostly for home mortgages and home equity loans, without any serious evaluation of the borrowers' financial conditions. American consumers need an effective regulatory institution to protect them from abusive practices in the lending business. Too much credit is extended to people who cannot handle it. It is deliberately and maliciously extended with the full expectation that the debtors will get in arrears and in default. Then they will get hit by penalties and finance charges at usury rates. It has happened in the mortgage field, it has happened in the credit card field and now it is happening, in a very threatening way, in the student loan field. It happened to us and we accepted full responsibility for the mess we had created for ourselves.

With the help of the court-appointed trustee and the bankruptcy judge, we created a plan by which all of our creditors got repaid in full over five years. The important benefit we derived from declaring Chapter 13 is that it stopped the clock on interest, finance charges, and penalties. Without the Chapter 13 protection, we would have continued to accrue interest, finance charges, and penalties over the amount of our debt and the burden would have become insurmountable. Also, through Chapter 13, we were able to protect the equity in the house we had built and the retirement funds in our IRA and 401K.

There is little doubt that this painful personal experience has, forever, colored my view on getting in debt, including my view on the reckless disregard for good management the nation has displayed in ratcheting up the national debt over the last couple of decades.

———

It is impossible to pinpoint how our personal lives would have developed differently if we had not decided to make America our home. We can look at the lives of our many siblings, who all stayed behind in the Netherlands, and the lives of our Dutch friends and it does not give us a conclusive answer on who is better off. Our siblings and their children have had no trouble to stay gainfully employed in the Netherlands and I have no reason to believe that our children would have fared any less in that respect, had we stayed in Europe. Clearly, the communist threat that loomed large in the 1980s has completely evaporated. But Holland has become very crowded and it struggles with the effects of consumerism much like we do here.

It also has an immigration problem in that it finds that the integration of waves of "guest workers" from Turkey and North Africa, mostly

Muslim, followed by influx from Poland and the Balkan countries, is not as successful as the assimilation of earlier waves of immigrants. Tolerance appears to have also waned in the place where it was born!

The Netherlands has paid a price for having been a colonial power until shortly after World War II, in that it had to offer citizenship to residents of its colonies, Indonesia, New Guinea, the Dutch Antilles, and Suriname before these nations became independent. That has led to waves of immigrants who were poorly prepared for life in the cold and dampness of the Low Countries and would never have come if it was not for Holland's colonial past and the loyalties developed at that time in its history. As a result, the Dutch population is a lot less homogeneous today than it was at the time I grew up there.

Since our decision to make America our home, we have moved five times to different country destinations (and a few more times locally), almost certainly more than we would have done if I had stayed with NSM, even though, under Norsk Hydro ownership, NSM became part of a multinational operation with offices in Oslo, Brussels, Moscow, Hong Kong, Singapore, Qatar, and the U.S. and I would probably have been asked to spend time at some of them. Moving, as we did, from Tampa to Philadelphia, to Geneva, Switzerland, to London, England, back to Tampa and, ultimately, to Cleveland we never settled anywhere long enough to put our roots down and that has undoubtedly cost us in some respects, financially and socially. Financially, it cost us because we lost more than we gained in the multiple times of buying and selling a new residence. And, because we never had an opportunity to build much equity by seeing the value of our property appreciate over an extended period of time.

Socially, because we uprooted ourselves again by the time we had settled in somewhere and begun to make friends. Cleveland, OH has become our last destination, because that is where my career path brought me. And there, we now have lived longer (twenty-two years) than any place else, without any intent to move again. But arriving here in our middle age, we found that it was not as easy as it was before to make new friends. And some of the best friends we made left the area as their careers changed.

One of the motivations behind our decision to "try out" America the first time around, in 1976, was that the demands from our social- and family-life had become so strong that it began to impinge on my priority of making a career. All of my life I felt that, because I did not come from a business environment and had made a late decision to go in that direction, I had to prove myself. One of the ways in which I did so was by making sure that my job came first and that I never ran out of time to attend to my business obligations. The first victims of that attitude were our social contacts.

Many were held at arm's length, although Christie and the kids worked very hard and successfully on making up for my shortcomings. But now, with the benefit of hindsight, it is easy to conclude that my single-minded focus on my job also short changed my wife and my children. The more so, because for most of the time that the children were living with us, I was frequently traveling overseas for long periods of time. Like many American males, I saw it as my first obligation to provide for my family and in our case that meant providing at a level that kept up with the Joneses'.

To this day, this very American concept of "keeping up with the Joneses' ", has haunted me. The nature of my business, as an executive for a distribution business, has brought us in contact with many people who owned their own businesses or were top executives for companies with which I did business. As I got to look inside these peoples' lives, I discovered a world of material wealth and comfort that I could only dream about. What I saw was, in most cases but not always, wealth that had accumulated over generations and that displayed itself in large mansions, vacation homes, private education, boats, cars and lavish lifestyle spending. Thankfully, most of these displays were so far out of my reach, that I did not even try to keep up. But, surely, it caused us to put our best foot forward when it was our turn to reciprocate the hospitality received in these quarters. In that sense, our lives in America developed differently from what they would have been on the other side of the ocean, where the pressure to keep up with the Joneses' is not felt the same way.

The biggest difference our choice for America made in our personal lives was the fact that we chose to have a second set of children, born in America. We were blessed with a girl and a boy early in our marriage and the thought of possibly having more children had not crossed our minds until we were well settled in the house we bought from Ben Geradts in Eastchester, N.Y., where Christie was a full time home-maker with the help of an au-pair. We were living the expatriate life with lots of outdoor space, lots of sunshine, and a bright future. We were looking ahead to the time that Nienke and Pim would be leaving for college and we asked ourselves if we were ready to become empty-nesters so soon. And the unanimous answer was "no". Having seen Nienke and Pim grow up together, with only a year and a half between them, we also knew that we would not have a third child stay unaccompanied. Thomas was born in Tampa in January of 1981 and Michael followed in March of 1983. It is most unlikely that these two would have ever seen the light of day if we had stayed in Europe.

As much as our son Pim questioned what the merit was in having to share everything, space, time, wealth, with two more children, I will say that our personal lives have been enriched by doing the parenting thing twice. The second time with a lot of help from Nienke, who, other than her brother, saw nothing but fun in having two little brothers around and quickly became a competent and devoted surrogate mother before she became a mother herself.

While living in America was conducive to our family expansion, it paradoxically meant that I was not as involved in the upbringing of our children as I might have been, had we stayed in Europe. I missed numerous birthdays, games, and performances and other functions for which children expect their parents to show up. In fact, I probably missed more than I attended and I'm not too happy about that now. I never coached any of my children in soccer, baseball, swimming, tennis, or anything else and that cannot be entirely explained away by the fact that I was not very talented in any of these activities myself. I cannot be sure that I would have set priorities differently in Europe—my experience in Switzerland and England puts that in doubt—but I definitely would have had more free time, including vacation time, there than I ended up having in the USA. The mindset is very different when it comes to finding the right balance between work and family. No excuse, but it is an explanation. There are plenty of fathers in the USA who have demanding jobs that make it hard to free up time for family commitments, but they find a way to coach a baseball or a basketball team and they certainly find time to attend school graduations and ceremonies. I doubt that I would have lost my job or got paid less if I had set my priorities differently. My children all show me how that can be done.

———

Nevertheless, there is little room or reason for regrets. Our life's experience is somewhat unique, at least by American standards, in that it has exposed our family to life in many different countries and cultures. Particularly our two older children, Nienke and Pim, will tell you that they feel like citizens of the world and no stranger on either side of the Atlantic.

There is no doubt that having made the decision, against all odds, first to make a career in business and later to make that career in America, I have put pressure on myself to vindicate those decisions all the time and at all costs. I was not about to fail in what I set out to do. And I have found that I am not the quickest wit around and need a lot of time to think things through before I do or say anything. I am fond of Jorge Luis Borges' saying *"Don't talk unless you can improve the silence."*

One resource we all have in the same measure is time in a day. I am not at ease unless I have freed up the time it takes for me to get my work done and plan for the next step. I get flustered when there is too much demand put on my time from different angles. I know how to stay the course but am not very adept in multi-tasking.

This combination of stubborn determination and a slow, but methodical, approach to going about my business has exacted a price in a less than desirable involvement in family life and the upbringing of our children. It did not help that my job in the international trading business meant that I was traveling much of my time and traveling far away and for extended periods of time. Under those circumstances, parenting was done solely by Christie, who had given up her career in education when Nienke was born and had chosen to remain a home-maker after our move to the USA. She was so good at it, and had all the time to dedicate to raising children, that it took the pressure off me and provided me with a free pass to mind my business.

This aspect of my life, struggling to find an optimal work/life balance, almost certainly would have developed differently if we had never pursued our American dream and settled for life in the old country.

What this boils down to is that, from a personal, family, perspective our move to America has been a mixed bag. It has made us miss out on the development of life-long friendships that come with shared experiences starting with school life, family building, church, and work. We have found out, to our detriment, how hard it is to maintain meaningful friendships from a distance. Most all of the friendships that we have nevertheless been blessed with, were either coming from my work connections, the neighborhoods we were living in, or the friendships our kids developed. And most of them have been of passing significance as times and circumstances changed. If we are honest with ourselves, we have to conclude that, while we have many acquaintances and maintain communication with a number of people we have come to know and appreciate along the road, we have maybe only one couple that we are friends with in the deepest and truest sense of the word: Nancy and Ralph Rocco, the parents of Adam Rocco who is best friends with our youngest son, Michael.

They lived in the same neighborhood in Westlake, Ohio, where we lived for five years during my tenure with Lesco and our friendship has easily survived our later move to North Ridgeville. For the better part of twenty years we have shared triumphs and tragedies with the Rocco's and there is no other couple that we spend more time with, socially. It helps that both Ralph and Christie are great cooks and we all enjoy good food and great wine. And we share our wedding anniversary date, the twenty-fifth of October.

While we have reasons to believe that our personal lives might have been richer, socially, if we had stayed on the other side of the Atlantic, if that is true at all, it only is true for Christie and me. Our children have no such handicap, having spent a much larger part of their lives in America and being much less nomadic in their own careers than we have been. And, I can just hear Dave Sullivan warn me to avoid hindsight as much as humanly possible. He told me that it is too often an audit of missed opportunities and always irrelevant (since it is water under the bridge).

So, on balance, as Terry Tempest Williams has warned us: *"It's impossible not to look back and wonder what would have happened if you had had the wit, or guts, or luck to go in some other direction."*

Goal achieved: Cleveland Jagers on U.S. soil. From left: Patrick, Nienke, Thomas, Reagan, McKenzie, Andrea, Christie, Abby, Frans, Emma, Kelsey, Liam, Michael (with Buc and Tina). Dressed to support the Dutch National Soccer team in the 2014 World Cup in Brazil.

The Richmond, Virginia Jagers, dressed to support Holland in the 2014 World Cup Soccer: From the left Molly, Robin, Kaelie, Pim, and Payton.

CHAPTER 4

IS AMERICA STILL EXCEPTIONAL?

"We can't solve problems by using the same kind of thinking we used when we created them." (Albert Einstein)

"*Y*ou only live twice" is what James Bond aficionados were told in 1967, when the fifth movie in the 007 series came out. It feels that way to me. It feels as if I'm now living my second life, very different from the life I was experiencing in the early 1980s, when we picked America over Europe as a place for permanent residence. Of course it may just be my age that is creeping up on me, but the fact is that I had much higher expectations at the start of our immigration process than what was delivered in actuality. In the early 80s, I was riding two waves of optimism: The optimism of the young professional who is just hitting his prime and is ready to conquer the world and the general optimism that Ronald Reagan inspired after almost two decades of malaise in America, which started

inertia and complexity of the Pentagon to internal conflicts within the executive branch, the partisan abyss in Congress on every issue from budgets to wars, the single-minded parochial self-interest of so many individual members of Congress, and the magnetic pull exercised by the White House and the National Security Staff, especially in the Obama administration, to bring everything under their control and micromanagement, all made every issue a source of conflict and stress – far more so than when I had been in government before, including as the Director of Central Intelligence. I was more than happy to fight these fights, especially on behalf of the troops and the success of their mission; at times, I relished the prospect. But over time, the broad dysfunction in Washington wore me down, especially as I tried to maintain a public posture of nonpartisan calm, reason and conciliation." The next Section of this book will address ways in which this this dysfunction, and the logjam it has created, can be broken.

SECTION III

CREATIVE DESTRUCTION

What can and should change in America if it wants to stay on top of the world in the twenty-first century? Suggestions from a first generation immigrant.

"It always seems impossible until it's done." (Nelson Mandela)

CHAPTER 1

THE ROOT OF THE PROBLEM

American business has been exceptionally successful in my lifetime, in part because it has continually mustered the courage to apply the principle of creative destruction. Creative destruction in business refers to the practice of destroying the economic viability of a product by creating a better solution, often before the existing product is completely obsolete. This happens all the time in business—at least at companies that are at the leading edge, of which America has more than its share—and it is one of the main reasons why investing in business is an inherently risky business. Classical examples of creative destruction in business are the replacement of horse driven buggies by automobiles, of propeller aircraft by jet engine aircraft, slide-projectors and overhead projectors by PowerPoint, and video rental by Netflix.

Often the creative destruction is perpetrated by the competition. It is the reason why Polaroid, Telex, and Kodak are either a thing of the past or only a shadow of their glorious past stature. But it is not unusual at all for a company to make its own product obsolete by launching an improved version. Apple is doing it all the time with its iPhone and iPad and so is Intel with its chips and micro-processors.

The benefit of creative destruction from a macro-economic perspective is that it keeps the economy fresh and competitive. It attracts creative talent and risk takers to business and it stimulates innovation. It also stimulates consumption, driven by human desire to have access to the latest and the greatest.

Government generally does not work that way, unless there is a revolution. Without a revolution, change in government—in terms of laws, regulations and policy—is almost always gradual and incremental, if it takes place at all.

Even with a change in the balance of power between the two parties in the American political system, changes in government policy and action come only slowly and gradually. This is mostly the result of the carefully crafted balance of power between the branches of government, the prevalence of a divided government in terms of which party holds the White House, the House of Representatives and the Senate, and the stabilizing force (call it inertia) of the bureaucracy.

A further, and possibly more relevant, difference between the embrace and implementation of change in business and government is the inevitable need for compromise in politics. In business, if a company finds a better solution for the consumer, there is nothing to stop it as long as it has the resources to develop and market that solution. In government, if the president of the United States wants to change the government policy on anything, be it immigration or gun control, he is constrained by countervailing forces in congress, the public opinion, pressure from interest groups, and political considerations (re-election). Given this reality can we really be surprised that the Beltway always settles for suboptimal solutions? The answer—of course—is no! Decision making in Washington is so much influenced by money, ideology, and pressure groups that straight thinking and doing the right thing are hard to come by. The reason for not reaching for the stars in government, but settling for suboptimal solutions, is not only found in the money influence and the pressure groups. It is the direct result of our political polarization and the fact that, if legislative compromises are found at all, they are based on the lowest common denominator, the politically feasible rather than the strategically desirable.

A legislative compromise is only good when it combines the best elements of what one party wants with the best elements of what the other party wants. What we are normally getting, if not stalemate, is a heavily compromised, watered down, version of what the political majority originally proposed.

Finally, legislation in America is, more often than not, done reactively rather than proactively. Congress typically does not jump into action until it has stared disaster in the face. That was true after 9/11, it was true after the bank crisis in 2008, and it was true after the massacre at Newtown. And then, in a hurry to be seen doing something, congress typically addresses symptoms of the problem rather than the causes for the problem.

If American business acted the way the American government acts (or demurs), it would face one bankruptcy after another and the American economy would be left in the dust by other, more enterprising, systems.

In the preceding Section of this book, I enumerated the imperfections that the American system has fostered and that should be addressed by a responsible government. Among them, unfortunately, is the imperfection embedded in the American political system. This system, as it operates today, shows symptoms of dysfunction. And it is this system that has to deliver the solutions to the problems the nation is facing. It has not demonstrated the capacity to rise above partisan bickering so that it can effectively address the nation's challenges and chart a course for a future for America on top of the world. I will argue that the dysfunction in the American political system impedes finding solutions for any of the other challenges, which, with the exception of inequality, are eminently solvable for a nation with the resources that America has at its disposal.

This suggests that all popular energy should go into an overhaul of our political system: Without a dramatic change in the rules of the game on the political side, none of the other, lesser, problems will get adequately addressed and overcome.

I am not alone in that assessment. Extreme dissatisfaction with the way our government, and particularly congress, operates shows up in poll after poll, on cable TV, and the opinion pages of our newspapers. Nicolas Berggruen and Nathan Gardels have written a book about this, titled *"Intelligent Governance for the 21st Century"*. In the book, the authors are searching for an effective model for governance in a hybrid between democracy and meritocracy. They correctly state[23] that *"For America, democracy is an end in itself."* And they continue that, in contrast, *"In the post-ideological pragmatism proposed by Chinese thinkers such as Eric X Li or Zhang Weiwei, democracy is only a means to the end of good governance."* *"If it helps deliver results, great. If not, who needs it?"*

I am not sure that we should seriously consider throwing the baby out with the bath water. More practically, I see no way, without giving up on the basic tenets of our Constitution, in other words without a second American Revolution, to effectively change the structure of public governance in America. As I will explain later in this book, I do not believe that a structural change is needed to give government the tools it needs to effectively deal with the challenges the nation faces.

What it will take is a popular consensus that "enough is enough" and that the voting public will want to see real results for the high price it pays for being democratically governed. Moises Naim was for over a decade Editor-in-Chief of Foreign Policy Magazine. In a new book titled *"The End of Power"*[24] he arrives at the same conclusion that I put forward in this book: That disruptive innovation has not arrived in politics, government and political participation. But, he says, it will. What is needed in Naim's view is nothing less than restoring trust, reinventing political parties, finding new ways in which average citizens can meaningfully participate in the political process, creating new mechanisms of effective governance, limiting the worst impacts of checks and balances while averting excessive concentrations of unaccountable power, and enhancing the capacity of nation-states to work together. No small task.

CHAPTER 2

TOLERANCE

U nfortunately, the American public is as divided and polarized as the two parties that currently control the political scene. In that sense it may be reaping exactly what it is sowing. The public is divided in watchers of Fox News and MSNBC and these networks work very hard and effectively on keeping us apart. What is getting eliminated from the American psyche is tolerance for the opposing point of view. We are quickly losing our capability to differ of opinion about politics and ideology without giving up on the respect we owe to our fellow citizens for their perspectives. Watching the 2008 and 2012 presidential election campaigns, it was striking how vitriolic the hate of the (extreme) left had become for the person and presidency of George W. Bush. And now that the shoe is on the other foot, it is again alarming to sense the depth of the hatred and despise the (extreme) right has for the person and presidency of Barack Obama. Under the guise of the First Amendment rights, we allow the media to broadcast lies, half-truths, and innuendo for the sole purpose of getting people riled up against "the other side". It is deeply distressing to me to see how we are losing the capacity to agree to disagree without allowing the disagreement to stop all further civil discourse. This may be happening on the other side of the Atlantic as well. I cannot gauge that because I do not live there anymore nor am I a frequent visitor of my home country.

But in my eyes, America had become the torch bearer for tolerance when it erected the torch bearing Statue of Liberty it was given by an admiring French nation. And to me, tolerance is an essential ingredient of the leadership of nations.

Allan Bikk pointed out in his 2007 presentation to the NEH (National Endowment for the Humanities) Seminar[25]: "*The Dutch imagine their Golden Age as not only one of economic prosperity and intellectual-scientific innovation but also as one in which their nation achieved an almost impossible civility between people of disparate faith and ideologies.*"

The Dutch had good pragmatic reasons to make that link between economic prosperity and tolerance between people of differing beliefs and ideologies. That same link drives the pursuit of free trade and open borders as a tool for global economic growth.

Bikk argues that is was indeed pragmatism that overcame bias and intolerance in the Golden Age of the Dutch Republic. Largely Calvinist—a religion not known for its tolerance—the Dutch came to the conclusion that their interests in trade, exploration, and science were incompatible with their innate desire to keep other religions suppressed and at bay. They saw that intolerance, discrimination, prejudice, and persecution would stand in the way of their personal prosperity and the nation's well-being. As Bikk says: Consider the expression "it's just business."

It was this pragmatism that set the Dutch Republic apart from the other major powers of the time: Spain, Portugal, England and France. It explains why so many people, mostly notably religious and political exiles or refugees, would seek shelter in the Netherlands.

It is easy to paint too idealized a picture of Dutch tolerance in the Golden Age. A collection of essays published by the Cambridge Press in 2002 under the title "*Calvinism and Religious Toleration in the Dutch Golden Age*"[26] makes that abundantly clear. Tolerance, then and now, is best judged on a relative, comparative, scale. The Dutch Republic of the seventeenth century was highly decentralized, leaving provinces and towns a lot of leeway to determine the treatment of people who were not members of the State-sanctioned Calvinist church. The one common denominator within these many jurisdictions was, however, that in the Dutch Republic one would not be persecuted for one's belief and that was a big deal in Europe at that time. At the same time people were well advised (and generally smart enough) not to flaunt their "deviant" beliefs too much in the open. There was a "don't ask, don't tell" kind of attitude in the Netherlands, long before it became policy in America.

In his previously cited 2007 presentation to the NEH, Bikk compares the contemporary Dutch and American notions of tolerance and he posits: "*The Netherlands today is seen as one of the most liberal societies on earth, one ready to accept a broad spectrum of human interaction, of virtue and vice. Dutch people take considerable pride in their historical legacy of tolerance and see it as evidence of a noble and progressive civilization. In contrast, that other Protestant civilization, the United States, seems hostile and Puritan, far too ready to pass judgment, far too ready to sacrifice good common sense for some moral high ground.*" I note that, even if this was true in 2007, tolerance for the norms and behaviors of immigrants from other cultures has diminished in the Netherlands under influence of the rise of xenophobic right wing political agitation.

Separation breeds intolerance. And, in spite of all the effort put into the civil rights movement in the United States, there is far too much separation in American society today; separation and polarization. The unfortunate people of Murray's Fishtown live light years away from the fortunate people of Belmont. Democrats are seated in opposite aisles from Republicans in Congress and people get their "news" either from the Fox News network or from MSNBC. And they get that news relentlessly, endlessly rehashed and regurgitated, 24 hours a day. We color the map of the United States with blue states and red states. Debate in Congress has degenerated to grandstanding in front of the C-Span cameras by senators and congressmen from both sides of the aisle—more often than not in a near empty chamber—kowtowing the party line on whatever issue is brought forward by the majority leader.

I am not sure if the fault is more with the public or with the government. In many ways the public gets the government it deserves. With the two-party system we have accepted the rule that one of the two parties calls the shots, at least until the next election. Other than in the parliamentary system in the Netherlands, there is no culture and history of coalition building in America. To get elected here, candidates and their campaigns are all focused on how they separate themselves from their opponents rather than being focused on offering a political agenda that can move the nation forward.

It does not help that in America social issues like abortion and gay marriage have infiltrated, if not hijacked, the political agenda. Nowhere is intolerance more in evidence than between the two sides on the debate on these highly charged social wedge issues.

All of the bickering, the intolerance, the polarization, and the push away from finding common ground are an offense to intellectual honesty and human dignity. It is also an impediment to the prosperity of the nation going forward. This book, and particularly this Section, is a plea for more common sense and less ideology. It is a plea for a victory of tolerance over intolerance, if only on pragmatic grounds. That served the Dutch Republic well in the seventeenth century and it will serve America well in the twenty-first century.

These thoughts on creative destruction and tolerance are merely the preamble to the heart of the matter. In the following chapters, I will go one-by-one through each of the challenges facing America that I have identified in Section II. And in each instance, I will offer suggestions for steps that could be taken and policies that could be enacted to overcome the challenge. We have too many armchair critics in this country. It is so easy to find fault with what is happening in America today, but it is a whole different challenge to come up with practical steps that can be taken to put America back on course of Exceptionalism. In my approach to solving the problems, I do not want to be held back by staying within the confines of the existing governance model. I see little hope that America can overcome its challenges without some degree of creative destruction applied to the governance model and the political system it has spawned. Whether that is feasible is a different matter. Change does not come easy and, more often than not, only when the pain of staying with the status quo exceeds the pain inflicted by the change process.

I will save addressing inequality and our political system for last, because they are of a different nature, a higher level of complexity, and a higher order than the other challenges, which should be fairly easily solved if the right political will and constellation is available.

I fear that inequality and a failing political system are intransigent and will take an enormous effort, a lot of patience and perseverance, and a long time to overcome. But we can't give up hope. After all, the nation has overcome more formidable obstacles in its short history. And, as Nelson Mandela showed us: *"It always seems impossible until it's done."*

———

Let me just say in advance, about inequality, that the rising inequality and the permanency, stubbornness, of the inequality in American society we experience today may very well be caused directly by the difference between the effectiveness of American business and the ineffectiveness of American government. The success of American business disproportionally benefits the upper quintile of American society, while the bottom quintile is largely dependent on an ineffective government to keep them from falling through the social safety net.

Wealth and success in America is almost exclusively created in business, where it is very visible, even ostentatious in many instances. I believe that the success of American business is creating expectations in the population at large that the government, in its current constellation and under existing rules of engagement, is not meeting. American business is ruthlessly results-oriented. And it achieves impressive outcomes in the process. American government is politically-oriented. It will underachieve in comparison with American business if it cannot break through the paralysis caused by the ideological divide between the left and the right and mobilize all of the nation behind a forward looking strategy that aims at preserving America's status as the global leader for good.

CHAPTER 3

UNEMPLOYMENT

The United States government works with very inadequate data about the real employment situation in the country. What is missing is a reliable data-base that measures the number of people that are employed in some capacity. All we have now is a metric called the "Employment-Population Ratio", which gets published monthly by the Bureau of Labor Statistics. This statistic measures the proportion of the civilian non-institutional population aged sixteen years and over that is employed. But what about the non-civilian population? And what about the institutional population (whatever that may be)?

Government cannot do its job if it does not know who is working and who is not; and, of the people who are not working, it needs to know the reason why not (too young, too old, full-time student, disabled, unemployed, retired, living off established wealth, etc.) How can the government craft effective policy if it has to guess at who is working and who is not and for what reason?

America will have to put new metrics in place that give it the information it needs to refurbish its employment policy.

My second suggestion is certain to be more controversial. But, I am intimately convinced that the nation's unfulfilled needs are so large and wide-spread that no able body, who applies for a hand-out from the government, should receive support without offering a public service in return. I cannot reconcile the fact that the government supports so many people (on unemployment, on disability, on welfare, in prison) who are not contributing to a productive effort with the many unmet or partially-met needs of the nation. We should be thinking of the government acting like a giant temporary agency in putting recipients of government safety net payments to work, even if the work needs to be created for them by the government. What I am thinking about is infrastructure projects, National Parks maintenance[27], staffing of homeless shelters, food-banks and soup-kitchens; but also providing government assistance in elderly care, medical research, data-entering and processing, education, rehabilitation, and environmental projects for which, otherwise, there would be no funding. Even foreign aid should be considered in this context. Are we living in a perfect world? Far from it, and that means that there is a lot to do. We should mobilize the disengaged to help getting it done.

In Section II of this book I have pointed out that the unemployment statistic put out monthly by the Bureau of Labor Statistics gives a false and significantly understated picture of the level of unemployment in the USA and I have argued that probably as high as 18 percent of the labor force is involuntarily disengaged from the labor process. A high and persistent level of unemployment is a sign of structural problems in an economy. Unemployment in the USA is in large part due to a mismatch, between the skills and competencies required for todays' jobs and the skills and competencies available in the labor force. At any time there are likely to be more job openings in our economy than there are job seekers, but the available job seekers, including youngsters looking for their first jobs, don't have the training or expertise required for the jobs that need to be filled. Our economy is moving fast in some respects. The pace of change has been accelerating significantly over my lifetime and even more so in the last two decades with the advances in computer technology in almost all work places. At the same time, the economy has been slow to condition the work force and individuals for the requirements of the jobs for tomorrow. The system is failing us. It was not long ago that people working for a company could have a reasonable expectation that they could finish their careers there. That is clearly no longer the case. But nothing in the system has been arranged to keep workers up to speed with the changing job requirements.

Neither companies nor the government underwrite a process of continuing education for anything more than a handful of fast track executives. Today, retooling and re-schooling waits until unemployment has hit and then it is only sporadically available and used. How much better off would we be if continuing education were to be widely available to workers who are employed but are facing changing and increasing job requirements? Isn't there a compelling argument for making continuing education obligatory for all Americans of working age?

Many professions require recertification on a regular basis to make sure that the public can have confidence in professional designations like CPA, CFP, PE, PHR, CPM etc. Shouldn't continuing education be part of everyone's life, but particularly for business employees and executives? The world moves too fast to allow for sufficiency of learning on the job. Life-long learning has become a matter of necessity.

The world has changed and America's position in the world has changed with it. America has insufficiently adjusted for the demands imposed on its people by the globalization that has taken place over the time of my residency in the United States. The result is that American Exceptionalism is further out of reach than it appeared to be in the early eighties, at least from an employment perspective.

CHAPTER 4

HEALTHCARE

In this chapter, I will address healthcare in the broadest possible sense. I suggest that a nation should be concerned with the living conditions inside its borders in a comparative sense, comparing itself with other nations in its realm. What is exceptional about living in the most powerful nation in the world if its population, or any segment of it, has a lower life expectancy and a lesser quality of life than the population of other developed nations? Healthcare, by my definition, and for the purpose of this book, is: *The sum of all conditions that contribute to or detract from the wellness of the population it is set up to serve.* That definition certainly includes mental health, which is one area of healthcare in which the nation deserves a failing grade. It is also behind many of the problems for which America has yet to find a solution, notably violent crime, inequality, addiction, and disability. Mental healthcare, more than any other area of healthcare, seems to take the brunt of budget cuts at times that we see the knee-jerk political response to economic downturns and public pressure to do something about deficits. And yet, we are paying an enormous societal price for inadequate access to mental healthcare. Will the publicity around the mental health problems of veterans returning from war, and around the mass shootings that we have had to endure with increasing frequency, generate enough political awareness that this segment of the healthcare system in America needs triage of its own? It may very well be that a significant increase in the public funding for mental healthcare could be financed by commensurate decreases in unemployment, disability, incarceration, and lost productivity.

As a nation, we need to explore why we are paying so much for healthcare, demonstrably much more than other advanced economies, and not getting better outcomes. There is evidence that the rapid increase in life expectancy that the U.S. population has experienced over the last three generations has come to a screeching halt and may even be reversing itself somewhat. America is far from the top when it comes to ranking countries by life expectancy. According to the OECD Better Life Index[13], life expectancy in the USA stands at 78.7 years. Twenty four OECD countries do better than that, including Slovenia, Portugal, Greece, the Netherlands (at 81.3 years), Canada, and Australia. Life expectancy is highest in Switzerland where it stands at 82.8 years (more than four years more than in the U.S.)

You would think that, since President Obama put healthcare on the top of his domestic political agenda, healthcare has been a focal point of the current administration and in some ways that has indeed been the case. Before and after its enactment, the Affordable Care Act of 2010 (ACA), has been at the center of domestic politics on both sides of the aisle, but as a bone of contention, not because of the importance of healthcare as an issue. The only attempt made by Republicans to address healthcare in America has been to repeal the ACA. The Democrats, and particularly the White House, see any criticism of the ACA as sacrilege. No attempt has been made to improve the clearly flawed initial design of the law by either party. It is important to note that Obamacare addresses only the question of who is paying for healthcare in America and how it is paid. It does nothing for the quality of healthcare available in America, for medical research, or for the control of cost of healthcare. Dr. Sherwin B. Nuland, in a 2010 update to his classic *"How We Die"*[28], phrases it this way: "*The new legislation (ACA) is all about economics, demographics and distribution, with a subtext of political accommodation.*"

Obamacare, just like Medicare and Medicaid, imposes limits on what health providers can charge the public for medical interventions, but it does little or nothing to promote healthier lifestyles, to improve medical efficiency, or to deliver cost containment.

In Section II of this book, I posited what's wrong with healthcare in America:

- It is too expensive
- It is unevenly distributed
- It is more curative than preventive
- The quality of healthcare is too locale-dependent
- For most people it is not of world class quality
- It is failing in finding the right balance between prolonging life and quality of life

Let's look at each of these flaws in some detail.

Too expensive

According to data[12] released by the Organization for Economic Development and Cooperation (OECD) which is comprised of 34 developed nations, the USA spent $8,233 per person on healthcare in 2010 versus an OECD average of $3,269. The next highest cost OECD nation is Norway at $5,388 per person.

As a percentage of GDP, the USA spent 17.6 percent on healthcare compared with an OECD average of 9.5 percent. The Netherlands spent 12.0 percent of GDP on healthcare and was in second place behind the USA. It looks like I traded one high cost environment for another. But the difference is significant: The healthcare part of GDP in 2010 was 32 percent less in the Netherlands than it was in the USA.

When you read these numbers the thought inevitably comes up that maybe the cost difference is explained by a difference in the quality of healthcare received. Like shopping at Nordstrom versus Walmart.

But that supposition is not supported by facts. According to the OECD, in the United States:

- There are fewer physicians per person than in most other OECD countries. In 2010 the U.S. had 2.4 practicing physicians per 1,000 people, well below the OECD average of 3.1.
- The number of hospital beds in the U.S. was 2.6 per 1,000 population in 2009, lower than the OECD average of 3.4 beds.
- Life expectancy at birth increased by almost nine years between 1960 and 2010, but that is less than the increase of over fifteen years in Japan and over eleven years on average in OECD countries. The average American now lives 78.7 years, more than one year below the OECD average of 80.0 years (2012 data).

According to research published in 2011 in the Journal Population Health Metrics[29], between the year 2000 and 2007 more than 85 percent of American counties have fallen further behind the international life expectancy frontier. In the study, life expectancy data for 3,138 U.S. counties and 10 cities are compared with data from a previous survey from 1987 to 1997. The study concluded that the U.S. has extremely large geographic and racial disparities, with some communities having life expectancies well behind those of the best-performing nations. At the same time, relative performance for most communities (as measured against international standards) continues to drop. What this study tells us is that, in judging healthcare quality in the U.S., we can't simply look at the national level data. The macro numbers mask the real picture of a system that is failing the less fortunate in our society.

International comparison makes clear that Americans pay a very high price for healthcare, but many of them don't get their money's worth. Unfortunately it is an issue that was not really addressed in the

ACA. It is another matter that has fallen victim to a dysfunctional political system.

Uneven distribution

Of further concern to U.S. healthcare is how it is unevenly distributed across the United States, which comes in focus when life expectancy is measured at the county level. Two studies from the Institute for Health Metrics and Evaluation at the University of Washington in Seattle demonstrate this defect in the U.S. healthcare system. The previously cited study from 2011[29] concluded that: *"Across U.S. counties, life expectancy in 2007 ranged from 65.9 to 81.1 years for men and from 73.5 to 86.0 years for women."*

For black men these numbers deteriorated to 59.4 and 77.2 years and for black women to 69.6 to 82.6 years. In summary, the gap in life expectancy for men between the "healthiest" and the "unhealthiest" county was 15.2 years in 2007. For women the gap was narrower at 12.5 years. The other study[30], titled *"Left behind: widening disparities for males and females in U.S. county life expectancy, 1985-2010"* and published in 2013 concludes that: *"In all time periods, the lowest county-level life expectancies are seen in the South, the Mississippi basin, West Virginia, Kentucky, and selected counties with a large Native American population."* That is hard and unpalatable evidence of uneven distribution of healthcare in the USA: If you live in the wrong place it may cost you 12-15 years in life expectancy! It represents another tough element of inequality.

It is interesting to note that, while we believe to be living in the mecca of medical care in Cleveland, Ohio, where the Cleveland Clinic and University Hospitals are competing for best performance in providing medical care, the county in which these institutions are located, Cuyahoga County, is not on the list of the top 20 counties with the highest life expectancy. This shows that the locational access to very good medical care does not directly result in higher life expectancy as it is apparently offset by a high percentage of "at risk" residents of the county which includes downtown Cleveland.

There is a link between the high cost of healthcare delivery in the USA and the uneven distribution of healthcare. An inordinate amount of money in healthcare is spent on a relatively small segment of society. For example, in Medicaid the top five percent of users of Medicaid services account for more than half of all the Medicaid spending. Similarly, a disproportionate share of the total healthcare spending goes to people who are in the last years of their lives. In the year 2000, healthcare expenditures for people of age 85 and older were three times as high as for people aged between 18 and 64.[31]

It seems to me that the United States government does not know where to start in an effort to bring the cost of healthcare down. I would say a good place to start is the opening up of competition in pharmaceutical trade and in healthcare delivery across state borders, tort reform as it pertains to medical malpractice, computerizing medical records, and reducing the administrative cost in healthcare. Focus should also be on the identified areas of higher than average healthcare consumption for the purpose of identifying new approaches to healthcare delivery that can take away or mitigate the causes for these high use patterns. Finally, the consumers of healthcare services should be restrained from indiscriminate use of healthcare facilities and providers by incurring a reasonable out of pocket cost for every doctor's visit and medical test or procedure.

With respect to the quality of healthcare we need to find a way to move towards the principle that healthcare providers should be paid for outcomes rather than for interventions. The Cleveland Clinic is rapidly moving in that direction and so should the nation. This is the kind of thing that people should expect from healthcare reform, but is missing from the ACA.

Curative rather than preventive.

The next defect in American healthcare to be addressed is that it is set up to be biased towards being curative rather than preventive. It is evident that a lot of health problems are a direct result of unhealthy behavior like smoking, drinking, drug use, poor diet, sedentary life style, sleep deprivation, and unprotected sex. With the exception of anti-tobacco measures, little is done effectively to steer people towards healthier behavior. In the current American healthcare system we are so protective of people's freedom to live their own lives that we let unhealthy behavior go way too far, when expensive medical intervention is the only solution left. Bariatric surgery to treat obesity is a prime example. We pay a very high societal price in the cost of our healthcare for not stopping unhealthy behavior in its tracks. The task for the government and the healthcare system in this realm is to discourage and penalize unhealthy behavior and support, reward, and otherwise encourage a healthy lifestyle.

While smoking tobacco has diminished as a health threat in the United States as a result of deliberate government intervention in the form of huge increases in the "sin" tax imposed on the purchase of tobacco products, by public awareness campaigns, and by banning smoking in almost all public places, other behavioral health threats have come up that are largely ignored in government health policy. A National Health Interview Survey[32] for the years 2005 and 2010 showed a drop in the percentage of persons aged 18 or over who were currently cigarette smokers from 20.9 percent to 19.3 percent. Of interest to note is that this survey unveils inequality also when it comes to cigarette smoking:

1. Smoking cigarettes remained high or even increased among American Indian/Alaskan Natives (31.4 percent); people with only 9-11 years education (33.8 percent); and GED holders (45.2 percent).

2. Much lower than average tobacco use is attributed to people over 65 (9.5 percent); Asian Americans (9.2 percent); undergraduate degree holders (9.9 percent) and graduate degree holders (6.3 percent).

3. Smoking among males dropped significantly more (from 23.9 percent to 21.5 percent) than smoking among females (from 18.1 percent to 17.3 percent) but remained higher than average.

Other health hazards, similar to the use of tobacco, that are all causes for and contributors to a costly and ineffective health system, are: Obesity, the use of illegal drugs, the overuse of pharmaceutical drugs, and abuse of alcohol. If unhealthy behavior cannot be legislated or regulated, it certainly can be taxed or penalized with higher insurance premiums like we already do with the use of tobacco. Public policy should encourage the concept of wellness and discourage unhealthy behavior in individuals; it should stimulate—by financial incentives and in public campaigns—vaccination and screening for preventable diseases, and it should step up the funding for medical research. It needs to focus on behavioral aspects like tobacco smoking, drug use, sedentary lifestyle, diet, and alcohol.

The previously cited 2011 study *"Falling behind: life expectancy in US counties from 2000 to 2007 in an international context"*[33] concludes that if the leading four risk factors (smoking, high blood pressure, elevated blood glucose, and adiposity) were addressed, life expectancy in 2005 at the national level would increase 4.9 and 4.1 years, respectively, for males and females. It continues: *"Addressing leading preventable causes of death could dramatically improve the international performance of a large fraction of U.S. counties for both males and females."* The ACA deals with none of this.

These findings indicate that healthcare insurance premium calculations should put less weight on age and gender and much more weight on lifestyle and behavioral factors. The promotion of preventative healthcare should have been enshrined in our national healthcare design much like the principle of paying for positive outcomes rather than interventions. It will pay out nicely in fewer emergencies down the road and it is the ethical, moral, thing to do.

Locale-dependent

A major flaw in the current healthcare delivery in the U.S. is the fact that it is too locale-dependent and apparently becoming more so. This, too, is an aspect that should have been addressed in a bill that purports to be a comprehensive approach to healthcare reform but is not.

As we have seen above[30], life expectancy in the U.S. varies significantly by county, by gender and by race. One quarter of all U.S. counties saw an actual *reduction* in life expectancy for women between 1997 and 2007, meaning that girls born in those counties in 2007 are expected to live shorter lives than their mothers. This trend has accelerated over the past two decades. From 1987 to 1997, there were 314 counties with either a loss of female life expectancy or no growth in it. From 1997 to 2007 the number of such counties had grown to 860 (out of more than 3,000). Madison County, MS, saw a staggering drop of two-and-a-half years in life expectancy for women just in the last decade.

Community level disparities in 2007 cover a wide range of global experiences, from counties with life expectancies better than the best-performing nations to those lagging behind these nations by more than 50 years. The extent of geographic inequality is substantially larger in the U.S. than in the U.K., Canada or Japan.

Not world class

We have to assume (but we found no hard data to confirm) that, in large part, the huge difference in life expectancy between counties in the U.S. has to be attributed to the uneven distribution of the location of medical facilities and quality differences between the medical care centers in different counties. Not every county has a Cleveland Clinic, a Mayo Clinic, or a Johns Hopkins Medical Center. In fact, quite a few counties have no medical care center at all. But that is not the whole story.

Any analysis of causes of disparities needs to also investigate the impact of poverty, inequality, race, and ethnicity. The fact that medical care is unevenly distributed across the U.S.—and top notch medical care more so than medical care in general—has for effect that most Americans do not have access to world class healthcare. Government can address this problem by putting policies in place that aim at increasing the number of primary care physicians and registered nurses and at the dispersion of them throughout the country, if necessary by offering incentives to practice in less sought after regions of the country.

Imbalance between length of life and quality of life

American society has a real difficulty coming to grips with death as a logical and inevitable counterpart of life. Driven by a huge, and politically influential, medical services and equipment industry and by the Hippocratic ethic to preserve and prolong life at the cost of almost anything else, we are now in a situation that in 2011 a full 28 percent of Medicare's annual budget was spent on medical care for patients in the last six months of life[34]. The percentage of people dying in a hospital is indicative of how far and long we are willing to go to extend life beyond the desirable from the point of view of the patient and the loved ones. Today that number is above eighty percent. In 1949 it was fifty percent and it has gradually risen from there[28].

Katy Butler, a writer and journalist, has brought up this topic in her hauntingly beautiful book *"Knocking on Heaven's Door"*[35], following in the footsteps of her journalist colleague Lisa Genova in her fictionalized book *"Still Alice"*[36]. Both books draw attention to end of life issues that most of us prefer not to dwell upon. Nevertheless, these issues are part of the fabric of our healthcare environment. In our current healthcare system we are almost mindlessly spending any amount of money on the use of medical technology and pharmacy to prolong peoples' lives without regard for the impact of that spending on whoever foots the bill. For good reasons, when it comes to saving lives, we don't first ask "what is that going to cost us?" But when it comes to prolonging lives, in instances where there is no realistic outlook on recovery, or where any quality of life is absent, maybe the cost of treatment should come into consideration.

The medical establishment will try to preempt these questions by intervening first and letting the patients and their heirs deal with the financial consequences. As Katy Butler points out[37]: *"Most of us don't want to die "plugged into machines", and yet a fifth of American deaths now take place in intensive care, where ten days of futile flailing can cost as much as $323,000."* Maybe, even more worrisome than the financial cost aspect, is the near complete disregard for the effectiveness of the intervention on the quality of life of the patient. And the denial of the emotional cost on the relatives of the patient resulting from a prolonged agony towards an inevitable end. Katy Butler argues, and I agree with her, that we have lost our way and need to think about how to help the stricken and elderly to be accepting of the inevitability of the end of life and to offer compassion, facilities, and services to assist these patients and their loved ones in making the transition from life to death meaningful and comforting for all involved.

From all of these perspectives, the conclusion emerges that while the capabilities of the medical establishment in the USA have increased measurably over the thirty years that we have called America home, the delivery of top notch healthcare to the population at large has not kept pace with the advances in medical technology. In those respects, other nations have done better and American Exceptionalism in healthcare appears to be further out of reach than it was thirty years ago.

CHAPTER 5

WASTE

I n Section II of this book, I posited that America, much more than any other country in the world, has become a disposal society. It wastes more resources, food, water, and energy than most any other country consumes.

In terms of energy consumption per capita it ranks second in the world behind Canada (where the climate and the distances between population centers are drivers of high energy consumption) at 7.3 tons of oil equivalent per person[38]. Other modern economies have found a way to consume much less energy per capita:

1. Australia with 5.9 tons per person is lower by 19 percent
2. The Netherlands with 4.8 tons per person is lower by 34 percent
3. Germany with 4.0 tons per person is lower by 45 percent
4. Japan with 3.7 tons per person is lower by 49 percent
5. Israel with 3.1 tons per person is lower by 58 percent
6. Hong Kong with 2.0 tons per person is lower by 73 percent
7. Mexico with 1.6 tons per person is lower by 78 percent
8. Brazil with 1.4 tons per person is lower by 81 percent

The difference with Israel is particularly striking. Just like the Israelis have learned to be frugal with water, they also manage to thrive with less than half the amount of energy we use per person in America. Without living any less comfortable!

The causes for the high, call it wasteful, use of energy in America are multiple. Most are lifestyle related. We use a lot of energy because we can, it is abundantly available, and relatively cheap. We find that out when we are traveling abroad and fill up our rental car at the pump. Gasoline prices are typically two to three times as high in Europe as they are in the USA. Our bad habits were instilled in us at a time that America was the largest energy producer in the world—a situation we may be in again before too long—and they have stayed with us. To any visitor or immigrant to the U.S. the causes for over-use of energy are immediately in plain view: Our houses are significantly larger than in other advanced economies and often not very well insulated. American cars gained envy and admiration in the rest of the world mostly be-cause they were much larger than European or Japanese cars, in size, horsepower and weight. But the first energy crisis of 1973 dampened that enthusiasm quickly, everywhere but in America. Many Americans drive a truck, where a car could easily do the job. We drive our cars and trucks everywhere, including for long commutes from the suburbs to the cities. Public transportation is much less developed and only available in the larger cities. No one thinks about using a bike to get from here-to-there and for a reason, it is simply too dangerous to bike on American roads.

Unique to America is also the use of air conditioning. It has always intrigued me that many Americans set their thermostat at home in the summertime at a lower temperature than they are comfortable with in the winter! The use of (hot) water per capita is higher in America than in OECD countries. Everyone has a dishwasher, which uses three times as much hot water than used in hand dish washing.

But energy is not the only resource that is poorly husbanded in America. Waste is everywhere. According to World Bank data[39], America generates 624,700 tons of municipal solid waste per day, high above China that, with more than three times as many people, generates 520,548 tons per day. Countries like Brazil (149,096), Germany (127,816) and Japan (144,466) stay far below these numbers.

In 1960, according to the Clean Air Council[40], each person in the U.S. generated 2.68 pounds of waste per day. In 1970 the number was 3.25. In 2008 it stood at 4.5 pounds per capita per day.

Bottled water is a major culprit in this waste scenario. Between 1997 and 2007, bottled water consumption in the U.S. more than doubled, from 13.4 gallons per person to 29.3 gallons per person. More than a million tons of plastic PET bottles were produced in the U.S. in 2006, requiring the energy equivalent of 50 million barrels of oil. Most of these bottles ended up in landfills where they will not decompose for thousands of years. End on end, plastic water bottles thrown away annually in the USA will circle the world 55 times!

The other main culprit is packaging. In too many instances the cost of packaging exceeds the cost of the product it protects. And large components of packaging like Styrofoam and molded plastics will stay in landfills forever. This is another area of our economy where the consumer is not confronted with the full cost of a product, including its disposal.

America is also wasting an enormous amount of energy in the form of food. According to the Natural Resources Defense Council[41] getting food to our tables eats up ten percent of the total U.S. energy budget, uses fifty percent of U.S. land, and swallows eighty percent of fresh water consumed in the U.S. Yet, forty percent of food in the U.S. today goes uneaten ending up in our landfills. USDA reports that, in 2010, 133 billion pounds of food was harvested but never eaten. The Natural Resource Defense Council calculates that food saved by reducing waste by just fifteen percent could feed more than twenty-five million Americans every year at a time when one in six Americans lack a secure supply of food. Wouldn't this open up a better, more efficient approach to food assistance than food stamps do?

In June of 2013, the U.S. Department of Agriculture (USDA) and the Environmental Protection Agency (EPA) have launched a plan, called U.S. Food Waste Challenge[42], which invites food producers, retailers, consumers, nonprofits, and government agencies to sign up and "list the activities they will undertake to help reduce, recover, or recycle food waste in the United States". As part of the program, the USDA is addressing food waste in schools, updating nationwide food loss estimates from retailers, pilot testing a meat-composting program, and working to make it easier for companies to donate misbranded meat and poultry and imported produce that does not meet U.S. quality standards. The Maryland Food Bank uses prison labor in a program to collect farm field gleanings that otherwise would go to waste.

A typical American waste is found in the casualness with which we abandon our cities and proliferate our suburbs. We much rather build new than renovate existing buildings and structures. Land is still abundant and relatively cheap and we love to build new in green fields. In the process we often forget to clean up what we left behind, resulting in widespread decay and blight which, in turn, attracts crime and societal breakdown. Just ask the citizens of Detroit.

Waste in all of its ugly forms is a sign of carelessness, inefficiency, and lack of discipline. It represents a huge societal cost that contributes to, or stands in the way of solving, other social problems like poverty, inequality, and poor health. A functional government that is concerned about America's status and reputation in the world would do well to combat waste wherever found. Combatting waste in government spending is on everyone's political agenda, without ever producing credible and lasting results. Waste elimination is another area where business is way ahead of government. Through disciplines like lean manufacturing and six sigma, American business has successfully cut out waste wherever it would find it and it has become stronger in the process. Admittedly it had strong competitive incentives to do so. But so does America if it wants to stay in the lead in the race of nations.

Government will have to sort out how to change wasteful behavior in a coordinated effort between federal, state, and municipal authorities. Consumption taxes and disposal fees on waste, particularly non-recyclable waste, would go a long way to discourage wasteful behavior. America cannot legitimately claim world leadership in efficient management of its affairs if it cannot get its waste problem under control. America was a wasteful nation when we first arrived here. In that sense, not much has changed. What has changed is the global awareness that we have to manage our resources and our environment better and the technology available to combat the types of waste addressed in this chapter. In that sense, America is underperforming against its capabilities and thus a long distance away from being exceptional.

CHAPTER 6

WORK/LIFE IMBALANCE

According to the previously quoted Better Life Index published by the OECD[13], Americans work 1,790 hours a year, more, but not much more, than the OECD average of 1,765 hours. Yet life in America feels more work dominated than for instance in the Netherlands. Maybe, it is because of long commutes that many American workers have to deal with. Maybe, it is because of the fact that two-income families are now more the rule than the exception. Maybe because Americans take their work with them, particularly now that most every management level employee remains tethered to the office by PC, smart phone and/or tablet.

The most striking difference between the U.S. and Europe in terms of work/life balance is the number of vacation days available to and used by workers in the two continents. It is well known that France is just about closed for business the whole month of August. It is my experience that most management level Americans don't use all of their vacation days and find it difficult to be away from the office for more than two weeks at a time. Even then they will stay in touch with the office by cell phone, text and email. They also typically pay a heavy price by working overtime to get ready to go on vacation and by—upon their return—catching up with what was dumped on their desks while they were on vacation. Dave Sullivan blames much of this phenomenon on what he terms "introspective arrogance". An ingrained belief that no one can do the job as well as you can and that you are truly indispensable to the success of an organization. This, of course, is immediately refuted when put to the test by divine intervention.

My personal experience with work/life balance is a mixed bag. In an earlier part of this book I have already conceded that I have probably given too much deference to my office obligations. I am sure that I could have done well had I occasionally insisted on claiming more time for the family and myself, particularly early on in my career in America. As I got closer to my retirement and more secure in my position and awareness of what I was bringing to the table, I got better at protecting my free time and my freedom to manage my time the way I liked it. Famously, during my tenure with PrimeraTurf, I "moved my office to the beach" in July/August when we had our family vacations in Low Country Carolina. Every situation is different. For most of my career I had the excuse that Christie was a full time Mom, so that our children were always guided and properly attended.

In the recent literature about work/life balance, the emphasis has moved away, from the time spent on the job versus the personal life, to the happiness and fulfillment gained with the two parts of our lives: Work and life away from the workplace. The reasoning is that Thomas Jefferson had it right when he stipulated that the freedom of pursuit of happiness is an unalienable right. The workplace can and should be a happy place where people can realize their dreams and ambitions even when it takes a large bite out of the twenty-four hours they have in the day to get things done.

On the other hand, people can have a well-balanced division of time spent on the job and with the family but be miserable because of being in a dead-end job or a bad marriage. A 2012 study conducted by the Society for Human Resource Management[43] found that the number

of employees who consider work-life balance important or very important to their overall job satisfaction stands at eighty-nine percent. But
what are these employees really after? Kristi Hedges asks this question
in a Forbes[44] article titled R.I.P. Work-Life balance: *"Is work-life balance the
goal, or is it enjoying the various aspects of your life?"*

For me it is clearly the freedom to enjoy all the various aspects of life.
There is always more than one solution and what is good for one person
is not necessarily right for another. It may all be about stress avoidance.
If we, or our family members, feel stressed out by the pressure of the job
and the time spent on it, it is time to seek a better balance. But I also
believe that it is necessary and healthy to build a certain level of tolerance for stress and that career-oriented people should accept that there
will be times in their lives that the demands of the job are out of kilter
with their desire for freedom to spend time on other aspects of life. The
expectations of the people who are near and dear to us play a significant
role in determining how we balance our work requirements with other
life's necessities. If the workplace is a happy place, where dreams are
fulfilled and ambitions satisfied, chances are that the contentment spills
over into personal life and family life.

I have found that, as long as work is fun and fulfilling, the matter of finding a workable work/life balance for yourself and everyone
around you is not particularly challenging. But that is a big qualifier
and a major hurdle to climb: Work places where having fun is part of
the culture and a way of life are few and far between. Companies will
start paying attention to this when they begin to find it difficult to attract and keep talented people, or when someone will conclusively and
consistently link a business culture of fun and happiness with superior
business results.

Government can and should be a facilitator of a healthy work/life
balance by legislating good family practices like family leave to attend
to the needs of family members who are unable to take care of themselves and by providing child care for children of two working parents.

Otherwise it should just get out of the way and let people make their own decisions about work/life balance choices.

In terms of work/life balance America was not a shining example when I first came to work and live here, and, thirty years later, it is no more a beacon of light in that respect.

CHAPTER 7

EDUCATION

Ifeel passionately about education for several reasons. First, as explained in the second Section of this book, I have had the privilege of a very good and inexpensive (to my parents and me) public education, all the way from kindergarten through law school and I recognize the value of a great education. There is no better preparation for a productive life. Second, because teaching is a family tradition—one that I sought to escape by going into business—touching many generations of family members and my wife. Third, because a great education opens up avenues that otherwise remain closed. And last, but not least, because a well-educated population is the surest guarantor of continued prosperity and world leadership for America.

Thomas Jefferson wrote[45] in 1818 in a report of the Commissioners for the University of Virginia about the objects of education: "*To give every citizen the information he needs for the transaction of his own business; to enable him to calculate for himself, and to express and preserve his ideas, his contracts and accounts, in writing; to improve by reading, his morals and faculties; to understand his duties to his neighbors and country and to discharge with competence the functions confided to him by either; to know his rights...... and, in general, to observe with intelligence and faithfulness all the social relations under which he shall be placed."*

This still, two centuries later, is a stunningly to-the-point summary of what education should do for us. How well have we done against this instruction from one of our Founding Fathers?

What do you want first, the good news or the bad news?

The good news is that at the top, American education is world class. The bad news is that only a minuscule part of the population gets to access it. Fears are founded that education, while it should be the great equalizer and the path towards greater equality, in America it is perpetuating and even increasing inequality.

In business we learn that, if an organization of generally motivated and well-meaning people does not produce the results it expects, chances are that the blame is not to be found with the people but rather with the system or the processes employed. In the case of education, if we, as a nation don't get the results we expect and need, we should not point the finger at the teachers, at the students, or even their parents as the culprits. Chances are, that they are the victims of a dysfunctional set-up in education (be it well understood that teachers, students, and parents include their share of bad apples who contribute to the malaise).

Problems that stand in the way of better education in America include:

- We are not sure who should be taught what
- We have allowed education to become a political issue
- We are controlling costs poorly and have not found a way to spread out the costs so that they do not impede anyone's access
- We are reluctant to demand much of our students
- We do little to attract the best available talent for teaching jobs
- We have not made training competent teachers a national priority
- We have not embraced the concept of continuing education

How can these fundamental and systemic flaws be addressed and where do we start?

Who should be taught what?

Education is not a goal in itself. Education prepares us for a productive life when we grow up. Young people need to be educated on how the world functions and on how to succeed in life (see Thomas Jefferson's instruction in the previous pages). Progressive education advocates make a case for more and better early childhood education and I agree with them. We can no longer rely on parents to be there night and day when learning starts and child care centers are no substitute for the learning environment that was traditionally offered by a stay-at-home parent or grandparent. Once schooling starts, the three "R"s, reading, writing, and arithmetic, are merely the fundamental prerequisites. A liberal arts education should be part of any curriculum in grades K-12 to stimulate children's creativity, critical thinking, intellectual curiosity, and to make them aware that they are part of a continuum that reaches far (back) and wide and that needs to be carried forward on their shoulders.

The Commission on the Humanities and Social Sciences of the American Academy of Arts & Sciences published in 2013 a report on education in the Humanities and Social Sciences under the title "*The Heart of the Matter.*" In it the Commission gives a passionate plea for keeping the Humanities and Social Sciences at the core of our K1-12 education. It argues persuasively: "*The humanities and social sciences teach us to question, analyze, debate, evaluate, interpret, synthesize, compare evidence, and communicate – skills that are critically important in shaping adults who can become independent thinkers.*"[46]

Having said that, the educational system also needs to be instrumental in sorting out how its students will be contributing to society in a vocational capacity. And then it should teach them whatever is required to hit the ground running when school is finished and work begins.

The reality is that we can't all be leaders of the pack. The education process should help children sort out what they are good at, what they enjoy, and what they can be productive and successful at doing. A handyman will continue to be in high demand, but does not require the training and education a nuclear scientist or a CPA needs. The reality is that organizations like companies, non-profits, and government agencies need labor and management. It takes different levels of education to be successful at different levels of an organization. The American system, where all children are expected to complete a high school education of essentially the same curriculum, and then decide if they go to a two-year college for a vocational training, a four-year college to get an undergraduate degree, or find a job, does not offer nearly the flexibility and differentiation required to prepare students for their vocation. Even though states offer vocational training programs for high school age students, they do not take away the requirements for obtaining a high school diploma. There is no national structure for vocational training and even at the state level I found that there is a hodgepodge of solutions that may vary by county.

American children and young adults would be much better served with a secondary educational system that offers choices that are tailor-made to prepare them for whatever their next step on the ladder of social mobility is.

Education as a political issue

Politics pervade education in the U.S. From the school levies to the election of school boards at the local level, to the State Boards of Education, to the federal Department of Education, politicians have their hands on education at every level.

Unionization of teachers is guaranteeing that the policy debate with respect to education is subject to ideology and thus, highly polarizing. None of this is helpful in a situation where the education system as it runs is not producing the results the nation needs.

Education is no less important to the national security than our military. I would like to see a rethinking of the American educational system along the lines of our military organization. Including thinking of and treating our teachers—at all education levels—like an educational corps that gets trained at special academies, reports to Joint Chiefs of Staff, which in turn reports to the president as the Commander-in-Chief. And, I would like to see a rethinking of the financing of the operation. Other aspects of the military model that could be applied to education include a ban on unionization, pay-scales, ranks, and promotions.

The merits of following the military model in education include: 1) Elevating education to a matter of security interest; 2) shielding it from too much political intervention; 3) creating a framework for better merit-based compensation; and 4) offering a platform for merit based career advancement so that the cream of the crop will rise to the top. I am not advocating putting our teachers in uniform. The critical role of parents in education should be acknowledged in this military model and can be preserved through parent-teacher-organization (PTA) and by delegation of specific oversight responsibilities.

Cost control and access

Cost control and access have become huge issues, primarily in higher education. For the first time in history, Americans have good personal reasons to wonder if the cost of higher education is worth it. The cost of the very best higher education is now so high that only very wealthy parents can afford to fund it for their children. And the tools to provide smart children from low or middle income parents access to this education are too few and imperfect. At the more mundane level, where the large majority of colleges and universities dwell, the cost has also risen to levels where the cost effectiveness needs to be questioned. And these schools typically have less financial aid available than the richly endowed Ivy League schools and their equivalents.

Student loans have long been the vehicle by which low or middle income students have been able to complete their higher education. But, in the process, the burden of student loan debt has become so huge that the question if it is worth it is very legitimate. The Federal Reserve Bank of New York reported[47] in early 2013 that student loan debt was higher than credit card debt and had been growing at alarming rate, doubling since 2007. In the third quarter of 2013 total outstanding student debt crossed the $1 trillion line and the delinquency rate stood at 11.8 percent. This burden—which cannot be discharged in bankruptcy—hits particularly hard the students who drop out before finishing college. And the ones who graduate from poorly performing colleges or in disciplines they are either not suited for or which offer only poor career prospects. It condemns many young, but well-educated, Americans to a life at or near the poverty level. It stunts the very much desired upward mobility. This phenomenon will also have considerable long term negative effect on the economy. Confronted with their student loan burden, young entrants to the workplace economy hold off on buying a house, buying a car, and starting a family. It is anybody's guess how many of them hold off on starting a business because of the debts they have already incurred.

The cost of higher education, and the widening discrepancy in the quality of education received from the best performing and the worst performing colleges and universities, contribute largely to the increasing inequality and the vanishing mobility between residents of Fishtown and Belmont.

In part, this problem is the result of a lack of choice in educational systems that prepare for life in the workplace. A college education is only productive if it offers a curriculum that builds the skill and competency required for a chosen career path. Just getting a college degree does not cut it anymore in a globalized world, where our children compete with their peers from all over the planet in a knowledge-based society. If you are not good at something that needs to be done, then someone else will do it!

The prevailing mindset of students and colleges alike is: Let's get a degree. Other than where there is a specific partnership between a business and a local college or university, there is too much emphasis on graduation as a goal in and of itself and too little on preparation for a meaningful and productive participation in the future workplace.

Education and healthcare suffer from the same problem. They are both far too expensive for what they deliver and access to the best forms of it is very unevenly distributed among income classes and—correlatively—among ethnicities. Both have been growing in cost at levels far above the rate of inflation. If that should not be seen as a signal for government intervention, I do not know what will. The richest nation on earth should easily have the capacity to offer better healthcare and better education to its entire population than any other. It is just a matter of political will and national priority.

Demands on our students

By international standards we don't put enough demand on our children's attention to education. Very few children—when left to their own devices—will do of their own free will what is necessary to assure them a good education. Distractions are everywhere and widely available and accessible. Electronic tools, that can provide children with knowledge sources, offer other applications that most children will find a lot more exciting.

Here, too, is a direct link with inequality. In Charles Murray's Belmont children go to college prep schools that attract the best teachers, maintain great class discipline, and have high expectations from their students. Parents are involved—they have the luxury of freedom to decide how and where to use their time—and, if everything else fails, there are always tutors. In Fishtown, however, the children go to the local public school that is constantly plagued with funding issues, has trouble attracting and keeping the best teachers because everything is a battle, and where the environment is not safe and conducive to learning. When the kids get home, there is no-one there to guide them to homework. And there is no money for tutors.

Although many believe that school vacations are excessively long, there is no evidence that in the U.S. hours of classroom instruction per year fall short of international standards. Jal Mehta, assistant professor at the Harvard Graduate School of Education, points this out in an excellent 2013 article in "Foreign Affairs"[48]. He informs us that "*structurally, U.S. teachers spend more time in the classroom and less time planning and working with one another than do teachers with high-performing schools. Secondary school teachers in the United States teach an average of nearly 1,100 hours a year (actual hours differ some from state to state), compared with an average of 660 hours across the countries of the OECD and fewer than 600 hours in Japan and South Korea.*"

This leads to the inevitable conclusion that time in the classroom is not as well spent in America as it is in some of the countries we compete against. Apparently teachers and students fail to make the most of the time they spend together in the classroom. That flaw can have many causes, one of which being that the expectations we have of our children attending school are not high enough.

Then there is the typical American culture of extra-curricular activity that competes with the primacy of academic development. Sometimes it seems to matter more to students, parents, and educators alike how their school competes on the football field, in a band contest, or with their cheerleaders, than with other schools in academic performance. It is uniquely American—or North American—to have schools involved in competitive sports. In Europe, if you want to play soccer, you join a soccer club. There the sports franchises are completely separated from the education franchises. Educational institutions—and their student body—in Europe have no excuse for not being completely and narrowly focused on academics.

The teaching profession

Jal Mehta, in his previously mentioned article for *Foreign Affairs* that he titled "*Why American Education Fails*", puts the blame for our relatively poor educational performance primarily on the way we build, guide, and support our teacher corps. He traces the origins of the currently existing model back to the turn of the previous century when, in one generation, a network of one-room schoolhouses was transformed into a set of district school systems. For building these systems the best knowledge of business organization was applied, which at that time implied a top driven system that empowered mostly male superintendents to act as CEOs of school districts, where mostly female teachers would follow the rules and programs that their superiors chose. Mehta then posits that "*Teachers received minimal training, the assumption being that they did not have a complicated job. The top education schools mostly avoided training teachers, seeing teaching as carrying the stigma of low-status, feminine work; they instead focused on cultivating the male administrators who would govern the system.*"

He also observes that, "*Teachers were mostly women, who had few other employment options and were generally not the breadwinners in their families, so their low pay did not provoke significant resistance.*" For a long time, these female teachers had short careers with most of them giving up their calling when they got married and had children. Such was the culture of the American educational system a century ago and Jal Mehta argues that it has not fundamentally changed.

It is time to break the mold and recognize the teaching profession for what it is. A pillar of our national security and prosperity. Our teaching corps should be held in no less esteem than our military officers' corps. Of course that presupposes that our teaching corps is well trained and of world class quality.

Teacher education

Where else to look for the reasons behind a relatively poor performance of U.S. education, if placed in a global perspective? There is no reason to assume that American children are inherently less talented, gifted, than Finish or Japanese children and that their test scores merely confirm this handicap. If we rule that out, then it comes down to the quality of education the children receive and the culture of the educational environment. In 2006 Arthur Levine, then the president of Teachers College at Columbia University, issued a report[49] that termed teacher preparation programs in the U.S. "*from inadequate to appalling*". The *New York Times* columnist Bill Keller, in a column published October 20, 2013, termed the teacher education business "*An industry of Mediocrity*"[50]. For the quality of education we need to look at how our teachers are trained and how their training is kept up to date during their tenure. The United States has a dazzling array of facilities for teacher education: At least 1,300 college level faculties, a good number of alternative certification providers, city-sponsored residencies, and some grade schools that run their own training programs.

In other words, there is no concentration of teacher education in centers for excellence. That's why I think there is merit in following, for teacher education, the military model for officer training in our five Federal Service Academies. Doing so would serve the purpose of standardizing the quality and content of teacher education, it would elevate the standing of the teaching profession by making the education more competitive, and it would instill an "esprit de corps" with a national reach. This esprit the corps would enable the spread of a culture of excellence and urgency in education that is missing in the current model that, as we have learned, is now more than one hundred years old. As a nation, we need to learn to revere education as the cornerstone for our national primacy. Arthur Levine, in his previously cited report[49], advocates a less radical approach in proposing a "Rhodes Scholars" type program for teacher education. On this issue of improving teacher education, I am leaning again on observations made by Mehta in his previously cited article in *Foreign Affairs.*

Mehta refers to a recent study by the Bill and Melinda Gates Foundation of more than 3,000 classrooms in the United States that found that over 60 percent were competently managed, meaning that the students were not unruly and did the work assigned by the teacher, but that only 20 percent were engaged in ambitious learning that challenged students to think, reason, and analyze texts or problems. Mehta then states—and I agree with him—that, *"any attempts to reform American education would have to start with attracting better teachers, retaining them, and helping them develop their practice."* He continues: *"The most striking finding of comparative international research is that the best-performing school systems draw their teachers from the top third of college graduates, whereas lower-ranking school systems do not."* A recent McKinsey report[51] found that most U.S. teachers come *"from the bottom two-thirds of college classes, and, for many schools in poor neighborhoods, from the bottom third."*

With quality and competitiveness of teacher-education comes respect for the profession. The kind of respect that Americans have for the graduates from our military academies. In Finland, teaching is the single most preferred career for 15-year olds. How enviable is that? Kids, who are still in school, like the educational environment so much that they want to make a career there. The result is that in Finland only one in ten applicants is accepted for teaching education. In the U.S. even the most prestigious education schools commonly accept 50 percent or more of their applicants.

The last component of better success in teaching is the support the teachers get over their careers. From the government, in terms of creating and maintaining standards for academic achievement and in terms of offering a system of continuing education and certification to assure continuous improvement and motivation. From the nation at large, in terms of respect for the profession, willingness to pay for value received, and recognition of the vital importance of a superior educational system and performance measured by international standards. We owe it to our teachers and ourselves to give them all of these levels of support. If kids succeed through education, the nation succeeds.

Continuing education

If our existing educational system fails our children by allowing them to fall behind their peers in other industrialized nations, it fails our adults even more, by not offering an institutionalized platform for continuing education and re-education that is now required for most workers to keep up with the changing and increasing demands of their careers. We have all long accepted that the days of a life-long job with one employer are over, but we have left it to companies and industries to provide a permanent education platform for re-tooling and upgrading the skill and knowledge base of their employees. Unions, industry trade organizations, and professional associations should be the drivers of incorporation of continuing education in our social contracts. Cost would need to be addressed, but, other than with respect to who initially foots the bill, should not really be an issue, because the continuing education would pay for itself by increased productivity and reduced unemployment. It should not be left to the government to spearhead this, although government could help. Just like we have laws that prescribe rules for family leave, we could and probably should have legal requirements for employees to spend part of their annual work hours on maintaining their career prospects by attending classes for recertification, refreshing, and upgrading their technical competencies or adopting new skills for a career change. In almost everyone's vicinity there is a community college offering a low cost, easily accessible, avenue for continuing education. This network of educational institutions is eminently situated to help knowledge workers keep up with the demands of their time and the global competition. Making continuing education a regular part of adult life would stimulate the motivation for active engagement with and in the workplace. It would provide increased opportunities for career advancement and instill in children the notion that learning is a life-long process. The previously cited Commission on the Humanities and Social Sciences—in its report, *"The Heart of the Matter"*[52]—addresses the merit of continuing education as follows: *"As citizens, we need to absorb an ever-growing body of information and to assess the sources of that information. As workers, we need to adapt to an ever-accelerating rate of technological change and to reflect on the implications of these changes. As members of a global community, we need to look beyond our borders to communicate and interact with individuals from societies and cultures different from our own. As a nation, we need to provide an educational foundation for our future stability and prosperity – drawing on all areas of knowledge."*

Peter Gilbert, executive director of the Vermont Humanities Council, puts it this way: *"If learning stops when formal school stops, then the knowledge and understanding of America's workforce and citizenry will be inadequate by any measure."*

John Kasich, the governor of my State of Ohio, in his 2014 State of the State address appealed to the Ohio legislature to support his plan to institutionalize "life-long learning" as a tool to keep Ohio competitive in the battle for job creators.

I leave it to you to decide if, considering all the elements of this evaluation of American education, American Exceptionalism is alive and well when it comes to education.

CHAPTER 8

DRUGS

We may as well admit it. We have lost the "War on Drugs" that Richard Nixon started and has been waged now for over forty years with no appreciable result. Come to think about it, this experience should cause future administrations to think twice before declaring war on anything. Lyndon Johnson's "War on Poverty" has yet to make a difference after fifty years and George W. Bush' "War on Terror" is in danger of going the same way as Nixon's war: Nowhere. America would be better off never declaring war of any kind it has no intention of winning nor one that it simply cannot win. War should really be the last resort settlement of a conflict of any kind. If you think about it, America has not really won a war since World War II, which ended with an unconditional capitulation by the enemy. The Korean War ended in a stalemate resulting in a cessation of hostilities rather than a peace. The Vietnam War we outright lost. The first Gulf War we won, but it turned out to be a Pyrrhus victory, because we had to fight it all over again thirteen years later. And the outcome of Afghanistan War is yet to be determined, but we cannot possibly claim to have defeated either Al

Qaida or the Taliban. We don't need to add to the list by continuing to use war terminology in fending off the threats of drugs and terrorism.

I do not know of any formal measurement of the negative effect that illicit drug use has on the nation's psyche, its productivity, and its safety and security, but we all know from experience that it is devastating. We see personal tragedies all around us that are drug-related. From the armed robbery of our bank or neighborhood convenience store, from broken marriages and families, from overdose deaths and suicides, from mob and gangster wars, and from lost jobs and productivity. The most recent federal data show 19,154 opioid drug deaths in 2010, with 3,094 involving heroin and the rest painkillers. Heroin deaths of teenagers and young adults tripled in the first decade of this century. We are spending billions of dollars on interdiction with no appreciable success and of the almost 2.5 million people populating our prison system a high percentage, probably as much as 50 percent, is jailed for drug related offenses.

What does it tell us when we have fought the battle with all means at our disposal for more than forty years and not won the war? It tells me that it is time to change course. To do the same thing over and over again and expect different (better) results is generally interpreted to be dumb. Warren Buffett calls it the definition of insanity. I may go off a limb here, but I seriously think that it is time to decriminalize the use of major mind altering substances just like we have done with the other one, alcohol, after the prohibition. At the same time, I would control the distribution and sale of these drugs through licensing, just like we do with alcohol, and then impose very high sin taxes (we sure can use the revenue!) Such decriminalization could be combined with a regulatory control mechanism and a ban on products that are simply too dangerous to be allowed. And it should be combined with effective outreach programs that can help young victims break the deadly spiral of addiction.

The weekly magazine *The Economist*, in its February 8, 2014, edition addresses America's epidemic of heroin overdose deaths in the wake of the death of actor Philip Seymour Hoffman. (How often does it take a celebrity death to draw the nation's attention to a major societal problem?)

The Economist reports that *"Switzerland and the Netherlands have pioneered the "heroin assisted treatment" (HAT) approach and evidence suggests that HAT slashes heroin related deaths, since users are shooting up under medical supervision. HAT also drastically reduces heroin related crime, since addicts have no need to steal or sell their bodies to get money for their fix. Heroin use is falling steadily in both Switzerland and the Netherlands; by the late 2000s the Dutch incidence of new heroin users had fallen close to zero."*

We need to decriminalize the trade, so that our kids no longer drop out of school or stop looking for legitimate work because they find enticement in dope peddling for drug lords and end up in jail.

We need to decriminalize the trade, so that we put the Mexican and Columbian drug lords out of business because the growers of marijuana and opium then have legitimate outlets for their crops.

And, we need to decriminalize the trade and save billions of dollars now spent in the war on drugs that are better used to address infra-structure requirements, education, and deficit reduction. Decriminalizing the trade would allow us to trade prisons for schools and jailers for teachers. Decriminalizing would no more solve all the drug related problems than ending the prohibition solved all alcohol-induced problems. But by taking drugs out of the criminal context it would bring the effects of drug abuse out in the open, where they can be treated and healed.

America had a drug problem thirty years ago. It knew so and it had declared war on drugs ten years prior to our immigration decision. But the problem has only gotten worse. Not exactly an area in which to find exceptionalism.

Chapter 9

Terrorism

The president of the United States, not just the 44th but any president, past, present, or future, will say that protecting Americans from harm is his first and most-sacred duty. However, protecting Americans from harm, all the time and in every situation, is more than any president can deliver. He can no more prevent fatal car accidents or deadly shootings from occurring than he can prevent a suicidal pilot from crashing his plane into a packed football stadium or an ammonia storage tank. Not to speak of his helplessness in preventing earthquakes and tornadoes.

So, the best we can expect from him and his administration is that they take all reasonable steps and precautions to keep such events from happening, and—if they nevertheless do happen as they inevitably will—to minimize the damage inflicted upon the citizenry.

George W. Bush did us a disservice when he dubbed his response to 9/11 the "War on Terror". Americans expect to win their wars and, unless you vastly expand the usual meaning of victory, this is not a war that can ever be won. History is replete with acts of terror and fighting terrorism is like slaying the mythological Hydra: You chop off one head and another one pops up somewhere else. In fighting terrorism it is counterproductive to raise expectations that cannot be fully delivered upon. That is what you are doing when you declare War on Terror. War may last longer than you like, but it is never unending like our need to suppress terrorism. A war that you cannot win encourages your enemies and demoralizes your citizenry and your allies. The twenty-four hour news cycle, with its sensational and penetrating coverage, empowers the enemy and alienates the population from the just cause.

Intelligence and technology are the weapons we need to use to better advantage in the struggle against terrorism. Every time I go through airport security, I shudder to think of the waste of money and effort that goes into passenger and hand-baggage screening.

Our authorities clearly do not believe in the current set-up either, because Disney puts them to shame when it comes to screening and crowd control. Just look at the flimsy array of equipment and personnel used in Transportation Safety Administration (TSA) operations at our airports, and it becomes clear that all we do is make a halfhearted attempt at catching the bad guys, while thoroughly inconveniencing the rest of us. Smart use of the combination of intelligence and technology should allow us to screen only a fraction of the airline passengers and those much more thoroughly than the TSA does today.

A good part of our insecurity stems from the fact that our government does not have the information it needs to protect its borders. It is my belief that a responsible government, that is truly concerned with the security of its people, needs to know at any time who resides within its borders, for what purpose and under what title (citizenship, visa, Green Card). That can only be achieved if the law requires (and the Constitution is interpreted to permit) a forge-proof, biometric, identity card for entry in and exit from U.S. territory as well as for obtaining a job, bank account, credit card, driver's license, and other similar life necessities. The database collected with the issuance of such identity card should record the purpose, duration, and conditions for entry to the country and should raise an alarm if any of these conditions for entry are no longer met. With this type of technology and its applications, we no longer have to build fences along our borders and maintain an army of border patrol agents that, together, have proven to be incapable of keeping illegal immigrants and other undesirables out. Combined with good intelligence, new technology leverages the advantages America has as a rich, technologically advanced, and innovative nation and offers a much higher degree of national security than the measures we currently have in place. This is an area where government can learn from the business practice of creative destruction: Forget what does not work and start from scratch.

The United States government has a huge spending problem but its biggest problem is that it spends big on the wrong things. It does not spend enough on new technology that can deliver better results. It is not easy to judge America's performance in the fight against terrorism. For good reasons, most of the work gets done behind the scenes and out of the limelight. America certainly makes an exceptional effort, in terms of money and resources, combatting terrorism. But does it deliver exceptional results? We can only hope that the U.S. already taps into the best available technology to fend off the threat of cyber warfare, which is probably the largest and scariest security threat of our times.

CHAPTER 10

IMMIGRATION

The same forge proof biometric identity card (a chip would even be cooler), I am proposing in the previous chapter for the purpose of enhancing our national security, would go a long way towards solving the problem we have had in this country with illegal immigration: If illegal immigrants without a forge-proof biometric identity card cannot get a job, open a bank account, get a driver's license, attend school etc. they will not be here for long. As it is, we are paying an inordinate amount of money for immigration enforcement. According to the Migration Policy Institute[53], federal spending on immigration enforcement amounted to $17.9 billion in fiscal 2012. By comparison, federal spending on all other principal law-enforcement amounted to $14.4 billion. Is it possible that we have our priorities wrong and need to go about immigration control in a different way?

Opponents of comprehensive immigration reform harp mostly on two objections:

1. That it would hang the "welcome" sign out and perpetuate, without floodgate control, the problem of illegal immigration;

2. That it would translate to "amnesty" for breaking the law and unjustly put illegal immigrants in front of people who seek citizenship through legal immigration.

The first objection falls away if we have the courage to require everyone who legally resides in the country to carry a forge proof biometric identity card.

The second objection can be addressed by denying illegal immigrants citizen status but allowing them permanent residency, after paying a fine for breaking the law. That penalty could be assessed in the form of a permanent surcharge on income tax, including payroll tax.

As I posited in Section II of this book, the problem in the U.S. today is that legal immigration is too hard and illegal immigration is too easy. I will not go deeper into the arguments for immigration. They have been well-documented in books, columns, and articles that do not have to be repeated here. Orderly large scale immigration is essential to the future of the nation. We need migrant workers to harvest our crops and to do our grounds maintenance and landscaping. We need migrant workers for a whole host of entry level positions that will lead to productive careers. If anyone doubts the importance of immigrants in the daily functioning of our economy, he/she should watch the 2004 movie "A Day without a Mexican", which is funny and deadly serious at the same time. We don't realize anymore how deeply dependent we have become of migrant workers in so many aspects of our lives. We need youth to offset our graying population. We need workers to shore up our payroll taxes. And—most of all—we need entrepreneurial talent and skills to advance our technology and economy. Paul Taylor[18] has elaborated on this in his book "*The Next America*" and he phrases it perfectly: "*Immigration is the engine that makes and remakes America.*"

America has a problem with engagement. Too many people are standing on the sideline, relying on the safety net deployed by the government to pick them up. That is not typically the case with immigrants. Legal or illegal, they come to this country to improve the lives of themselves and their families. They are willing to do just about any work that needs to get done. As Paul Taylor points out: *"They're also our face to the world, and their life stories embody the values our nation holds most dear: pluralism, dynamism, tolerance, entrepreneurship, achievement, optimism."* With immigrants there is no lack of motivation and they will be actively engaged, if only we allow them. America is a nation of immigrants. It is in our DNA and you have to believe that the constant influx—over many centuries—of people willing to risk everything for a chance to build a new life in America has had an impact on the gene pool available in America today. Controlling the process is one thing. Trying to stop or hinder immigration has proven futile in the long run; it is counterproductive and a refutation of the American heritage. Immigration will only stop if America no longer offers the promise of a better future. We should all hope that it never gets to that point!

The only thing we could possibly be debating is how to prevent illegal immigration and convert it to legal immigration. Nothing would be more conducive to reaching that goal than a legal requirement to present this forge proof identity card for all of the civil transactions required in modern day life. People could still cross our borders with Canada or Mexico clandestinely, but they could not do anything of substance and they could not possibly be here for long. Intelligence and conventional border controls would have to protect us against terrorists who might want to cross our borders clandestinely for committing a terrorist act. But they could not rent a car, take flight lessons, book a flight, check into a hotel, or draw any money out of an automated teller machine (ATM).

It seems to me that the only public interest in controlling and limiting immigration is in the need to keep undesirables out.

In the preceding chapter, dealing with the War on Terror, I have already acknowledged that every sovereign nation has a need and, in fact, an obligation to control its borders and a legitimate need to know at any time who is residing within its borders. Thankfully, modern day information technology (much of it developed by immigrants) provides the government with the tools to make this a very doable undertaking. A comprehensive overhaul, modernization, and streamlining of America's immigration policy and practices is long overdue. In the interest of the nation, legal immigration should be encouraged and opened up for:

- Foreign Students as long as they show academic results,
- Knowledge Workers,
- Entrepreneurs,
- Investors,
- Unskilled workers as long as they are willing to work.

The question of how to deal with illegal immigrants already in America, while politically explosive, is practically not very hard to answer. The main task and challenge would be to separate the chaff from the kernels. What would be wrong or difficult with requiring illegal immigrants currently in the country to appear before an immigration panel which should determine if their legalization is in the best interest of the country, with a presumption of qualification? Non-qualifiers would then need to be deported to their country of origin. Qualifiers would be allowed legal status, short of citizenship, that permits them to reside and work in this country. By not addressing immigration with badly needed new legislation, America is missing an opportunity to remain exceptional as a welcoming nation that is the dream destination for the brilliant, the destitute and the ambitious alike.

CHAPTER 11

INFRASTRUCTURE

merica is paying a price for the fact that it invested early—long before its current competitors outside of Western Europe— and heavily in the key components of its infrastructure, like water supply, the power grid, the railroad system, airports, bridges, and tunnels. Major parts of these systems are now so old, unsafe, and insufficient that they need to be overhauled or replaced. Unfortunately, the nation has not saved, like a prudent household or business would do, to fund the maintenance and investment cost it is facing. On the contrary, it has put itself deep in debt without spending the money needed for the upkeep of its lifeline systems. Someday soon it will have to bite the bullet. It will have to do the deferred maintenance and it will have to bring its infrastructure components up to par with the exigencies of global competition. In Section II, I already commented on the fact the any major storm hitting any part of the nation, immediately causes the power to go out for millions of people and businesses. In terms of the power grid, America resembles a third world country and in terms of several other components of infrastructure, the country is not much better off. The American Society of Civil Engineers (ASCE) issues every four years a report card on the state of the infrastructure in the country and it gave the nation a D+ in its report for 2013. It also estimated that a $3.6 trillion investment in infrastructure improvement will be needed by 2020. Admittedly, this number may be biased, as the civil engineers of the nation stand to benefit from such investments, since they would do most of the work.

Let's look at individual components of the U.S. infrastructure.

Ports

The U.S. Army Corps of Engineers estimates that more than ninety-five percent (by volume) of overseas trade produced or consumed by the United States moves through the nation's ports[54]. And yet, *"America is the only industrialized country that does not have a comprehensive freight strategy"*, says Robert Fuentes, a senior fellow with the Brookings Institute. That may prove to be a fatal miss, because major changes in trade patterns are coming, resulting from new shipping lanes opening up. By the end of 2014, the Panama Canal is scheduled to complete a major expansion project that will allow the canal to double its capacity and accommodate the world's largest cargo ships (that currently have to go around Cape Horn to travel from the Atlantic to the Pacific). The other development that will dramatically alter the world's shipping routes is the opening up of the Arctic Northwest and Northeast passages for summer traffic between Asia, North America, and Europe. How will these structural changes in shipping lanes, and the resulting change in vessel size and configuration, affect the viability of U.S. ports and who is going to put a strategy in place that protects America's interest in participation in world trade?

Inland waterways

The 2013 Report Card for America's Infrastructure[55] gives this gloomy assessment of the condition of this part of our logistical system: *"Our nation's inland waterways and rivers are the hidden backbone of our freight network – they carry the equivalent of about 51 million truck trips each year. In many cases, the inland waterway system has not been updated since the 1950's, and more than half of the locks are over 50 years old. Barges are stopped for hours each day with unscheduled delays, preventing goods from getting to market and driving up cost. There is an average of 52 service interruptions a day throughout the system. Projects to repair and replace aging locks and dredge channels take decades to approve and complete, exacerbating the problem further. Inland waterways received a D- grade once again as conditions remain poor and investment levels remain stagnant."*

Levees

Levees along the inland waterways are in no better shape than the waterways themselves. And we don't do anything about it until after the horse has left the barn. Case in point New Orleans. It took the Katrina disaster, and more than 1,800 fatalities, for the levee system of the greater New Orleans area to get upgraded and reinforced. This seems to be the modus operandi for much of the public service sector: It takes a catastrophe to break through the apathy and inertia of the bureaucracy and get things done, even if the public safety is clearly at risk. Even today, there is no comprehensive plan for dealing with the projected rising water levels and more extreme high water crests that are likely to result from global warming. Not surprisingly, the ASCE gives our levees also a failing grade D-.

Railroads

Recent accidents with railcars carrying oil across the country have heightened the scrutiny on the condition of the railroad tracks and the tank cars carrying flammable products. Only because of these accidents has it become clear to the public that safety is threatened not only by operator error, but also by outdated equipment and insufficient track maintenance. The trans-continental rail systems, together with the inland waterways, have the potential to give the U.S. a decisive competitive advantage when it comes to the speed, cost, and efficiency of domestic transportation of goods, but only if these systems are well maintained and operated. As it is, America relies way more on truck transport than effective from a cost perspective and desirable from a sustainability point of view. Another miss in the rail infrastructure is, that compared to other advanced economies, the USA is far behind in the availability, reliability and sophistication of its passenger rail systems. Glaring is the complete absence of a high speed commuter rail service around and between the larger metropolitan areas.

Roads and bridges

Maybe the roads are not so much to blame for our traffic woes. It may be more the relentless dependency on our cars and our roads when it comes to getting from A to Z. And that dependency, in turn, is of course the result of the lack of a comprehensive public transport plan and strategy for the U.S. But, whatever the cause of the trouble, the result is that forty-two percent of America's major urban highways are congested, costing the economy an estimated $101 billion in wasted time and fuel annually[56]. Not to speak of the stress and aggravation it causes the commuters of the nation. The Federal Highway Administration estimates that $170 billion in capital investment would be needed on an annual basis to significantly improve conditions and performance.

With respect to our bridges, the ASCE informs us that one in nine of the nation's bridges are rated as structurally deficient, while the average age of the nation's 607,380 bridges is currently forty-two years. The Federal Highway Administration estimates that to eliminate the nation's bridge backlog by 2028, we would need to invest $20.5 billion annually.

Airports

World travelers know intimately that, in terms of passenger convenience, the U.S. Airports cannot stand in the shadow of the much more modern and user friendly airports in Europe and particularly in Asia. The airports in the United States are still struggling to adjust their layout and passenger handling to the new security demands resulting from the events of 9/11, now 13 years ago. The time wasted and the aggravation caused as a result of the user unfriendliness of our larger airports makes many of us decide to take the car, rather than fly, for distances of up to four to six hours in driving time. This, in turn, exacerbates the road congestion and causes us to burn more fossil fuel than we have to.

Power Grid

The power grid in the USA is a complex patchwork of some 6,000 power plants, 450,000 miles of transmission lines and regional delivery systems. The nation's electric grid is one of the great engineering achievements of the twentieth century, but it is old and about at the limit of its capacity. ASCE estimated in 2012 that, unless $673 billion is invested in the system, it could break down by the year 2020. More than two-thirds of the system's transmission lines a power transformers are more than twenty-five years old and most circuit breakers are older than that. But, the greatest vulnerability of the grid is that it is almost entirely above ground, where it is exposed to the impact of violent weather of any kind, winter, summer, spring, and fall. In addition it is vulnerable to sabotage, terrorism, and cyber-attacks.

Water Supply

Much like the power grid, the water supply system in the USA is also old—with many parts of it dating back to the 19th century—and vulnerable to sabotage, terrorism, and cyber-attacks. In addition it is leaking. There are an estimated 240,000 water main breaks per year in the United States. The American Water Works Association (AWWA) asserts that the cost of replacing the existing water pipeline system could reach more than $1 trillion.

Broadband

While much of the problem with the previously reviewed components of America's infrastructure stems from the fact that they were designed and built more than a century ago to meet demands that were very different and much less stringent than today's, that cannot be said for our mediocre broadband system. The availability and quality of broadband services in the U.S. is highly locale dependent.

According to OECD Broadband statistics, the United States ranks seventh for wireless (mobile) broadband penetration on a per capita basis, lagging Australia, Finland, Sweden, Japan, Korea and Denmark and it ranks 15th for wired penetration with a percentage of 29.3 versus 40 percent or higher for the Netherlands and Switzerland. For the richest nation in the world and the nation with the ambition to be leading the world in communication and connectivity, it is distressing that we still can't drive along our interstate highways, or be riding Amtrak between our major cities, without experiencing dropped calls and losing internet access.

———

Reviewing all of these components of American infrastructure, one can only come to the conclusion that the country, largely due to an early start, runs on an infrastructure that is keeping things moving (most of the time) but not at world class levels. Much of it is antiquated, poorly maintained, and stretched to capacity. It is certainly not of a scope and quality that supports America's leadership among nations. The ASCE, in its 2013 report card confirms this assessment when it states that *"our infrastructure systems are failing to keep pace with current and expanding demands."*

There is no short term fix for this problem. It is so broad in scope, consists of so many sub-segments, and requires injection of so much money, that it would be foolish to start upgrading any part of the system without a national plan. What is needed most is a vision of what America expects from its infrastructure twenty or thirty years down the road. Will it remain a nation that largely relies on the automobile to move people around? Should anything be done to reduce the need for people to move around for the only purpose of functioning in the economy? If the automobile remains at the core of the system, will it continue to be fueled by fossil fuels? Each component of the system requires an assessment of the needs for the future and a strategy for how to get from where we are today to where we want to go tomorrow. In each case, such assessment should ask the question if, with modern technology, we can do more with less. If we can trade quantity for quality. And how we can enhance the sustainability of the system. The strategy should focus on creating the planning and decision making platform for cooperation between the various levels of government and the private sector and it should address the question of funding the required investments. At some level, the planning for each of the components, needs to be brought together in a national infrastructure plan that sets priorities, avoids duplication of effort, streamlines the permitting process, and assures the internal consistency of the deliverables of the aggregate of the component plans. ASCE has it all right when it states[57]: *"Infrastructure is the foundation that connects the nation's businesses, communities, and people, driving our economy and improving our quality of life. For the U.S. economy to be the most competitive in the world, we need a first class infrastructure system – transport systems that move people and goods efficiently and at a reasonable cost by land, water and air; transmission systems that deliver reliable, low-cost power from a wide range of energy sources; and water systems that drive industrial processes as well as daily functions in our homes."*

CHAPTER 12

DEBT AND DEFICIT

I would be bullish on America, if only I saw signs of political will to put the nation's fiscal house in order. In 2013 we have gone through another government shut-down and, at one minute before midnight, we have twice avoided, for now, a default on the federal debt obligation, but all we are doing is kicking the can down the road. How many more chances will we get and forego to solve the serious challenges the nation is facing, of which the burdensome and unsustainable national debt is one of the more intransigent?

The lack of political courage to deal with the debt and deficit of the federal government raises the specter of a serious sudden debt crisis and a total collapse of the economy that we barely avoided in the 2008 recession. It has every potential of hitting us hard, but if allowed to fester, it is sure to hit our children and grandchildren even harder. If I'm convinced of one thing, it is that the U.S. economy would resume its historical growth path and that many more well-paying jobs would be created, if the business world, the investors in the American economy both at home and abroad, saw clear and convincing evidence that Washington is serious about eliminating the deficit over a reasonable time of say five years and is serious about attacking the herculean task of whittling away at the national debt.

There is a legitimate discussion about the desirable level of national debt. Borrowing—it seems to me—is justified when it is a means to spurring economic growth, paying for disastrous events, like unsolicited wars, or natural disasters, and for infrastructure investments. Most households find it desirable to take on debt at certain times, when expenditures exceed current income, or to invest in real assets like a home. But households get worried when repayment of the debt moves beyond their capacity of future earnings. And we should be worried about the size of our National Debt at $17 trillion.

With the National Debt at $17 trillion, has anybody calculated what the debt service would add to the budget deficit if interest rates would go up by only a few percentage points? How long can we expect to be living with near zero interest rates, while we continue to pile up debt? As if a National Debt at $17 trillion and growing is not serious enough, it hides the awful truth that the sum of our future obligations is more like $200 trillion, if you add in the commitments the nation has made to its citizens under its major entitlement programs, Social Security and Medicare.

The administrations responsible for the debt explosion were Republican and Democrat, so neither party can claim the moral high ground. Their actions and inactions, that have led us to the brink of a debt crisis, are both economically detrimental and morally decrepit.

Economically detrimental, because we did not go into debt to invest in a better future for Americans, but simply because we allowed the expense of running the business of the country to exceed, year after year, the revenues we were collecting. We accepted year after year a budget deficit and, for many years, we abandoned the principle of budgeting our expenses altogether and we just funded our runaway expenses with a series of continuing resolutions (finally in February of 2014 Congress passed a federal budget resolution after four years of funding the government by a series of continuing resolutions). In the process, Congress has let it come to the point that our national debt now just about equals the size of our entire economy.

Morally decrepit because our generation has selfishly spent to accommodate its bad habits and utter lack of fiscal discipline. It protects ad nauseam the interests of its senior citizens in programs like Social Security and Medicare that were last written into law in a different day and age and with a very different outlook on demographics and economic realities. And, unless Congress and the administration reverse course and negotiate the comprehensive action package that is now required, we will present the bill for our spending spree to our children and grandchildren.

The two branches of government responsible for creating the debt by means of accumulating annual deficits are the legislative and executive branches. Neither one can possibly say that they are at a loss how to go about solving a problem that has festered for so long and has grown so large: Simpson/Bowles have created an excellent blueprint that contains all elements required for a solution, leaving only to decide how much of what medicine the patient should take. How healthy do we want the patient to be when all is said and done?

And there are plenty of other good recommendations for a clear path out of the morass. We all know that what is needed is what has been termed a "grand bargain". Congressional action that addresses all of the major challenges at one time in a bi-partisan overarching compromise. Think tanks have been active in offering frameworks for the kind of "grand bargain" that is required. Prominent amongst them is "Third Way" publishing a discussion paper titled *"The Bargain"*[58]. This document spells out a practical guideline for putting America back on a path of sustainable growth at an average 3.3 percent rate that has brought prosperity to the country between the end of World War II and the start of the 2007-2008 recession. The Bargain advocates seven areas of political action:

1. Re-balance the budget
2. Become an export giant
3. Reform corporate taxes and business regulations

4. Boost the productivity and educational attainment of the American workforce
5. Become a global magnet for talent
6. Improve infrastructure
7. Spur breakthrough innovation

We have been borrowing for four years, from 2008-2012, more than a trillion dollars per year to fill the gap between federal revenues and federal spending. This is the equivalent of a family taking out credit card debt every year, from year-to-year, just to keep consuming at a level that is beyond its means. That results in bankruptcy and some people believe that we already are a bankrupt nation.

Economists at the International Monetary Fund (IMF) warned in 2011[59] that funding America's long term obligations will require an immediate and permanent thirty-five percent increase in all taxes and a thirty-five percent cut in all benefits! Whether the IMF has it right or not, there is no argument that we are spending way beyond our means and we are not spending on structural improvements of our infra-structure or on our competitive advantage in an increasingly globalized environment. We are spending to meet expectations that we have raised, but now find that we cannot fully fund without mortgaging our future. These expectations reside in the entitlements (including healthcare), in government retirement programs, and in the role of our military as a global policy force. The first task at hand, therefore, is to put a stop to running up an annual budget deficit. There is no acceptable reason for the federal government to run a deficit under normal circumstances. If it happens routinely, it means that spending is out of whack with revenues and the two should be brought back in balance. In fact, revenues need to exceed spending going forward to start reversing the growth of our national debt. We don't have to try to bring it back to zero debt—although that would be nice—but we should agree on a reasonable number, as a percentage of GDP, bring down the debt to that level and hold it there.

NEITHER HERE NOR THERE

The national debt has exploded during the last twenty-four years from $4 trillion in 1990 to $17 trillion right now. As a percentage of GDP the debt has also increased, particularly under the administration of Barack Obama. While the debt has moved over time in a range from fifty-six percent of GDP in 1985 to eighty-one percent in 1996, it has now peaked at about 115 percent of GDP and is projected to go higher from there. In other words, our national debt is now fifteen percent larger than the size of our economy. (In comparison, the national debt of the Netherlands stood at sixty-nine percent of GDP in 2012).

It seems to me that the further task at hand is to design and codify a plan and a strategy that will, over a reasonable amount of time (like 5-10 years), bring the national debt back to within a range of 50-80 percent of GDP by stimulating economic growth, while reducing government spending. Thereafter the task should be to keep the national debt in that range, reaching the lower limit in good times and the higher limit in times of economic distress or national emergencies.

None of this can be done without tax reform, which is long overdue anyway. And when we speak of tax reform we need to think of real reform, not just tinkering at the margin. Simplification needs to be a core element of tax reform. It should not be necessary for ordinary citizens to retain H.R. Block or a personal CPA to do their income tax returns. Tax reform needs to ask the question: How many different taxes does America need? Personal income tax, corporate income tax, estate tax, capital gains tax, sales tax, inheritance tax, sin tax? Tax reform needs to be guided by the principle of fairness and needs to protect economic growth. We should not kill the goose that lays the golden eggs. But the bottom line is that the tax system will have to be designed to generate enough revenue to allow the nation to operate on a balanced budget and meet its national objectives.

Tax systems can and should be used to reward productive behavior (investments, research and development, hard work, charity) and penalize unproductive behavior (over-consumption, milking versus building a business, or behavior that is detrimental to good public health). In this context,

166

Congress would be well-advised to study the merits of a consumption tax (on products and services other than elemental needs like food, shelter, education and medical care) to alleviate the burden of income tax.

In dealing with personal income tax, reformers should start at the principle of zero tax expenditures: All credits and deductions go away, unless elimination would unduly hurt specific vital economic goals. This principle has been embraced by the Senate Finance Committee Chairman Max Baucus and ranking committee member Orrin Hatch and has also been advocated by Simpson/Bowles. The savings, generated by the elimination of tax expenditures, can then be used for tax rate reduction and debt reduction. But don't hold your breath; it will be a big ticket to get this principle accepted by Congress. The even bigger ticket is the work that needs to be done to put the major American entitlements on a sustainable footing as required by current and foreseeable demographics. In 1950 the average American reaching age 65 lived an additional 13.9 years. By 2010 this number had increased to 19.1 years. This meant the need to fund an additional 5.2 years of Social Security and Medicare payments for a quickly growing number of recipients. In 1950, there were 16.5 workers supporting one retiree. In 2013 that number had decreased to 2.8 and is projected to further decrease to 2.1 by 2035. You have to be blind not to see that significant changes to the entitlement programs will be required to keep them viable and sustainable. As it stands the combined Social Security trust fund will run dry by 2033, unless Congress takes action.

The picture is bleak, but it is also unambiguous. Our debt and deficit problem has been allowed to fester and grow to the point that tinkering in the margin or taking incremental steps in the direction of either spending cuts or tax increases will no longer suffice. What is called for is a comprehensive strategic approach to putting our fiscal house in order.

Such approach would be one that encompasses budget control, tax reform, and entitlement reform. And an approach that shows courage to stop paying for things that clearly don't work (e.g. drug interdiction and border control) or are no longer opportune (like many of our defense systems dating back to the cold war). The previously quoted article "The Bargain" provides a plausible pathway for such strategy. I would add three steps to the seven outlined in the article:

1. Complete tax overhaul, including flattening of tax rates, simplification and possibly introduction of a value-added tax on consumption with low or zero rates for necessities and high rates for luxury items and products that threaten public health, like tobacco, alcohol, soft drinks, and snacks.
2. Tort reform.
3. Achieve energy independence from sources other than North America.

These ten steps all fall in the purview of the federal government. They demonstrate that there is a legitimate role for the government to play in stimulating economic growth. Government isn't all bad; only an overreaching and ineffective government is intolerable. But wouldn't it be fair and useful to ask, in everything the executive branch and the legislative branch will be prescribing: "Will this fit the budget and will it promote economic growth?" And, if the answer is "no", shouldn't there be a compelling and overriding need of another kind (like national security, public safety or environmental protection) to move forward?

Government works best when it is an "enabler" rather than a "doer". Enabling is generally a lot less expensive than doing. Herein lays another avenue towards reduced government spending.

There is a lot of talk in Washington about a "grand bargain". There is a lot of talk in Washington, period. In fact, there is a lot more talk than action. And it has been that way for too long. But if there is serious inclination towards a grand bargain, then the question becomes: "What is truly grand"? Grandeur is—like beauty—in the eye of the beholder.

The fear is not misplaced that, in the eyes of most members of Congress, even a little tinkering at the margin will be considered a great leap forward. Let's help them out. The grand bargain, required to liberate our economy from the shackles of a burdensome government and, conversely, to liberate government from the tired ideological meddling by election-driven politicians, will have to bring about a veritable reformation. It will have to bring reform in three critical areas:

1. Entitlement Reform
2. Tax Reform
3. Tort Reform

1. Entitlement reform is required, because our demographics have changed to the point that all previous assumptions about the financing of these programs are now obsolete. In fact, Congress should not create or revise any entitlement programs—Social Security, Medicare and Medicaid—without building in the requirement that the premises behind the program are reviewed and reset by Congress at set intervals. The private sector thrives on creative destruction. It throws out the way we have always done it, and starts all over again. In the public sector that does not happen nearly enough. The world is changing fast, but our politicians seem to assume that we can live with the same decades old programs in perpetuity.

Congress' prerequisite in any effort to reset entitlements should be to safeguard the programs for the next generation by funding them, within the parameters Congress is setting for long term budgets and for the control of the national debt. Since there is little good news in the demographic direction of our population from a program perspective, it is time to make means-testing a standard feature of all of our entitlement programs. In fact, we should give up on the notion of entitlements. These programs were designed—and should continue to serve—as a safety net. To keep the less fortunate members of our society from falling through the cracks. Not as an unalienable right for every member of society, regardless of income or wealth.

2. Tax reform should aim for simplification, transparency, and fairness. It should look at personal and corporate taxes. And it should

address the question if the time is not right to shift part of the revenue generation from taxing income to taxing consumption. To the extent that income remains to be taxed it should be done in only a few rate steps (looking at payroll taxes and other income taxes combined) and with the fewest possible exemptions while preserving the stimulus of important societal objectives like charitable giving, education, infrastructure investments, and research and development.

3. Tort reform speaks for itself. The threat of litigation, and the lack of reasonable limitations on awards given by juries in tort cases, are holding back growth and innovation in multiple ways. In the first place by the cost and availability of liability insurance for most any kind of productive human endeavor. The fear of being sued is holding otherwise responsible professionals back from experimentation and innovation. And the cost of liability insurance—if available at all—adds significantly to the cost of doing business, which is getting past on to the consumer. Tort reform is complete when we rid ourselves from the ambulance chasers that interrupt our TV viewing pleasure and are a blemish on the legal profession. The money spent in litigation, and much of the money spent on liability insurance premium, should be redirected to productive use. But the most compelling reason for tort reform is that we need to rid ourselves from anything that keeps us from reaching for new frontiers in science, creativity and productivity.

These three reforms, entitlement reform, tax reform, and tort reform, are required to address the deficiencies in the current modus operandi. But more than that, they are required to keep the U.S. economy competitive in the global environment. A grand bargain is required for the good of the nation. And it will only truly be "grand" if it addresses each of the three reforms advocated herein. The common thread connecting the three reforms should be the objective to: 1) Create optimal conditions for economic growth; and 2) Assure that implementation is within the financial means of the nation for all current generations. If this can be accomplished we can speak of the second reformation. Many pundits claim that it is unrealistic to expect that such grand bargain can be reached in the current political constellation, and that the more realistic approach would be to cut the task into a long sequence of small individual legislative initiatives. I hope not. Just because of the current political constellation, I see any small step in any particular direction strand in a divided Congress (even if the 2014 or 2016 elections put the same party in control of the House and the Senate).

The thought behind a grand bargain is that, for the good of the nation, both parties accept that they get some, but not all of what they would like to achieve on the topics of entitlements, taxes, and tort. It is worth trying. The question is: Where is the leadership that will make it happen? And how do we keep the special interest groups from torpedoing the effort?

In the ongoing debate about reducing the deficit and bending the curve on the national debt, attention will have to be paid to the effectiveness of the safety net that a series of social programs have knitted underneath our social structure, to prevent our poorest and weakest from getting lost in the shuffle.

A nation that was founded largely on the guiding principles of the Christian faith and mints its coin with the inscription "In God We Trust", does well abiding by the biblical words of Deuteronomy 15:11: *For the poor will never cease from the land; therefore I command you, saying, 'You shall open your hand wide to your brother, to your poor and your needy, in your land.'*

Arthur C. Brooks, the president of the conservative American Enterprise Institute, quoted that Bible text in the heading of an article he wrote for *Commentary Magazine* in February of 2014[60], and in which he made a strong case for a conservative social-justice agenda. He advocates a strong safety net as long as, "*It is designed and administered in ways that fight fiercely against dependency.*" He also points out—correctly in my view—that "*the safety net's ultimate goal cannot be the perpetual subsistence of poor Americans in barely tolerable lives.*" And he adds: "*We can aim at nothing less than real human flourishing.*" Amen.

John F. Kennedy had it right when he said: "*If a free society cannot help the many who are poor, it cannot save the few who are rich.*" Nobody can argue in good conscience that the richest country in the world cannot afford to take care of those who are incapable of taking care of themselves. If only we can find out, without ambiguity, who in America is deserving of being saved by the safety net!

We have a Rubik's cube of complexity. On one side of the cube we have a plethora of programs, like Social Security, Medicare, Medicaid, food-stamps, welfare, disability, unemployment, you name it.

On the other side of the cube you have the authority in charge, the federal government with several services like the Social Security Administration, the Veterans Administration, the Department of Housing and Urban Development (HUD), the Labor Department, the Department of Agriculture, the state, the county, the town, the church. At the bottom of the Rubik's cube you have the conditions requiring the application of the safety net: Old age, young age, disability, veteran, unemployment, poverty, homelessness, or disaster.

Finally, at the top of the cube, you have the parameters within which the law offers assistance, which can be limited in time, by financial resources available to the applicant, or by the degree of seriousness of the conditions requiring the application of the safety net. To add to the complexity, virtually every aspect of this Rubik's cube is subject to constant change.

In addition, the money involved in the payout of the safety-net programs is so huge (hundreds of billions per year), that it attracts fraud of all kinds, including fraud perpetrated by highly sophisticated criminal syndicates. Where is the bureaucracy with the capability and the motivation to manage this complexity for tens of millions of citizens and residents with the result that only the deserving get the benefits and only for as long as they need them?

For all these reasons, it should not be a surprise that voices are being heard[61] that advocate to guarantee every American resident a minimum income and do away with all other kinds of government support. It may sound hard to swallow for a nation that used to believe in rugged individualism and personal responsibility, but, combined with my advocacy of a national service system for recipients of government assistance, it should get some serious consideration. If—and this is a big if—this would be a way to do away with a monstrous bureaucracy and large scale fraud, it should not be as farfetched as it appears at first blush.

An April, 2014[62] report for the Partnership for Public Service by Booz Allen Hamilton sounds the alarm that *"the American Federal Civil Service system, the foundation for effective government, is in crisis."* If it has to be reorganized, why not shrink it significantly at the same time. The savings can then be used to flow directly to the people who would otherwise not reach the minimum income level. Who wants to support a charity where a large part of the contributions are used to maintain the charity, its organization and staff? Why would we want to support a similar public charity?

In a very well-reasoned article in *National Affairs*[63], Steven M. Teles, a Johns Hopkins University professor of political science, makes a compelling case for simplifying government and making it more transparent. He coins the word "kludgeocracy" to describe the current state of complexity in U.S. governance and his article is a forceful appeal to reduce the kludge. I agree with Steven Teles that, if well presented, a less kludgey government is an immensely attractive goal, and should appeal to Americans of all parties and ideologies.

Teles writes: *"The politics of that world would be neither more "liberal" nor more "conservative" in any simple sense. Government would be bigger and more energetic where it clearly chose to act (and received public sanction for doing so), but smaller and less intrusive outside of that sphere."* Complexity, kludgeocracy, hampers the transparency of governance and brings with it an enormous cost of doing business, resulting in waste and duplication. In his article Teles does not specifically advocate for replacing the existing labyrinth of social safety net programs by a single federally-administered minimum income scheme, but all of his reasoning points in that direction.

In a very different time, now forever gone, we had communities. In most instances, the churches were the focal points of these communities and they provided the only safety net available. It was a time where we were aware of how our neighbors were faring and who needed help. The problem at the time was that resources were scarce and the distribution of assistance subject to biases and prejudices. Today, these social controls have entirely evaporated. We have to take people at their word when they say they need public assistance and there is no bureaucracy in the world that can consistently, and without prejudice, apply the appropriate standards to tidal waves of applications and verify. This would be difficult under static circumstances, it is virtually impossible under fast-changing conditions for the applicants, beneficiaries, and eligibility criteria. Case in point is the shift from welfare payments to disability payments. Since the Clinton Welfare Reform, the number of families on welfare has declined from five million to less than two million. But at the same time, the number of low income people on disability has risen from five million to seven million. Have you ever dealt with the government? Whether it is with the Motor Vehicle Department, the IRS, the INS, the Post Office or the Social Security Service, the bell curve is in full force and effect: The government employs a small percentage of conscientious, competent, and motivated workers; a large percentage of fair-to-average workers; and a significant percentage of incompetent, unmotivated workers. That is the force that has to straighten out the Rubik's cube!

The safety net is failing. It is failing the people it is supposed to protect and it is failing the tax payer. Good governance requires that public funds are spent wisely and only on legitimate public causes. Is there any chance that this reasonable requirement can be met? No sure thing, but it will have to be tried. It will be a test of our constitutional democracy to see if it can forge fundamental changes in the way government operates. If, like we have to assume, America is not ready to move in one step from the current hodgepodge of safety net programs to a federally administered minimum income program, there are other steps that can be taken to come to a more efficient and more equitable safety net system. I can think of the following steps to consider when reconstructing the safety net to make sure it serves only the truly needy and protects them effectively:

- Centralization of all programs, other than Social Security, Veterans Administration, and Disaster Relief, at the state level.

- Creation of a cadre of highly trained and equipped public servants to manage all aspects of the safety net.
- Use of technology, like the forge proof biometric ID card, to eliminate identity-based fraud.
- Compelling recipients of any type of government assistance to file, under penalty of perjury, a semi-annual census of their need for assistance including their financial conditions.
- Diligent law enforcement and heavy penalties (including forfeiture of all future benefits) for fraud and abuse.
- Enlisting able safety net beneficiaries in a national service program (no more free rides).

America has the financial wherewithal to protect its truly needy from the vagaries of life. But it cannot afford, for moral and fiscal reasons, to not administer the assistance with targeted precision.

It is hard to believe that thirty years ago, America's debt and deficit were not problems that needed to be addressed. America was exceptional in that it had its fiscal house in order. The conclusion is inevitable that such exceptionalism is now far out of reach, at least with current policies and under the current political constellation. America has spent like the proverbial drunken sailor without buying anything of lasting value with the money.

CHAPTER 13

INEQUALITY

What does inequality really mean? The Declaration of Independence states that, "all men are created equal", but it is open to various interpretations as to what was really meant by the signatories with that statement. Thomas Jefferson certainly was not blind to individuality, human frailty and strength.

We are all unique human beings and no two of us are equal in every respect, not even "identical" twins. So, inequality is, to some degree, a given and any attempt to eradicate it is doomed to failure. At the time of the Declaration of Independence the phrase certainly did not mean "equal before the law". The inequality I'm addressing here is the social and economic inequality that Murray wrote about in his book *"Coming Apart"*. It is more than just income inequality and wealth inequality, although both are important components of the inequality challenge the U.S. is facing. It is the inequality of opportunity that is most worrisome.

Some argue that inequality is good. The argument is that inequality gives the less fortunate greater aspirations. That may be so. It hardly matters. Inequality will be with us, regardless of what we do, politically, and economically, because it emanates from human nature. The question is:

At what point does inequality become socially untenable and economically counterproductive?

Finis Welch, emeritus professor of economics at Texas A&M, had an answer to that question. In his address to the Richard T. Lily Lecture of the American Economic Association in 1999, Welch said that he believed inequality was destructive only *"...when the low-wage citizenry views society as unfair, when it views effort as not worthwhile, when upward mobility is impossible or so unlikely that its pursuit is not worthwhile."* [64] My response to that is that we should never let it come to that point. When inequality becomes destructive it is too late, we have let it come too far. The challenge is to let a degree of inequality provide the motivation for people to seek upward mobility without letting it come to the point that it becomes unbridgeable in the eyes of the aspiring movers. We want to stay far clear of the tipping point, where the degree and scope of inequality becomes demotivating. The question is: Have we not crossed that line already?

Emmanuel Saez is an economics professor at the University of California, Berkeley and expert on income inequality. In a report issued in January of 2013[65] he examined how real family incomes have changed in the U.S. from 2009 to 2011, the first two years of the recovery from the 2008 recession. He found that the richest one percent of Americans saw their incomes grow by more than eleven percent on average, while for the other ninety-nine percent incomes shrank by nearly half a percent.

Sheila Bair, former chairwoman of the Federal Deposit Insurance Corporation (FDIC), commented on this report by Dr. Saez. She wrote in a February 26, 2013 column in the *New York Times*: *"I am a capitalist and a lifelong Republican. I believe that, in a meritocracy, some level of income inequality is both inevitable and desirable, as encouragement to those who contribute most to our economic prosperity. But I fear that government actions, not merit, have fueled these extremes in income distribution through taxpayer bailouts, central-bank engineered financial asset bubbles and unjustified tax breaks that favor the rich."*

Who can say it any better than that?

The most disquieting part of inequality in our time is that it shows up everywhere the U.S. faces a challenge. In this book, we have just gone through a litany of problems the nation faces and—without exception— in each of them there is an element of inequality. In Charles Murray's parlance, the unfortunate people in Fishtown experience higher unemployment, lower life expectancy, more and more serious drug-related problems, worse education, higher terror threat from gangs, higher exposure to illegal immigration, and worse effects of budget cuts than the fortunate people living in Belmont. Inequality creeps up in just about every aspect of modern day life in America. And here is the rub: Our generation has been building in the perpetuation and deepening of inequality by placing more and more burdens on the younger generation.

The youngsters who are entering the workplace now not only have to overcome the handicap of the demographic tectonic shift that is taking place, but they are also presented the bill for the debt we have been running up at their expense, and for the fact that our generation has refused to fully fund the entitlement programs we have in place. On top of that, they will be asked to make up for our failure to timely invest in the drivers of our future prosperity like, infrastructure and R&D. A triple whammy! They, as the largest component of the working population, will have to pony up (after paying off their student loans) the money required to pay the interest on the national debt and any amount of debt reduction; as well as the money required for the funding of our entitlement programs, infrastructure improvement, education overhaul, healthcare overhaul, and the cure for other ills that currently plague the nation.

Stan Druckenmiller, the retired hedge fund manager most known for predicting the subprime mortgage collapse, and certainly not part of the "at risk" generation, has gone on the road to impress upon college students that they are getting ripped off and need to find their political clout to fight the trans- generational income (and wealth) transfer that has been built into the system under pressure from the senior lobby in Congress, spearheaded by the all-powerful American Association of

Retired Persons (AARP). Will our Y generation get the message and start organizing themselves politically to provide a counter force to the senior lobby?

Why is inequality a threat to the future of the United States as a nation? Joseph E. Stiglitz, a Nobel Prize winner in economics and chairman of the Council of Economic Advisors under Bill Clinton, devoted a whole book, titled, *"The Price of Inequality,"* to this question[66]. His central argument is that widely unequal societies do not function efficiently and that their economies are neither stable nor sustainable. Stiglitz also points to the lack of fairness. He sees as a symptom of unfairness that, in our current economic model, there is no more correlation between individuals' contributions to society and their income, specifically at the very top of the income scale (the top 1 percent).

I agree with Stiglitz that no democracy can survive when a sense of fairness is completely absent from the system, or perceived to be absent. When this happens, it becomes the proverbial nation divided within itself. I see the threat a little differently. I see it primarily in the lack of cohesiveness the inequality creates. We are no longer E PLURIBUS UNUM. Inequality may have reached a threshold level from where the people at the lower ranges of the inequality scale remove themselves from participation in the productive process that propels the nation; and we cannot afford to run on less than all cylinders. Unassailable inequality is not only unfair, it is detrimental to the highest ambitions and aspirations we have for our nation.

In his book, *"The Great Divergence"*[67], Timothy Noah points to a factor that makes the current state of inequality in the U.S. much more problematic than previous episodes of high levels of inequality. He writes that *"economic inequality is less troubling if you live in a country where any child, no matter how humble his or her origins, can grow up to be President."* Notwithstanding the origin of the current occupant of the White House, Noah is no longer sure that Americans still live in such a country. There will always be exceptional individuals, who, with drive, luck, and patronage will escape from their milieu, but upward mobility is no longer built into the American system. In this, Noah concurs with Charles Murray who holds out little hope that children from Fishtown can ever move to Belmont. I see little to refute their pessimism. In the population that circulates in and out of the criminal justice system without ever having a realistic opportunity to rejoin the mainstream, in our public high schools, in the ranks of the unemployed and the disabled (by drugs, mentally and physically), and in the foot soldiers returning from our foreign wars unable to re-adjust to the civil society, we see evidence of inequality that has every appearance of being endemic. Unfortunately, the public at large does not want to see this and the government is too dysfunctional to fundamentally address the symptoms of inequality.

Under ideal conditions, social mobility is a two way divided highway: There is a lane open for people to move up the social ladder based on talent, hard work, and perseverance; and then, there is a lane for people to move down the social ladder based on the lack of these same attributes. The greatness of America is demonstrated in the preparedness of the most successful, like Warren Buffett, Bill Gates, Larry Ellison, Steve Case, Michael Bloomberg, Ted Turner, Mark Zuckerberg, and many others to donate the bulk of their accumulated wealth to charity. The Giving Pledge[68] shows 115 of the richest people willing to address the world's most pressing needs with the money they have earned or accumulated, rather than passing it on to their heirs. Hopefully all this money will serve, in part, to give other talented and motivated people, who are born in underprivileged circumstances, a chance to climb the road to success. And, by denying a good part of their wealth to their heirs, these philanthropists will lessen the perpetuation of privilege merely on the basis of birth.

This is the way business operates in America. Companies make it to the top and, more often than not, fall back because they are surpassed by newcomers. Equally so inside companies. People climb the corporate ladder, but only few reach the top and, of the ones who do, many fall back down the ladder and have to try all over again, somewhere else.

Here, too, exists a glaring difference between business and government in America. If businesses, or their chief executives, fail to perform for their shareholders, they will be held accountable and punished by loss of market value and their jobs. People rising to the top in government are set for life, regardless how well or poorly they performed. By speaking engagements, book contracts, lobbying, or placement on boards of corporations, non-profits or foundations, they are assured of perpetual high income even after they have left the political scene. The revolving door between government and Wall Street is very well documented.

Social mobility serves a nation optimally when it shows vibrant movement both up and down. Only then does it create a true meritocracy, where the most deserving (not the most privileged) reach the top and the least deserving (not the most under-privileged) hit bottom. But that appears to be missing in America today.

Arthur C. Brooks, in his previously cited article for *Commentary Magazine*, observed that "*The Federal Reserve Bank of Boston has shown that in 1980, 21 percent of Americans in the bottom income quintile rose to the middle quintile or higher by 1990. But those who started off in the bottom quintile in 1995 had only a 15 percent chance of becoming middle class in 2005. That is one-third decline in mobility in under a generation. Other analyses tell a similar tale. One 2007 Pew study measured relative mobility in Canada and Scandinavia at more than twice America's level.*" The conclusion is inevitable that America has lost ground when it comes to inequality, both in terms of where it was thirty years ago and in comparison with other advanced economies and the question needs to be asked: "How can the inequality problem be addressed and the logjam, that impedes the required social mobility, be broken?"

The solution is the mirror image of the problem. We need to address each of the major challenges outlined in this Section of the book, because they are all facets of and contribute to inequality. Inequality can only be alleviated and restored to the "normal" level, which is a reflection of inherent inequality of capability and motivation, by dealing with the persistent unemployment and disengagement from the labor process, the healthcare problems, the education flaws, the immigration problem, the drug problems, the obesity problem, and the fiscal crisis.

What this means, of course, is that there is no solution for the inequality challenge without a political consensus about the action the nation needs to take to get back on track and lead the world again in economic growth and development and in freedom and prosperity for all of its people. That sounds self-evident, but, if recent past experience is any guide to what we can expect going forward, it will prove to be a major obstacle. The political system is the topic for the next chapter of this Section of the book. In that chapter we will address both the inadequacies of the current political system and the changes that could be considered for the elimination or mitigation of these inadequacies.

Ultimately, the position of America in the global constellation will depend on the political will exhibited by the legislative and executive branches of government and the effectiveness with which the government can express this political will in solutions to the challenges enumerated herein.

CHAPTER 14

THE POLITICAL SYSTEM

Nothing wrong with the fundamentals

I chose for America for all the right reasons. I fit right in with the American spirit in the sense that I am an incurable optimist when it comes to the natural capacity to step back from the brink and find another, safer, way ahead. It is quintessentially American to believe that, when it comes down to brass tacks, America will do what it has to do to avoid hitting the slippery slope. I, too, refuse to believe that a country, built on such strong democratic principles, and blessed with unparalleled wealth and untapped resources, will not find a way to rid itself from the shackles that hold it back from seriously addressing the challenges that it faces in the global competition. America is not facing a challenge it cannot meet. In spite of what the OECD Better Life Index suggests, there is not a country in the world that is better positioned to be (and remain) a dominant force in the world than the United States of America. China has a much larger population, but that is a mixed blessing, particularly with the current demographics where the graying population vastly outnumbers the young. China will pay a hefty price for hanging on for too long to its misguided "one child" policy. This policy has kept the population growth under control and helped the great leap forward in terms of per capita income, but it has been kept in force for too long and drawn a big check on the future of the country. China will also pay a hefty price in the form of corrective action it will soon have to take to deal with its environmental challenges. And, in spite of all the progress the Chinese economy has made over the last couple of decades, it will have to deal with the friction resulting from a much larger degree of inequality than we experience in America. The only "advantage" China has over the United States is that its political system will allow it to take and enforce top driven decisions to throw money at solving these problems without being constrained by a balance of power and the paralyzing effect of discord between political parties and branches of government. I place the word "advantage" in quotation marks, because I believe that this advantage will turn out to be a disadvantage in the long run. The economic liberalization of China has far outpaced the political liberalization and to correct that may turn out to be the biggest challenge that China will be facing, a challenge that is unique to that country. The process to meet that challenge is likely to bring with it periods of instability and economic and political uncertainty.

On the surface, then, there is plenty of justification for optimism. Optimism, though, does not solve any problems and has the nasty habit of morphing into naivety and complacency. I will say that America resembles in many ways its prototypical citizen, who continues to drive his Cadillac or pick-up truck everywhere, even if he could easily walk or bike; who continues to stop for lunch at McDonald's and supersizes his meal even though he knows he shouldn't; who talks about losing weight and going to the gym, but puts it off until tomorrow, next week or next year; and who, as a result, keeps gaining weight slowly and steadily, one pound at a time, but decides that he still has time to deal with it later and reverse course. Political America is indulgent and un-disciplined, probably because it believes that, in the absence of clear and present danger, it still has time to make the hard choices later. Popular voices in the media like Paul Krugman in the New York Times lend credibility to this dangerously flawed attitude by endless repetition. Who does not want to believe that everything will come out fine in the end? I am a firm believer in the dogma that not much good happens without careful planning and timely action, even if that action will be painful, politically and monetarily.

The flaws are in the system and the process

If a building is structurally flawed and unsafe, it gets condemned. America needs a similar solution for its current political system, because it is deeply flawed, and unfit for the purposes it is supposed to serve. The biggest structural flaws that I see are (in no particular order):

- The two party system
- The money influence
- The election system
- The absence of a national strategy

I see these flaws as interconnected and believe that they each need to be addressed simultaneously, if we want our political house to be re-designed to absorb the shockwaves that our nation is enduring now and will have to endure in an uncertain future. Having said that, I realize the enormity of the challenge to get anything of this nature implemented. It is no sinecure to turn a battleship around! But I see the existing structure falling apart; and I see the current political constellation in America as unsuited for future use. It ought to be condemned. There is some serious creative destruction to be done. Let's look at each of the flaws separately.

The two party system

The polarization between the two parties in our current political system has come to the point that it is rendering the whole system dysfunctional. It has become political suicide for a Republican member of Congress to support a Democratic initiative and for a Democratic member of Congress to underwrite a Republican legislative proposal. Governor Christie of New Jersey gets chastised by the right for hugging President Obama when he came out to see for himself and address the devastation caused by hurricane Sandy. The Republican Party will not allow the Democratic Party to be seen solving the nation's pressing issues and vice versa. The end-result is that nothing of importance gets done in Congress or, if something gets done, like the "2010 Patient Protection and Affordable Care Act" better known as Obamacare, it is ill considered and ideologically biased. The jealousy and hatred between Republicans and Democrats is such that neither one can stand the thought that their nemesis might have contributed to, if not crafted, a solution to a public problem. This explains why Congress has not taken the first step towards solving the most prominent challenges our nation faces:

- Deficit elimination and debt control
- Entitlement reform
- Tax reform
- Tort reform
- Immigration reform
- Energy policy
- Global warming
- Cyber space protection
- Infrastructure renewal
- Education reform
- Health Care reform and wellness policy (obesity and drugs)

The obvious solution to the problem is the creation of a centrist third party, that is less ideological, and more pragmatic, and that can govern by forming a coalition either with the right or the left, depending on the outcome of Congressional elections. A centrist party that could attract moderate Democrats and Republicans who want to be freed from the shackles of the ideological extremes within their parties as well as a large proportion of declared independents. Such centrist party would, if not by itself, in a coalition with either the Democrats or the Republicans, produce a large enough majority in Congress to break through the existing stalemate and get our top level issues addressed.

The money influence.

Money, not competency, is now the critical success factor for any national elected office and for most of the high profile state and municipal elected offices. In 1950, senators could get elected by spending 100,000 dollars on their campaigns; by 1980, that number was typically several million dollars; by 2010, many senate candidates spent 20-30 million dollars to win or retain their seats[69]. It should not surprise anybody that, in just about the same timeframe, the number of registered lobbyists in Washington has risen from below 100 to almost 14,000. These 14,000 lobbyists spend more than $3.5 billion annually. Combined with the freedom of speech, which allows any interest group or political action committee (PAC) to craft any commercial, pro or con a candidate for office, without regard to truth or material content, money has taken control of the political process in the USA, starting with the election process.

Only in America! Nowhere else in the democratic realm of nations has money taken such a commanding control of the political process and its outcomes.

The only saving grace—if you can call it that—is that there are so many rich purses fighting for control that there are off sets and countervailing balances. Be it what may, the result is that hands are tied, our elected representatives are beholden, not to their constituents, but to their campaign contributors and nothing of importance gets done. Nicholas Stephanopoulos of the University of Chicago wrote in the 2013 *Columbia Law Review*: "*There is near consensus in the empirical literature that politicians' positions more accurately reflect the views of their donors than those of their constituents.*" We are so far along this corrupting road that it is hard to imagine that we are capable of freeing ourselves from the influence of money on the outcome of our political system. But we should try with all of our might and the following steps would go a long way towards removing the controlling influence of money:

- Limit the period during which the media are allowed to run political advertisements in similar ways as currently practiced in Canada and the U.K.
- Prohibit private funding of election campaigns and replace it with a system of public funding in equal amounts for each candidate.
- Pay members of congress an honorarium of a million dollars per year and prohibit them from earning or accepting any money (other than from existing investments) from private sources for the time of their tenure.
- Prohibit members of congress from lobbying the government for a period of five years from leaving congress.

There is so much the federal government, legislative and executive branches, could do to keep America competitive, but it is not happening. The system is paralyzed. Washington is immobilized by interest groups and petty jealousy between Republicans and Democrats. It is as if the army of politicians inside the Beltway is under control of the mob and scared to death to do anything that the boss will not condone. The boss, of course, in this case is the lobbyist for whatever special interest group rules the roost. It is demoralizing to see how much the legislators are beholden to institutions like the National Rifle Association (NRA), AARP, National Education Association (NEA), United Auto Workers (UAW), American Civil Liberties Union (ACLU), not to speak of the lobbies for major industries like defense, banking, oil and gas, pharmaceuticals, healthcare, financial services, and communications.

The voting public should be the boss, but its influence has been hijacked by individuals and institutions with pockets deep enough to buy the subservience and vote of the peoples' representatives. The net result is that the nation's business no longer gets done. The federal government can no longer proclaim that it sets the rules of the game by which all constituents have to play. It is incapable of creating optimum conditions for free enterprise and citizens to shape conditions for a brilliant, sustainably competitive future.

One has to be blind, blinded by the lightning strike of the obvious, not to see how even the most common sense solutions to America's challenges get stopped in their tracks because of the sway the money-men and special interest groups hold over our legislators on both sides of the aisle. So, the question becomes: How much longer are the American voters going to tolerate this perverted façade of representative democracy?

The election system

Many flaws in the current political system are the result of the high frequency of national elections in this country. Congressmen have to go to the mat every two years. The president has barely time to get familiar with the office before he has to get back in a campaign mode for re-election. And, as long as private money is allowed to be used in election campaigns, fund raising rather than governing becomes the most time-consuming job for the incumbent.

If, like proposed above, we pay our elected officials royally for serving the nation and provide public funding for their election campaigns, they have no more excuse not to focus exclusively on the job they have to do for us. We should also extend their terms so that they are not distracted all the time by the need to get re-elected. Finally, the system would be served by term limits, which would prevent congress from being dominated by career politicians rather than by citizen servants, like the Founding Fathers intended.

Another major flaw in the current system is the absence of any statutory requirement to address, in a national election campaign, the most important challenges presented to the nation for which the political system will have to provide solutions. Case in point, in the 2012 elections, was the total absence of any discussion among the candidates for national office about how to eliminate the deficits and bring the national debt under control. How can the voting public determine who they want in office, if it has to wait and see how the elected official will deal with the most pressing needs of the nation? For these reasons I believe that the nation would get much better results from Washington, DC if, in addition to the changes proposed above, the following changes were implemented in the election process:

- Have a committee of wise men/women with national credentials establish a list of the major issues facing the nation and require each candidate for national office to publish a position to be taken on each of them. This will help providing a mandate for the elected officials and increase accountability.
- Decrease the frequency of national elections by limiting the office of president to one term of six or seven years and by limiting the office of members of Congress to four terms of four years for the House and three terms of six years for the Senate.

The absence of a national strategy

America has too many people standing at the sidelines rather than playing the field. Nations are successful when they engage the whole population—with hardly anybody left out—behind a clearly articulated vision of the desired place of the nation in the global environment. But a vision is merely that—a fata morgana—if it is not accompanied by a solid strategy outlining how to reach the desired outcome. America is lacking a national strategy policy. American governance has no tradition or statute for the creation of a binding strategic plan that is built on broad consensus and transcends the shifting balance of power between the Republican and Democratic parties. How much sense would it make if there was a constitutional requirement on the president and the leadership in Congress to establish a national strategy, much like companies develop a strategic plan for their business that then becomes the compass by which investment decisions and other resource allocations are made? Such plan should have a long time horizon, transcend the term limits imposed on politicians, and be formally reviewed from year to year to adjust for changes in the external environment.

What's required is a clear articulation of some overarching bipartisan national objectives and a popular buy-in of these objectives. America has not had a clearly articulated national objective since John F. Kennedy decided that America was to be the first nation to put a man on the moon and bring him back safely to earth. We can borrow a chapter out of the book of my country of origin, which—after the flood of 1953—made it a national objective to protect its low laying areas from a 500 year flood. Public policy in the USA is too much influenced by the perpetual election cycle. Big strategies take a long time to be developed and implemented and don't fit in with the election-driven decision making practices of our politicians. Here, too, comes to light a major difference between the public and the private sector. In business nothing survives without a solid strategic plan and careful, methodical implementation. In public life, politicians get slaughtered if they don't cater to the immediate needs and fancies of their constituents.

But, without a long term plan there is no expected outcome and it is, therefore, not surprising that we are beginning to hear voices[70] calling for a national strategy. The articulation of such strategy is the role and responsibility of the federal government. Note that recent administrations have declared "war" on a number of national challenges, but they have not bothered to rally the nation behind any particular national objective. Can we think of any highly worthwhile broad national objectives? I would suggest that the following would make a good place to start:

1. **Wellness and productivity**: Creating the conditions and environment whereby most, if not all, of our residents can lead healthy lives for at least 95 percent of a lengthening lifespan and productive lives for at least 75 percent of the same lifespan;
2. **Response to climate change**: Determine the positives of climate change and take steps to capitalize on them like with a comprehensive Arctic strategy; and defense against the negatives of climate change by protecting people and property from its adverse consequences.

Let's look at these two possible pursuits a little closer. With respect to the first objective:

We are not running on all cylinders. Innovation and creativity comes from too few of us. It would be in the national interest, and a tremendous boost to our chances to maintain world leadership, if we were able to mobilize each and every resident to be productive citizens for a long span of his/her life. That requires making sure that they have unfettered access to life-long education and that they are in a mental and physical condition fit for peak performance for most all of their adult life. Today, we have too few producers and too many consumers. Humans, by nature, will always be facing a limited lifespan.

Thank goodness! Can you imagine what the world would look like if we just kept procreating and none of us ever went away? Given this limited lifespan, medical research should be focused on keeping people in a positive frame of mind, pain free, fit, and productive, accepting the fact that one day we all must die from something. Healthcare that aims to achieve just that is a political and sociological imperative. It deserves an all-out scientific, technological, and political effort and commitment.

With respect to the second objective:

Too many people see the issue of climate change as a politically motivated, ideological matter. It is, however, beyond doubt that icecaps are melting around the globe and glaciers are retreating. What we are arguing about is, if and to what extent human intervention is driving this phenomenon. Winning or losing that argument is of little interest to people who stand to lose their livelihood, if not their lives, as a result of climate change. Climate changes are older than mankind. But never before in history have as many people and as much private property been threatened by the effects of climate change. Close to home, where beach erosion already challenges the irresistible desire to live at the ocean's edge, just imagine the consequences of the sea water level rising a few feet or hurricanes increasing in frequency and intensity. The lack of a national strategy is glaringly missing in the government's neglect of the American interest in the Arctic. If there is any good news in global warming, it may be that it is opening up the Arctic to new permanent shipping lanes that significantly reduce the transportation distance between Asia, Europe, and North America. And, that it is opening previously ice covered lands up for cultivation, exploration, and exploitation of natural resources like hydrocarbons, precious metals and stones, and rare earth materials. America, as it stands, has no strategy in place to safeguard these assets, with the help of friendly Arctic nations like Canada, Denmark, Norway and Iceland against intrusion by Russia and China. Doesn't that look like a missed opportunity?

The case for a centrist third party

The existing two-party system is blocking the progress the USA badly needs to stay ahead in the race with emerging economies like Brazil, China, and India and competitors like the EU and Russia. Technically, the major impediment to congressional action on required strategic decisions on entitlement reform, energy, education, immigration, taxation, regulation, infrastructure, and tort reform is the Senate's filibuster rule that commands sixty votes to get a law passed in the Senate. With a nation so evenly divided between Democrats and Republicans the inevitable consequence of this rule is a permanent deadlock.

Common Cause, a Washington-based watchdog group, is suing the U.S. Senate over the constitutionality of its filibuster rule that enables a 41-member minority to block the debate of bills. However, chances that the courts will step in to force a change in the inner workings of another branch of government are remote for very good reasons. At any rate, one should think twice before asking the Senate to change this rule more than it has already done, in November of 2013, by eliminating the filibuster rule for the Senate approval of judicial appointments (other than for the Supreme Court) and for government appointees. The filibuster rule has the merit that it puts Senators on notice that rash and partisan decisions are to be avoided. The whole reason for the bicameral system of the U.S. Congress is to have one chamber, the Senate, which looks at the nation's affairs more strategically, contemplatively, and deliberatively, than can be expected from the House of Representatives. The filibuster rule also has the merit that it forces proponents of a legislative initiative to reach across the aisle to find support. The fact that this hardly ever happens anymore is not a verdict against the rule as much as it is a verdict against the polarization of public opinion and the narrow partisan mindset in the U.S. Congress these days. Rather than forcing a rule change in the Senate, the effort should be directed towards changing the dynamics of the political process by entering a third, centrist, party that attracts Independents and could pick up moderate Democrats and Republicans. While such party would, by itself, not muster the representation in the Senate to meet the 60-vote rule, it would almost certainly control enough votes that, in coalition with either the Republicans or the Democrats, legislation could pass the Senate with the required sixty votes. This would mean that suddenly there would be a competition of legislative initiatives between the parties in Congress from the left and the right, each with an incentive to secure the support of the third party in the middle. It would open the door to a lot less ideological and more practical approach to addressing the nation's major challenges. Some laws could pass by a majority of centrists and Republicans while others could pass by a coalition of centrists and Democrats.

Any president would have a tough time vetoing a measure that had passed both chambers of Congress by a wide margin and sustaining such veto.

According to a Gallup poll[71] released the first week of January of 2014, a record high percentage of Americans identified as political independents. The survey found that, in 2013, 42 percent of the people in the survey identified themselves as Independent, 31 percent as Democrat and 25 percent as Republican. And there are reports that, ever since the 2008 election, there has been a shift of registered voters away from both established parties to the Independent column. It is true that Independents are not all of one mind, but neither are the Democrats or the Republicans. The one thing that all Independents share in common is their discomfort with the two established parties and the desire to break the gridlock and get things done in Washington. They should not be perpetually forced to choose between the lesser of two evils.

The role of government

Name one thing that the government is efficient in running. Do you ever deal face-to-face with the federal bureaucracy? What is your experience? I find it hard, as a general rule, to find more unmotivated people than the ones who work for the government and yet they all retire on tax payer funded defined benefit pensions.

The role of the government should be to put policies and incentives in place that will enable human ingenuity, not human indifference, to lead the charge. Where can the government make a positive difference? As an enabler rather than an operator. In the role of enabler it should focus on creating the right framework, platform, for its citizens to propel themselves and their nation forward. As an enabler, the government can mobilize and energize its citizenry by:

- Setting direction for the nation by designing a national strategy, sell the strategy to the public, and allow state and local government together with private enterprise to implement the plan.
- Expecting personal accountability from its citizens for solving society's challenges and rewarding the contributors to society at the expense of the hangers-on, who milk the system without contributing.
- Providing a strong safety net, but only for the truly incapable, including the very young, the sick and the elderly.
- Making sure that America will continue to attract and welcome the best and the brightest talent in the world.
- Establishing policies and incentives that make sure that American education—including continuing education—is world class, accessible, and affordable. And that young Americans find means and motivation to tailor their education to match their God-given capabilities.
- Establishing policies and incentives that are directed towards supporting investments in bringing American infrastructure to world class levels.
- Establishing policies and incentives that are directed towards supporting research and investments in liberating technologies in the health care, environmental science, communications, and energy fields.

- Promoting a healthy lifestyle for its citizens and incentives for them to stay engaged in the work force for as long as people can make valuable contributions.
- Eliminating disincentives, including excessive litigious challenges, to investments that need to be made and policies that need to be enacted.
- Getting out of the business of running things.

To right the ship it will have to take a combination of personal accountability and political will and leadership. If America cannot provide that, others will.

Here is the good news: Let's assume for a moment that, miraculously, the Beltway pulls it off and puts together the grand bargain required for a way out of the quagmire we're in; what then are the reasons to be bullish about America? Here is my read:

- If Washington can effectively deal with the elimination of the deficit and bring the debt back under control, it can surely tackle just about anything else.
- The energy picture has changed dramatically in our favor in a few short years and it now appears that independence from Middle East oil is within reach.
- Our demographics, while not ideal, are a lot better than for many of our competitors like China, Japan, and Western Europe. As long as we keep our borders open for new young talent and we keep birthrates where they are, we are not graying nearly as fast as the competition. The fact that almost half the children in the U.S. are born into single parent families is a cause for concern.
- U.S. exports are on the rise and consist in large part of sophisticated goods and services for which there is an increasing demand as third world economies benefit from globalization.

- U.S. universities and colleges, at least the best of them, are still the envy of the world and are incubators of new technologies and applications.
- Scientific discoveries—in genetics, molecular biology, nano-technology, 3-D printing, space exploration, and artificial intel-ligence—abound; scientists claim to have discovered the Higgs boson, sometimes named the "God particle".
- The U.S. is leading in the development of man/machine tech-nology, whereby computers are used to enhance human capabili-ties like in flying, driving, or surgery. It will also show up in the use of meta-data in research and applied science.
- Labor cost in the USA is gradually becoming less of a competitive disadvantage as labor cost in the third world and China contin-ues to rise and as labor, specifically in manufacturing, continues to be replaced by technology in the form of robotics, software and micro-chips. The result is that America will be re-shoring rather than outsourcing.

All of this demonstrates that there truly is plenty of reason to be bullish on America. It has essentially come down to this: We are in much bet-ter shape than the nay-sayers will make you believe; if only politics in America keep pace with progress in all other areas.

The disconnect

In business, we have learned that when reality deviates from the ex-pected outcome, the reason for the disconnect is, more often than not, found in the process rather than with the people involved in the pro-cess. Might that be the case here too?

Glenn Hubbard and Tim Kane in a well-reasoned article in *National Affairs* titled *"Regaining America's Balance"*[72] argue that the main char-acters in the Beltway behave rationally and are very much in tune with popular demand as to be expected in a democracy.

While just about every serious student of the predicament of the future funding of the major social programs—Social Security, Medicare and Medicaid—knows that the future obligations under these programs are under-funded under current rules, AARP and other interest groups have made it clear that changing the rules equals political suicide. Similarly, Grover Norquist has instilled the fear of God into all Republicans who, otherwise, might think that raising revenues by tax increases might be required for a balanced and lasting solution to our debt problems. Can American voters really expect from their chosen representatives that they jeopardize their whole political career by going against the popular demand? The disconnect, I'm afraid, is with the citizenry. It allows interest groups like AARP, NRA, Chamber of Commerce, Americans for Tax Reform, and others to speak for all with broad statements that typically equate to "over my dead body". How are elected officials going to ignore that pressure?

Francis Fukuyama is a professor of political science at Stanford (he is a third generation immigrant) who has written extensively about the American political system. In an article he wrote for the December, 2013 edition of *The American Interest* about what he terms the *"Decay of American Political Institutions"*[73] he observes: *"Neither major party has an incentive to cut itself off from access to interest group money, and the interest groups fear a system where money can't buy influence."* And he continues: *"A reform coalition has to emerge that unites groups without a stake in the current system."*

It is hard to see any of that happening without the emergence of a centrist third party, combined with a public demand that money gets taken out of politics as advocated above. Francis Fukuyama is right when he states, in the same article, that it may require a major shock, or shocks, to the system! The disconnect is between a *general* consensus that something needs to be done to address the challenges the nation is facing and an *individual* refusal to contribute to the solution by giving up something that seemed to have been secured (be it a tax advantage, an entitlement, or cherished government program).

The nation is in the same dilemma that the "Big Three" auto makers were in only a few years ago. They were confronted with the realization that they had made insupportable long-term promises to their workers and that these promises, if kept, were threatening to put them out of business.

In business, the way out of this type of predicament is bankruptcy. That is the path GM and Chrysler had to follow; Ford escaped, but benefitted from the concessions that the UAW had to make in the bankruptcy proceedings of its competitors. The nation is bankrupt in the sense that its future obligations, under the entitlements it has created, far outstrip its capacity to raise revenues under the existing rules. For years now it has had to borrow more than a trillion dollars per year to meet its current obligations. But nations can't go to the bankruptcy court and ask for a reset. Nations have to find a political solution. So do the states. The State of Illinois has near one trillion dollars in unfunded pension obligations—literally bankrupting the state—but the only way out is a political solution.

The disconnect stems from the "not at my expense" attitude of the voting public. It is not dissimilar to the dilemma of nuclear waste disposal or the location of a maximum security prison: It needs to be done, but not in my backyard. Will enough Americans speak up and break the disconnect?

The American National Election Studies group has been asking Americans since 1958: "*Do you trust the government in Washington to do what is right, all or most of the time?*" Until the mid-1960s, seventy-five percent of Americans answered yes, but by 1980 that number had dwindled down to twenty-five percent and the last three decades the yes answers have ranged from twenty to thirty-five percent. Jessica Mathews, the president of the Carnegie Endowment for International Peace has brought these numbers to light in a presentation[74] she made at the Gerald R. Ford School of Public Policy at the University of Michigan, titled "*Can America Still Act?*"

She rightly asks: *"Think what it means for the healthy functioning of a democracy that two-thirds to three quarters of its people do not believe that their government does the right thing most of the time."* Somehow we need to find a way to restore peoples' trust in government and, once we do, we need to give government more power to address the needs of the nation and keep America competitive. That will not happen unless we take the corruptive power of money and special interests out of our politics and get back to a government that is not only from the people, but also by the people and for the people.

Unfortunately, the Supreme Court has time and again—most recently in its April 2, 2014 ruling in the McClutcheon v. the Federal Election Commission—held that election campaign financing by individuals, corporations, special interest groups, and Political Action Committees is an expression of the right to free speech and protected by the First Amendment to the Constitution.

One has to read the text of this important part of our Constitution to realize how far we, or, rather, the Supreme Court, has strayed from what was written into our Constitution in 1791:

"Congress shall make no law respecting an establishment of religion, or prohibiting the free exercise thereof; or abridging the freedom of speech, or the press, or the right of people peaceably to assemble, and to petition the government for a redress of grievances."

Can anyone, in good conscience, assert that the framers of the Constitution wanted to enshrine, with this First Amendment, the right of wealthy citizens to throw whatever money they chose behind their favorite candidates for public office and for these candidates to pocket that money for their campaigns? Of course not. Chief Justice John Roberts Jr. is right when he writes in his majority opinion in the McClutcheon case that, *"There is no right more basic in our democracy than the right to participate in electing our political leaders."* We do that by voting and campaigning for our favorite candidates. But should that include the right to throw money at the candidate(s) of our choice?

We only got to where we are by a long creep of wider and wider interpretation, by successive High Courts, of what the right to free speech means for the freedom of individual citizens. In many instances, and certainly in the case of campaign financing rulings, the Supreme Court has protected the right of individuals at the expense of a compelling and very legitimate public interest.

Our democracy would work much better, and be in full compliance with the principles laid down in the Constitution, if we had a system of public financing of election campaigns—like most all other Western democracies have—that banned all other sources of campaign financing.

Former Senator Alan Simpson said it best when he testified in an earlier campaign-finance case: "*Who, after all, can seriously contend that a $100,000 donation does not alter the way one thinks about—and quite possibly votes on—an issue?*"

How much more effective would our politicians be if they did not have to run around all the time to collect campaign contributions? Without campaign contributions from private citizens, corporations, interest groups, and Political Action Committees, how much less beholden would our representatives in public office be to anyone but their true constituency and the public interest?

Justice Stephen Breyer, in his dissenting opinion in the McClutcheon case, hit the nail on the head when he wrote that, "*The anticorruption interest that drives Congress to regulate campaign contributions is a far broader, more important interest than the plurality [of the Court] acknowledges. It is an interest in maintaining the integrity of our public governmental institutions.*" And then he wrote: "*Where enough money calls the tune, the general public will not be heard.*" In his dissent he accuses the deciding majority of the Supreme Court of failing to recognize the difference between influence resting upon public opinion and influence bought by money alone.

As a public we can complain forever about how dysfunctional our political system has become, but we have to realize that one of the root causes of this breakdown in our democracy is that the moneymen have come between the citizens (voters) and their representatives. What counts is not what you and I think that needs to get done, what counts is what the large campaign donors want our representatives in Congress to say and do. No-one gets elected to Congress anymore, unless the candidate is rich enough to finance the election campaign entirely on his own or, unless the candidate is willing to cater and pander to the whims of the campaign donors.

Only Congress can lift us out of this morass. It can do so by changing the election laws to only permit public financing of election campaigns. But that would require pulling itself out by its own bootstraps, which—as we all know—is one of the hardest things to do. Admittedly, the hurdles for the members of Congress to effect the required change are phenomenal. First, it would have to muster the courage and moral fortitude to ignore what the moneymen want them to do. And, if they can pull that off, they would have to have the courage of conviction that cutting the moneymen out of the election process can be done without infringing upon citizens' rights under the First Amendment.

The Supreme Court, in its rulings about the constitutionality of campaign finance laws, has done us a supreme disservice, that now only Congress can undo.

Is America condemned to live with the flaws in its current political system and accept the consequences of undue influence—politicians who are beholden not to their constituents but their campaign contributors and the resulting dysfunction and paralysis—or will the voters exercise the people power to condemn the political structure that has evolved over time and bring it "up to code" for the exigencies of modern times? To those who would argue that this would be too much heavy lifting, I say that this nation has dealt with tougher challenges, when it had to. Remember what Nelson Mandela said: "*It always seems impossible, until it is done.*"

CHAPTER 15

TECHNOLOGY IS THE ANSWER

You don't have to look all the way back to the first appearance of mankind on earth to marvel at the progress made in human creativity and problem solving capability. Just check how people lived in this country a mere 400 years ago—a blip on the radar screen of time—and compare it with how we live our lives today. And think about all the human creativity and problem-solving that was brought to bear to get here from there. When the development of nuclear weaponry and missile technology was determined to be required to beat the Axis in WW II, it was done, and it saved the world not only from fascism but, later on, also from communism. When John F. Kennedy announced this nation's determination to put a man on the moon and bring him safely back to earth, it got accomplished in an astonishingly short time. All this innovation proves what we like to believe but not always practice: That human ingenuity knows no borders or limits. It just needs to be directed towards the right purpose.

These days, the pace of innovation is happening on an exponential scale. Not much changed in the world in more than a millennium, between the fall of the Roman Empire and the Renaissance, in a manner that had an appreciable effect on peoples' daily lives. Now, by advances in technology—from medical technology, nano-technology, artificial intelligence, to communications technology and astronomy—the way we live changes faster than ever before. While up to the First World War most innovation originated in Europe, the United States has since become the lead horse in the technology race and should be concerned with staying in the lead in the face of global competition. What is required and what is at stake?

What's at stake is the leadership role of the United States in the world and the sustainability of the global pace of innovation. It is not impossible, but hard to see, that the pace of innovation can be sustained if we, in the United States, don't challenge ourselves to stay in the lead and take the steps that will enable us to do that.

What's required is: 1) World class education; and 2) engagement and motivation of the largest possible component of the population; together with 3) proper resource allocation; and 4) the collective will (determination) to make it happen. We need a "refuse to lose" attitude to pervade all social strata. Our people should be concerned about bigger things than who wins the Super Bowl, the Stanley Cup, the World Series, or the National Basketball Association (NBA) championship. This means that we have to get better at educating people and putting them at work in circumstances and positions where they sense that they can make a difference and, in fact, make a contribution to the sustainability of our leadership position. There is plenty of work to do. For one thing, we have been largely sticking our heads in the sand and ignoring the threats posed to the environment.

We are burdening the earth with many more people—and all they bring to bear—than ever before. Nature's way of dealing with that burden is to produce cataclysmic events, wars, plagues, meteorite impacts, earthquakes, and you name it, to rebalance the situation. That's not how we like to solve our problems in this day and age. Our challenge is to create conditions under which the earth can accept the burden and people can go on with their lives. Technology will have to be the answer.

Any technology that the United States can develop, that will serve to address the following challenges, will have great global commercial value and enhance both the prestige and the world ranking of the United States:

- World shortage of accessible fresh and clean water and its global distribution
- Nuclear waste processing
- Risks associated with the recovery of fossil fuels and gas
- Alternative energy development
- Environmental impact of any other kind of human activity

Herein lays the key. We should embrace the challenge presented by the current wave of global warming rather than arguing if it is even happening. We should embrace the challenge to find ways to sequester CO_2 from our emissions, even if we are only half-certain that these emissions are causing the apparent climate change. And we should embrace the challenge to find economically feasible alternatives for fossil fuels. Which nation is better equipped than the USA to find solutions for these problems? If we don't find them some other nation will, and we lose the opportunity to maintain our leadership of nations. Conversely, if we do find technological solutions for the challenges presented by climate change and the need for greater human productivity, these solutions will be very marketable all over the world and enhance not only our economic prospects but also our prestige in the world.

Why would the United States government not consider to issue worldwide challenges to find answers to some of the unresolved questions that stand in the way of further and more rapid progress? In 1714, England's Parliament offered a king's ransom of 20,000 pounds sterling to anyone whose method of measuring longitude at sea could be proven successful. In an age of exploration, precious time, cargo, and life was lost at sea because ships, on their voyages, were able to determine latitude by the length of the day or by the height of the sun or known stars above the horizon, but not longitude. It took an English clockmaker, John Harrison, fifty-nine years and five prototypes before he collected the prize with a chronometer that worked. Given all the money the government spends futilely, what would be wrong by paying another king's ransom (which would have to be a little more than 20,000 pound sterling) for finding answers to the most pressing issues of our time, like clean affordable energy, suppression of drug addiction, or boosting individuals' propensity towards positive attitudes?

Earlier on, I have argued that technology should also provide the answer in the raging debate about (illegal) immigration. The United States needs immigrants as much as it has ever needed them. If some political zealots actually found a practical way to send all illegal immigrants home, our economy would be in desperate straits. The issue that needs to be addressed is not keeping *immigrants* out. We probably need every one of them. The issue is keeping *undesirables* out and knowing who's in the country and for what purpose. The technology exists to give every resident of the United States a bio-metric identity card that establishes a forge-proof identity. There is a lot more security in a bio-metric identity card than in the biggest wall or largest electric fence we can build along our borders as a symbol of misunderstood interests.

Technology should also serve to bring our business performance and service levels to the next level. Let's face it. Most of us already work as hard as we humanly can and we may assume that we are about as smart as humans will ever be. Progress, in any field, will have to come from two sources: Participation by a higher percentage of the population and new and better ways of doing things, i.e. technology. Technology is the preeminent tool of creative destruction. New technologies, new and better ways of doing things, are allowing us to forget about what was and to focus on what can be. They allow us to dispense with the tools and ways of the past and relegate them to the waste pile of irrelevance. The fumbling with the implementation of Obamacare shows how inept government is in acquiring and implementing technology. And yet it is in this realm, of how our government works and how the political system functions, that the country needs creativity and innovation in the worst way. It needs to have the courage to use creative destruction in keeping our democracy fresh and functioning for this day and age. That may require giving the letter of the Constitution a close hard look.

Robert Gates, in his previously cited memoir *"DUTY"*, reminds us that, *"The Founding Fathers had created a system of government designed primarily for the preservation of liberty, not for efficient or agile government."* The question is if, more than 200 years later, it is time for a shift in emphasis.

Could it be possible that the Constitution—which was designed by its authors (James Madison more than anyone else) to provide us with a prudent, balanced, republican form of government consisting of three separate branches and with a citizens' bill of rights—has gradually been turned against us in some of its provisions? Turned against us, as a result of changing times and conditions that could not have been imagined more than 200 years ago, and as a result of interpretations of provisions of the Constitution by the judiciary branch, particularly the Supreme Court. What raises that suspicion in my mind?

1. **For starters, the gun-control debate**. All opponents of gun-control throw the second amendment, "the right to bear arms", at the policy makers who want to protect the public at large from the unbridled proliferation of the most sophisticated weaponry. And the courts have been very reluctant to allow reasonable limitations on the second amendment right. This reality, combined with a fiercely combative attitude from a large part of the U.S. population, frustrates just about any attempt to keep guns out of the hands of those who cannot be trusted with them and keep military or gangster type weapons out of the hands of everyone, except trained professionals who are sworn to protect us.

2. **The stranglehold money has on politics**. Corporations' right to lobby members of Congress and fund their election campaigns is being protected by the Supreme Court's interpretation of the freedom of speech afforded us under the first amendment to

the Constitution. The framers of the Constitution wrote their document to institutionalize the best form of government they could come up with. The veracity and effectiveness of our government would be greatly enhanced if we managed to keep money out of the governance process. We would be much better off if elections would be exclusively funded with public funds and if public office holders would be highly compensated, but forbidden to accept any money from other sources. But current interpretation of the Constitution stands in the way of moving in that direction.

3. **The corrupting content of media**. The Supreme Court's deference to the first amendment keeps us from shielding ourselves from all kinds of propaganda, misinformation, brainwashing, and dumbing down. The framers of the Constitution and their contemporaries were only exposed to the verbal and written word. They had no inkling of the intrusiveness of large screen TV images, retina tablet displays, or smart phone instant imaging. Even radio broadcasts were still a century away. What public good is being served—other than excessive deference to a law that was established more than two centuries ago in a completely different world—with advertisements of pharmaceuticals that nobody but medical doctors should decide if we need them or not? Or with advertisements for ambulance chasers? Or with the dissemination of video games with violent content? What public good is being served with seemingly interminable political ads that are under no test or obligation of veracity? Yet, all of these "rights" are protected by the current interpretation of first amendment to the Constitution.

4. **The undue influence of pressure groups**. Again under protection of the first amendment, pressure groups like AARP, the NRA, Labor Unions, the U.S. Chamber of Commerce, and large public pension funds like CalPERS, have gained excessive influence on the election process and the behavior of our elected

officials, once they are in office. These pressure groups frequently take political positions without ever checking back with their constituents to see if, and to what extent, these positions are fully supported. Much less are they concerned with the greater public interest. Maybe, the real problem is, that too many of our Congressional representatives lack the courage of their own convictions and just bend to the pressure of the interest groups that helped them into office. We better recognize that our elected officials are not immune from human frailty and greed. The Constitution should not stand in the way of eliminating undue influence.

5. **The curse of too many elections**. The president of the United States should be elected for one term—I suggest six or seven years—and not be eligible for re-election. The frequency of elections, particularly for the presidency and the House of Representatives, exacerbates the polarization of the voting public; it keeps those who should govern in a near permanent election campaign mode; it is extremely costly in financial terms, making it harder to keep the money influence out of politics; it does not allow an office holder to complete an agenda. The process would also be greatly enhanced if—by law—election campaigns were limited to running for no more than three months. It would save large amounts of money and keep politicians focused on their job with much less interruption.

If the Constitution, as it is written and interpreted today, stands in the way of addressing these five hurdles to a better functioning of our government—a government for and by the people—then it is time to amend the Constitution. It is not so sacred that it cannot be changed. The framers of the Constitution realized the need for adaptation over time, which is why they provided, in Article V, for the way in which the Constitution may be amended. After, in 1791, the Bill of Rights was incorporated in the first ten amendments to the Constitution, it was further ratified to be amended seventeen more times, the last time in 1992. It can be done. And it should be done again.

We are a nation of laws and should, by all means, keep it that way. But that does not mean that we should not amend or scratch laws—parts of the Constitution included—that no longer serve a public good that has been democratically expressed in our time. The task of keeping our laws "up to date" falls on the legislative branch. It is too sacred to be left to the judiciary. This is very much the position taken by former Supreme Court judge John Paul Stevens in his recently published work *"Six Amendments: How and Why We Should Change the Constitution."*

Democratic systems are ideal to foster ingenuity and creativity, because they allow equal opportunity to all to think for themselves, and find their own way rather than a path that may be laid out for them by their government. Democratic systems also make education more freely available to all who care for it. This is why so much innovation in the twentieth century has come from the United States. There is no good reason for us to lose that edge. We can only defeat ourselves. We need to have the courage to apply the method of creative destruction not only in our business life but also in our public life. Science and technology need to provide the answer. But it is not enough. We will also need to maintain and protect a society where the quality of life for virtually all is better than anywhere else in the world. Because innovation and ingenuity need to find a fertile soil in which to grow and innovation and creativity still need to be nurtured.

—

SECTION IV

THE FINAL ANALYSIS

How do we get from There to Here? Will America resolve to be truly exceptional again? Will the people in America come back together and retake control of governance, so that America will live up again to its old motto E Pluribus Unum?

"The world needs dreamers and the world needs doers. But above all, the world needs dreamers who do." (Sarah Ban Breathnach)

Thirty years later the journey has not been completed. I am still neither here nor there. And I am still in search of American Exceptionalism. I have definitely left the Netherlands and immigrated to the United States. My family is here. My children and grandchildren are here, and I have long passed the point of no return. And yet, it does not feel like I have arrived at my destination. It feels like I've started a journey that I may never complete and I embarked on a quest for something that remains out of reach.

Thirty years ago, I was convinced that I knew where I was heading. I was ready to experience American Exceptionalism for myself. The grass looked definitely greener on this side of the ocean and Serendipity had completed the puzzle for me. All events conspired to make the decision for me. Lady Liberty beaconed as the new torch bearer for tolerance and the doors behind me were closing. But now I wonder if I was chasing a mirage. Was I heading towards a fata morgana? Was I immigrating to an imaginary America that I could visualize but that would stay beyond my reach?

It is as if there are two Americas: The one that caused the world to speak of American Exceptionalism and then the one that exists today. The one of E Pluribus Unum and the one of E Pluribus Duo. The core of my disenchantment with America, as it functions today, is in the fact that the forces that pull America apart seem to have overwhelmed the forces that bind America together. Not unlike the dawn of the Civil War.

We are split and polarized in just about every way you can imagine: Belmont versus Fishtown; right versus left; Republicans versus Democrats; liberals versus conservatives; Caucasians versus non-whites; pro-life versus pro-choice; union versus non-union; gun control proponents versus opponents; lesbian, gay, bisexual, and transgender (lgbt) versus straight; immigration proponents versus opponents; tax payers versus benefit recipients; young versus old. And never the twain shall meet. We demonstrate and propagate, but the opposites never engage in a meaningful dialogue. If we can't get it our way, we don't play. We withdraw to the sideline.

What is missing in all of these confrontations is tolerance and civility, the willingness to try to understand the other side, and acceptance of more than one world view. The right thinks that the bottom dwellers do not do their fair share in pulling the wagon. And the left thinks that the people at the bottom do not get a fair chance. Both have a good argument, but being right does not solve anything. The real question is: What will we do to get the bottom dwellers engaged and how do we give them a real chance to participate?

America has too many players on the sideline. It is just not conceivable that, in the globalized environment we live in, the nation, any nation, can represent world leadership if not all of its people pull the wagon and pull it in the same direction. The sideline is killing us.

First, we have the many millions who are not engaged, because they are too old, too young, unemployed, on disability, on welfare, in prison, on probation or on parole, or incapacitated because of illness, drugs, or alcohol. America will have to do some serious social experimenting to move a good percentage of these disengaged from the sideline to the playing field. The nation would do itself a tremendous service if it were capable of rehabilitating most of its drunks, addicts, mentally ill, and criminals and turn them into productive, participative citizens. Society would have to be prepared to help their rehabilitation by removing stigmata and welcoming the rehabilitated back onto the playing field and into the productive process.

Then, we have yet to address the income inequality between the genders. Women are outnumbering men in attending higher education and graduating from our colleges and universities, but for many, a glass ceiling is preventing them from achieving their aspirations and their full potential and, in too many instances, they get denied the level of pay their male peers earn. If anything, society should find a way to remunerate women for often playing a dual role of leadership, at the workplace and at home.

Finally, we have the serious move to the sideline out of political calculation. Where the Democrats are in control, like they are in 2013 in the White House and the Senate, we see Republicans leave the playing field and go to the sideline and where the Republicans are in control, like in the House of Representatives, we see the Democrats return the favor. In business, saboteurs get fired.

In politics, sabotage is almost required to keep the job in our gerrymandered voting districts. In politics the scene is even uglier than in our society at large. Not only do we have roughly half of our politicians withdrawn to the sideline at any given time when they are in the minority, they are actually cheering for defeat.

America is like the smart kid that is so convinced of its superior talent that it is no longer interested in applying himself to get straight "A"s. Like this kid, America is grossly underperforming to its capabilities. This book would not have been written if it were different.

Citizenship is not the issue for me. It is not the missing last step in getting from there to here. I will know that I have completed my journey when I see that I have arrived at the destination of my imagination, at a safe harbor called America. For that to happen, the two Americas, the imagined and the real, will have to come together as one.

There is no doubt in my mind that America is blessed with the best of the most vital resources any nation could ever wish for: People, location, space, nature, water, minerals, and hydrocarbons.

America has enviable traditions in democracy, tolerance, freedom of thought and pursuit, entrepreneurial spirit, and self-reliance. All of that together justifies the sense of American Exceptionalism. But, having all the means does not mean much when the will, the desire, is not there to make the most of it every day. Glenn Hubbard and Tim Kane point out in their previously quoted article in *National Affairs*[72] that "*Great powers are rarely brought down by outside adversaries; they destroy themselves from within. Very often, they do it by falling victim to economic imbalances and the decay of once-vibrant governing institutions that prove unable to adapt to changing circumstances.*"

If America underperforms, as I believe it does, we need to look for the cause in the systems, in the processes, it deploys to serve and support its people and to mobilize its resources. It is political creep that has caused this nation to split apart in two Americas and it will take political action and leadership to put it back together. It will have to come back together for it to deliver on its promise and potential. It will have to come back together to prove the doomsayers wrong and keep America firmly in place in its leadership position in a world of human endeavor.

What poor governance has pried apart, good governance will have to put back together. In the final analysis, that means that the people who, together, form this nation have to reclaim their authority —wrest it away from the moneymen and the special interests—and select representatives who put achievement ahead of ideology and the nation ahead of the party they belong to. Today, America has a government of the people, but not a government by the people, nor a government for (all of) the people. America has allowed to let the moneymen, the special interest groups, come in between the people and their representatives. How can that be remedied? I have outlined some steps in this book that all have to do with taking the influence of money out of the political process. I am not against lobbying. The right to petition the government is an important constitutional right that should not be tossed out. Legislators need the input that comes from the people who will have to live with the laws that Congress passes. But I am fiercely against lobbying by people and organizations that finance the campaigns of our elected representatives. It is just unreasonable to expect that politicians can resist the temptation that comes with that: To please the donor so that he will give more when the next election comes around. The only people that have the power to change the paradigm are the voters. They will have to step up to the plate and shed their passivity. They have to retake control of the process.

A good place to start is for the voters to create a centrist third party, which is—I'm afraid—the only way to let the Republican and Democratic parties know that the game needs to change, if they want to count on votes in the future. The voters will have to demand action on the main challenges the nation faces and deny a seat in Congress to the representatives who are merely defending their seat at the table and the status quo. But the voters will also have to change their own mindset. They have to stop listening to the media that stoke our polarization and they have to be more accepting of the fact that there is always more than one way to skin the cat. They will have to become more tolerant of differing opinions and solutions and they will have to be willing to encourage and participate in a real dialogue aimed at finding the right solutions for the challenges the nation is facing.

There are two Americas in our time, an engaged America and a disengaged America, because the political system, as it functions today, has kept America from solving the issues that bring about inequality and that stand in the way of social mobility, up and down. The solutions to these issues are in plain sight: Education, healthcare, fiscal responsibility, safety net, environmental protection, resource management, budget control, immigration, and national security. All but two of the issues the country is facing are of a practical nature, meaning that there are known solutions available to solve them, if only we are willing to apply the resources and find the political will to deal with them. They are all well within the means of the richest nation on earth.

Two are systematic: inequality and governance.

Here is the catch 22: The practical issues will not be addressed and resolved unless our system of governance is restored to functionality and inequality will not be brought back to acceptable proportions unless the practical issues are addressed and resolved. It all hangs together and our destiny hinges on the linchpin of a functional system of governance.

It will, therefore, take the people's resolve and the right political constellation, will, and courage to tackle the issues the country is facing—the practical as well as the systematic issues—one by one. It may very well take some serious creative destruction, some letting go of rules and institutions we hold sacred because they served us so well in the past, before we can redesign them to serve us going forward. Most of all, it will take for the nation to develop a clear vision of what the American future should look like and then set some lofty strategic, long term, goals for how to realize such vision with the support of most all of the capable bodies and minds available. The Second World War was won—by America—because the American population rallied behind the cause. And everyone got engaged. The men went to war and the women produced the materiel the Allies needed to defeat the enemy. That is what made America exceptional at that time. We need again to get virtually all of the population engaged and all pulling the wagon in the same direction. Only then can we be confident that America will come back as one, true to its motto E Pluribus Unum. Only then will I finish my search for American Exceptionalism and only then will I complete my journey and arrive at my destination. I will finally be here and no longer there.

———

POSTSCRIPT

"We are a great country and we should be governed as a great country" (Olympia Snow)

As I completed my work on the manuscript for this book, the Bipartisan Policy Center published, on June 24, 2014 the report by its Commission on Political Reform titled *"Governing in a polarized America: A Bipartisan Blueprint to Strengthen our Democracy."*

Founded in 2007 by former Senate Majority Leaders Howard Baker, Tom Daschle, Bob Dole, and George Mitchell, the Bipartisan Policy Center is a non-profit organization that drives principled solutions through rigorous analysis, reasoned negotiation and respectful dialogue.

The Commission on Political Reform was launched in 2013 to investigate the causes and consequences of America's partisan political divide and to advocate for specific reforms that will improve the political process and that will work in a polarized atmosphere. The Commission had 29 members from all segments of society and from both parties, including 5 Co-Chairs: Tom Daschle, Dan Glickman, Dirk Kempthorne, Trent Lott, and Olympia Snow. In its report, the Commission concluded that: "It is clear that Americans are concerned about the lack of civil discourse and the increasing inability of the U.S. political system to grapple with the nation's biggest challenges." Then it adds, what I have argued in this book that: *"These shortcomings put the nation at risk of losing it standing in the world."*

The Commission proposes reforms in three specific areas: The electoral process, the process by which Congress legislates and manages its own affairs, and the ability of Americans to plug into the nation's civic life through public service.

Hopefully, the publication of this report and the work of the Bipartisan Policy Center and other similar initiatives will elevate the awareness in the American public of the need for engagement and convince the political establishment that time for change has arrived. On the surface, the recommendations by the Commission appear to be timid and too reverential of the existing order. But I will accept that change in the political system can only come in small incremental steps and that, as first steps, the recommendations are all steps in the right direction. I am particularly encouraged by the Commission's emphasis on the importance of civic education and participation, including the introduction of a one year civil service requirement for all Americans. The report gives little, if any, support to my much farther reaching proposals, but that can be explained by the fact that my book focuses more on the desired end-result, while the report of the Commission on Political Reform deals with practical first steps that can be taken to move the political process in the right direction. After all, the Bipartisan Policy Center represents the status quo in the sense that it tries to bridge the differences between the two existing political parties. The question is if these two parties, by themselves, can do the heavy lifting required or if they will need to be challenged by the catalyst of a centrist third party.

———

REFERENCES

Career Path

After graduation from law school at Erasmus University in Rotterdam and completing my military service as a first Lieutenant with the Royal Dutch Airforce, I took a job on the Commercial Staff of Nederlandsche Stikstof Maatschappij N.V. in Sluiskil, the Netherlands. The company was a manufacturer of nitrogen fertilizers and I joined the commercial staff, responsible for the sales and marketing of the product, as the junior partner of a chemical engineer and an economist. I stayed with the company until 1984 and served in several capacities, including two assignments with NSM's affiliate in the USA, Transnitro and an assignment with Centraal Stikstof Verkoopkantoor B.V. (CSV).

After serving a year as Vice President of International Raw Materials Ltd. In Philadelphia, I was recruited in 1985 by Continental Grain Company to set up a fertilizer trading business in Geneva, Switzerland for ContiChem, Inc. In 1987, I was promoted to Vice President and General Manager of ContiChem, Inc. in Tampa, FL.

In 1992, I joined Lesco, Inc. in Rocky River, OH as Vice President Purchasing, leaving the fertilizer trading and distribution business for the Green Industry where I worked for the next 18 years. From Lesco I moved in 2001 to PrimeraTurf, Inc. where I served for ten years as its Chief Executive Officer.

I retired in 2011 from PrimeraTurf and started Castnet Corp. a consulting company providing management support and executive coaching services to small privately owned businesses and their owners. My activities as an author of books, columns, and articles are also conducted through Castnet Corp.

Places where we lived

Born in Hummelo (near the German border), in the province of Gelderland in the Netherlands, I have lived in the following places:

1. Hummelo, the Netherlands
2. Groningen, the Netherlands
3. Rotterdam, the Netherlands
4. Sluiskil, the Netherlands
5. Grimbergen, Belgium
6. Eastchester, NY
7. Boskoop, the Netherlands
8. Scarsdale, NY
9. Eastchester, NY
10. Tampa, FL
11. Newtown Square, PA
12. Veyrier, Switzerland
13. West Byfleet, Surrey, England
14. Tampa, FL
15. Westlake, OH
16. North Ridgeville, OH

Dutch Governance

The Netherlands is a parliamentary monarchy. Under this system, the position of the monarch is largely ceremonial. The government is led by a Prime Minister, who typically emerges from the lead political party that was victorious in the national elections, which are held every four years or after the fall of a cabinet (whichever comes first). The Prime Minister forms his own cabinet from representatives of the parties that participate in his coalition.

The Dutch Parliament (Staten Generaal) is bi-cameral, like the U.S. Congress. The House of Representatives (Tweede Kamer) has 150 members, elected by proportional representation based on the election results. Proportional representation means that voters do not vote for a particular candidate but for a party. The number of votes that party collects determines how many seats it gets in the Tweede Kamer. In advance of an election, the party publishes a list of its candidates, ranked in order in which the party wants to see them seated. If the party collects fifteen seats in an election then the top fifteen candidates get seated. The Senate (Eerste Kamer) has seventy-five members, elected indirectly by the Provincial Administration on the basis of the outcome of provincial elections.

Twenty-one parties participated in the 2012 national elections, with eleven collecting enough votes to meet the threshold for gaining a seat in the Tweede Kamer. In post-war Netherlands, no party has ever gained enough votes to be able to form a government by itself. The Dutch are always ruled by a coalition government.

The twelve provinces of the Netherlands elect, every four years (but on a different schedule from the national elections), their own representatives (Provinciale Staten) to deal with largely administrative matters. The policy decision making process in the Netherlands is reserved for the Prime Minister and his Cabinet with blessing of the Staten Generaal.

In 1944, (the year I was born) the throne was occupied by Queen Wilhelmina. She had led the Dutch government in exile from London (and Canada when the German blitzkrieg threatened England) during the German occupation. Both Wilhelmina and her daughter Juliana, who succeeded her in 1948, were married to German aristocrats, but in World War II that did not affect the firm anti-German sentiment of the Dutch Royal family and it never caused a constitutional crisis (Wilhelmina's husband had passed away in 1934). Queen Wilhelmina played an active role in organizing Dutch resistance against the Germans. She was recognized by Winston Churchill and Franklin D. Roosevelt as an important war leader and was the first queen to ever address the U.S. Congress, which she was invited to do on August 5, 1942. Juliana was succeeded in 1980 by her eldest daughter Beatrix, who also married a German aristocrat, Claus von Amsberg. Queen Beatrix abdicated the throne, after a 33-year reign, in favor of her eldest son Willem-Alexander on April 30, 2013. Willem-Alexander became at that time, the first Dutch king in 123 years.

The Dutch Economy

The Dutch economy rests on three pillars: Its geography, its population, and its natural resources (mainly natural gas). Located as it is at the delta of the rivers Rhine, Meuse, and Scheldt, the Netherlands is a gateway for transport into and out of Germany, Switzerland, and parts of Central Europe. The port of Rotterdam is the largest sea-port in Europe and the sixth largest in the world, measured by tonnage moving through. This location has, for centuries, stimulated trade with other parts of the world.

The population is largely homogeneous, although less so these days than in the twentieth century as a result of increased immigration. It is extremely well educated by world standards, with a very high percentage of the population earning degrees from a large number of public institutions for higher education. It has a reputation for having an exceptional work ethic and it is used to speaking foreign languages as the Dutch language does not get them very far in the world. The combination of a trade based economy and a highly educated population with foreign language skills has meant that many Dutch work overseas for companies and in international organizations.

The third pillar of the Dutch economy is its natural gas reserve. The Netherlands is the second largest gas producer in Europe (behind Norway) and ninth in the world, accounting for more than thirty percent of gas production in the EU and more than 2.5 percent of the world total. The country exports about one-third of its annual natural gas output. With its domestic supply it serves the generation of electric power and the Dutch households with heating and cooking supplies. And, importantly from an economic perspective, it provides feedstock and energy for a sizeable chemical industry, which is largely situated in the river delta region of the country.

Based on these assets, the Dutch economy is currently the seventeenth largest in the world if measured by GDP. Its GDP per capita is approximately $42,000, which puts it in the top 10 richest nations in the world. The country is one of the five largest investors in the United States and it attracts significant foreign direct investments. It is home to a number of large and world class multinational enterprises like Royal Dutch Shell, Unilever, Philips, Akzo-Nobel, ING, AEGON, Ahold, Rabobank and Heineken.

A unique aspect of the Dutch economy is its flower business. The Netherlands is the center of production for the European floral market, as well as a major international supplier to other continents. The flower auction at Aalsmeer is the largest flower market in the world. Located near Schiphol, the large international airport of the Netherlands, it allows for daily shipments of fresh cut flowers all over the world. The production and distribution of cut flowers in Netherlands has grown dramatically since the 1970s and the export of cut flowers makes a significant contribution to the Dutch balance of trade. In 2013 the export exceeded the $7 billion mark.

Deltaworks

A good part of the Netherlands is situated below sea level and, historically, the Dutch have had to defend their territory against the ever threatening sea-water as much as against any other intruder.

It was in their fight against the water that the Dutch built their windmills. While some were used for the milling of grain and spices, most were pumping stations that kept the water out of the low laying areas. Not always with success. On February 1, 1953 a hurricane force northwestern storm whipped up the waters of the North Sea into the funnel created by the gradually narrowing English Channel to the point that ebb waters could no longer recede, pushing water levels in the critical river delta of the low country to over fourteen feet above normal. Some of the dikes in place to protect against the sea were in a state of disrepair and could not withstand the onslaught of the wind driven North Sea. Once some of them broke through, others followed and disaster was inevitable at that point. Nearly two thousand people died and more than 370,000 acres of mostly farm land were flooded.

The flood of 1953 was one of many that had hit the low country over the centuries. The southwestern sector of the Netherlands is a river delta for three major rivers, the Rhine, the Scheldt and the Meuse and all of the land along these rivers in the delta needs to be protected by dikes to keep the water out. The building and maintenance of these dikes had been the responsibility of the local communities, organized in "waterschappen", Water Boards, created specifically for the purpose of managing the water management for a specific area. The flood of 1953 caused the Dutch government to take charge of the problem on a national scale, without dismantling the regional framework of the waterschappen. Although nominally in charge of defense against the sea since 1798, the scope of the 1953 disaster caused the Dutch national government to make protection of its population and its territory against the sea a top national priority. It created a long term strategic plan to better protect the country and its population from continuing threats from the North Sea by means of a system of civil engineering works, collectively called the "Deltaworks".

The first Deltawork was put in operation in 1958, five years after the flood, and was a removable barrier designed to protect the densely populated western part of the Netherlands against future flooding. The final piece was put in place in 2003 when a new tunnel beneath the Western branch of the Scheldt was opened to improve traffic between the different parts of the Province of Zeeland and create a new gateway to the port of Antwerp in Belgium. There is a lesson in this for all of us today who live in a world of instant gratification: Major strategic initiatives need to be carefully planned and require a very long time horizon for implementation. It took the Dutch forty-five years to put in place a defense against the sea. Now they have in place an infrastructure they can build upon if rising water levels resulting from global warming tell them it's time to do so.

Dutch Education

Primary school in the Netherlands starts at four years of age and runs for eight years. Attendance is compulsory from age five. Children residing in the Netherlands must stay at school until their eighteenth birthday or until they have obtained a diploma. Every child in the Netherlands receives free education until the age of sixteen. The cost is borne by the government.

There are three branches of secondary education: Preparatory secondary vocational education (VMBO), senior general secondary education (HAVO) and pre-university education (VWO). A report from the primary school will advise which branch would best suit the child. Children undergo a test in eighth grade to assess their aptitude. This is called the CITO-test (*CITO-toets*). The report from the school will be based on the result of that CITO-test.

The VMBO (*voorbereidend middelbaar beroepsonderwijs*) trains pupils for secondary vocational education (*middelbaar beroepsonderwijs*, MBO) or, in some cases, to move on to senior general secondary education (*hoger algemeen voortgezet onderwijs*, HAVO). A VMBO education takes four years. After two years the pupil chooses the educational direction that best suits them.

There are four different directions varying in their practical and theoretical education balance, alongside general subjects:

- Basic vocational training (VMBO-B), with twelve hours a week devoted to practical subjects. The pupil can move on from here to MBO levels 1 and 2.
- Framework training (VMBO-K), with twelve hours a week devoted to practical subjects, aimed at a particular profession. The pupil can move on to MBO levels 3 and 4.
- Mixed training (VMBO-G), with four hours a week devoted to practical subjects and for the rest general subjects. The pupil can move on to MBO levels 3 and 4.
- Theoretical training (VMBO-T), with only general subjects. The pupil can move on to MBO levels 3 and 4 or to a HAVO education.

Pupils may also choose a sector in which to specialize and, within that sector, a particular department. There are four sectors:

- Technical, which is sub-divided into construction, graphics, metal, vehicles, electrical, installation, transport, and logistics.
- Agriculture, sub-divided into agriculture and natural surroundings, and food technology.
- Economics, sub-divided into administration, catering, commercial services, fashion, and clothing.
- Care and welfare.

A HAVO (*hoger algemeen voortgezet onderwijs*) education takes five years and is a preparation for university or a professional education (*hoger beroeponderwijs*, HBO). However, a pupil can also move on to pre-university education (*voorbereidend wetenschappelijk onderwijs*, VWO). At the end of the second year the pupil chooses a 'profile'- a package including both compulsory and elective subjects. The following profiles are offered:

- Culture and society
- Economics and society
- Nature and health
- Nature and technology

After the fourth year, the pupil will be in a period called the 'study-house' (studiehuis), where independent study is essential. In addition to traditional lessons, the study house offers a broad scope for individual approach.

A VWO (*voorbereidend wetenschappelijk onderwijs*) education has two separate branches: *Atheneum* and *gymnasium*. In the latter, pupils study Latin, ancient Greek and/or classical culture. The VWO takes six years and prepares the pupil for a university education. In the first two years, pupils study the fifteen subjects which form the basic curriculum. All VWO-pupils must study French, German and English up to the end of their third year. At the end of the third year the pupil chooses a 'profile' - a package including both compulsory and optional subjects. The following profiles are offered:

- Culture and society
- Economics and society
- Nature and health
- Nature and technology

After the fourth year, the pupil will be in a period called the 'study-house' (*studiehuis*), where independent study is essential. In addition to traditional lessons, the study house offers a broad scope for individual approach.

Higher education in the Netherlands is offered at two types of institutions: Research universities and universities of applied sciences.

Research universities include general universities, universities specializing in engineering and agriculture, and the Open University. Universities of applied sciences include general institutions as well as institutions specializing in a specific field such as agriculture, fine and performing arts, or teacher training.

Whereas research universities are primarily responsible for offering research-oriented programs, universities of applied sciences are primarily responsible for offering programs of higher professional education, which prepare students for specific professions. These tend to be more practice oriented than programs offered by research universities. In this binary, three-cycle system, bachelor's, master's and PhD degrees are awarded. Short-cycle higher education leading to the associate degree is offered by universities of applied sciences. Degree programs and periods of study are quantified in terms of the ECTS credit system.

The focus of degree programs determines both the number of credits required to complete the program and the degree which is awarded. A research-oriented bachelor's program requires the completion of 180 credits (three years) and graduates obtain the degree Bachelor of Arts or Bachelor of Science (BA/BSc), depending on the discipline. A bachelor's degree awarded in the applied arts and sciences requires 240 credits (four years), and graduates obtain a degree indicating the field of study (for example, Bachelor of Engineering, B Eng, or Bachelor of Nursing, B Nursing). An associate degree in the applied arts and sciences requires 120 credits (two years), and students who complete the two-year program can continue studying for a bachelor's degree in the applied arts and sciences.

A research-oriented master's program requires the completion of 60, 90 or 120 credits (one, one-and-a-half or two years). In engineering, agriculture, mathematics and the natural sciences, 120 credits are always required. Graduates obtain a Master of Arts or Master of Science (MA/MSc). A master's degree awarded in the applied arts and sciences requires the completion of 60 to 120 credits and graduates obtain a degree indicating the field of study (for example, Master of Architecture, MArch).

The third cycle of higher education, leading to a PhD, is offered only by research universities. The major requirement is completion of a dissertation based on original research that is publicly defended. All research universities award the PhD. In addition to doctorate programs, the three engineering universities offer technological designer programs consisting of advanced study and a personal design assignment in a number of engineering fields. The technical designer program requires two years of study to complete and graduates obtain the degree Professional Doctorate in Engineering (PDEng). The training of medical specialists is the responsibility of the professional group in an organizational setting at a university hospital.

ACKNOWLEDGMENTS

Thanks go out first and foremost to the many people who have enriched my life on both sides of the Atlantic. They are too numerous to be mentioned here by name—and I would be sure to overlook a number of them, if I tried—but they certainly include my wife of forty-five years, Christie, my children, Nienke, Pim, Thomas and Michael and my grandchildren to whom I have dedicated this book. You have been the very foundation on which I have built my life and you have followed me along and cheered me on in my journey from there to here. Thank you! Life would have been meaningless without you.

I want to single out for thanks in the same vein some friends we have been fortunate enough to make along the way and who have figured importantly in our lives: Dick Prins and Anneke Human, Norman Schreiner, Anton van Rossum, Frits and Agnes Goethals, Bert and Mieke van Dijk, Jacco Eltingh, Ed and Joannie Cavazuti, Jerry and Susan Crossan, Ted and Rose Schulte, Bob and Sue Yarborough, Jeff and Jennie Sims, Jeff and Lee Armbruster, Kip and Patricia Connelly, Randy and Beth Tischer, Ralph and Nancy Rocco and, importantly, our brothers (in law) and sisters (in law).

In helping me with the writing and editing of my book, I am deeply indebted to my daughter-in-law Andrea who did the cover design, to my son Pim, to Bob Rich and his son Rob Rich, who were among the first to read my original manuscript and gave me, separately, both the critique and encouragement I needed at that early stage; to Jeff Sims, Walter van

Driessche, Chris Ankersmit, Ted Schulte, and Dave Sullivan for reading later versions of the manuscript and making me rework it to the form in which it was ultimately published.

A special thanks to Garnette Bane who edited the manuscript for grammar and punctuation.

INDEX

NOTES

[1] Russell Shorto. *The Island at the Center of the World, the epic story of Dutch Manhattan and the forgotten colony that shaped America.* Published in 2004 by Vintage Books

[2] Alvaro Vargas Llosa in *Global Crossings, Immigration, Civilization and America,* Published in 2013 by The Independent Institute, page 295

[3] Democrat Senators Michael Bennett, CO; Richard J. Durbin, IL; Bob Menendez, NJ; Chuck Schumer, NY; and Republican Senators Jeff Flake, AZ; Lindsey Graham, SC; John McCain, AZ; Marco Rubio, FL.

[4] Alvaro Vargas Llosa in *Global Crossings, Immigration, Civilization and America,* Published in 2013 by The Independent Institute, pages 29-44

[5] Dan Morgan, *Merchants of Grain,* Viking Press 1979

[6] See www.aileron.org

[7] It is in fact Michael Gerber who coined this phrase first in his book E-Myth

[8] See www.classicalaskacharters.com with Captain Rob Scherer

[9] See castnetcorp.blogspot.com

[10] John D. Gartner, *The Hypomanic Edge: The Link between (a little) Craziness and (a lot of) Success in America,* published in 2005 by Simon & Schuster

[11]Robert Kagan, in a well-reasoned article in *The New Republic* of January 2012, warned against the risk of making this foreboding a self-fulfilling prophesy

[12]See www.socialprogressimperative.org

[13]See www.oecdbetterlifeindex.org

[14]Charles Murray in *"Coming Apart"* published 2012 by Crown Forum

[15]May 20, 2013 issue of *Fortune Magazine*

[16]See Amanda Ripley, *The Smartest Kids in the World (and how they got that way)*, published in 2013 by Simon & Schuster

[17]Saskia Sassen, *Expulsions. Brutality and Complexity in the Global economy, page 64*. Published in 2014 by the Belknap Press of Harvard University Press.

[18]Paul Taylor. *The Next America, Boomers, Millenials and the Looming Generational Showdown*. Published in 2014 by Public Affairs

[19]The Center for Disease Control pegs the birthrate in America at 1.3 percent for 2010

[20]Joel Kotkin, *The Next Hundred Million, America in 2050*, published in 2010 by The Penguin Press

[21]Richard T. Herman and Robert L. Smith, *Immigrant, Inc. (Why immigrant entrepreneurs are driving the economy and how they will save the American worker)*, published in 2010 by John Wiley & Sons

[22]Robert M. Gates, *Duty (Memoirs of a Secretary at War)*, published in 2014 by Alfred A. Knopf

[23]Nicolas Berggruen and Nathan Gardels, *Intelligent Governance for the 21st Century (A Middle Way between West and East)*, Published in 2013 by Polity Press, Page 65

[24]Moises Naim. *The End of Power, from Boardrooms to battlefields and churches to states, why being in charge isn't what it used to be*. Published in 2013 by Basics Books

[25]Allan Bikk, *Tolerance as Value-Neutrality in the Seventeenth Century Dutch Republic*, NEH Seminar 2007

[26]R.Po-Chia Hsia and Henk van Nierop, *Calvinism and Religious Toleration in the Dutch Golden Age*, Published in 2010 by the Cambridge University Press

[27]The National Park Service already has a Youth Conservation Corps that can serve as a model

[28]Sherwin B. Nuland, M.D. *How We Die*. Published in 1995 by Knopf Doubleday Publishing Group, Vintage Series

[29]*Falling behind: life expectancy in US counties from 2000 to 2007 in an international context*. Published in Population Health Metrics, September 2011 by the Institute for Health Metrics and Evaluation of the University of Washington, Seattle

[30]*Left behind: widening disparities for males and females in US county life expectancy, 1985 – 2010*. Published in Population Health Metrics, July 2013 by the Institute for Health Metrics and Evaluation of the University of Washington, Seattle

[31]*U.S. Health Care. Facts about Cost, Access, and Quality* by Dana P. Goldman and Elizabeth A. McGlynn published by the Rand Corporation, page 8

[32]Centers for Disease Control and Prevention, *Morbidity and Mortality Weekly Report*, September 9, 2011

[33]*Falling behind: life expectancy in US counties from 2000 to 2007 in an international context*. Published in Population Health Metrics, September 2011 by the Institute for Health Metrics and Evaluation of the University of Washington, Seattle, Discussion, page 9

[34]*Kaiser Health News*, June 4, 2013

[35]Katy Butler, *Knocking on Heaven's Door (The path to a better way of death)*, Published in 2013 by Scribner

[36]Lisa Genova, *Still Alice*, Published in 2009 by Gallery Books

[37]Katy Butler, *Knocking on Heaven's Door (The path to a better way of death)*, Published in 2013 by Scribner, Prologue page 5

[38]Source: *Economist Intelligence Unit*. 2011. Derived from International Energy Agency

[39]Urban Development Series – Knowledge Papers. MSW Generation by Country – Current data and projections for 2025

[40]www.cleanair.org. *Waste and Recycling Facts*

[41]www.nrdc.org. *Wasted: How America is losing up to 40 percent of its food from farm to fork to landfill*

[42]www.usda.gov/oce/foodwaste

[43]Society of Human Resource Management. *2012 Employee Job Satisfaction and Engagement Survey*

[44]Forbes. *Work in progress. Career talk for women.* July 11, 2013

[45]*Jefferson Quotations on Education.* August 4, 1818

[46]American Academy of Arts & Sciences. Commission on the Humanities and Social Sciences. *The Heart of the Matter.* Published 2013. Page 17.

[47]Federal Reserve Bank of New York. *Student Loan Debt by Age Group.* Released March 29, 2013

[48]Jal Mehta. *Foreign Affairs Magazine.* May/June 2013 Edition. *Why American Education Fails.* Pages 105-116

[49]Arthur Levine. *Educating School Teachers.* Published 2013

[50]Bill Keller. *New York Times,* October 20, 2013. *"An Industry of Mediocrity"*

[51]McKinsey & Company. *Closing the talent gap: Attracting and retaining top-third graduates to careers in teaching.* Published September 2010

[52]American Academy of Arts & Sciences. Commission on the Humanities and Social Sciences. *The Heart of the Matter.* Published 2013. Page 48

[53]Migration Policy Institute. *Immigration Enforcement in the United States: The Rise of a Formidable Machinery.* January 2013

[54]ASCE. *Report Card for America's Infrastructure.* Page 6

[55]Idem. Page 6

[56]Idem. Page 7

[57]Idem. Page 8

[58]Third Way. *The Bargain.* By Jim Kessler, Jon Cowan, and Ed Gerwin. November 2012

[59]In a report by IMF economists published on April 1, 2011

[60]See www.commentarymagazine.com/article/be-open-handed-toward-your-brothers-1/

[61]See Bruce Bartlett in the December 10, 2013 issue of the *New York Times* titled *"Rethinking the idea of a basic income for all."*

[62]*Building the Enterprise. A new civil service framework.* Published April 2014 by the Partnership for Public Service and Booz Allen Hamilton.

[63]See www.nationalaffairs.com/publications/detail/kludgeogracy-in-america

[64]Finis R. Welch. *In Defense of Inequality.* Published in The American economic Review 89, no. 2 (May 1999) pages 1-17

[65]Emmanuel Saez, UC Berkeley. *Striking it Richer: The Evolution of Top Incomes in the United States.* September 3, 2013

[66]Joseph E. Stiglitz. *The Price of Inequality, How Today's Divided Society Endangers our Future.* Published 2013 by W.W. Norton & Company

[67]Timothy Noah. *The Great Divergence. America's Growing Inequality Crisis and what we can do about it.* Published 2012 by Bloomsbury Press

[68]www.givingpledge.org

[69]Robert G. Kaiser. *Act of Congress.* Published in 2013 by Vintage Books.

[70]Michael E. Porter. *America's Test: A National Strategy for National Competitiveness.* In *No Labels: A Shared Vision for a Stronger America.* Published in 2014 by Diversion Books for No Labels

[71]Gallup Politics. www.gallup.com/poll/166763. January 8, 2014

[72]Glenn Hubbard and Tim Kane. *Regaining America's Balance.* Published in *National Affairs*, Issue # 14, winter 2013

[73]Francis Fukuyama. *The American Interest*, December 8, 2013. *The Decay of American Political Institutions.*

[74]Jessica Tuchman Mathews. *Can America Still Act?* Presentation made November 10, 2010 at the Gerald R. Ford School of Public Policy at the University of Michigan

with the Kennedy assassination and ended with the colorless one-term presidency of Jimmy Carter.

Times in America were very different from what they are now. America really had no equal in the world in terms of economic and military dominance and in terms of energy, drive, and motivation of its people. After Sputnik, it had quickly surpassed the Soviet space effort and it had been the first, and thus far only, nation to put men on the moon (and brought them safely back to earth.)

The Second World War had shown clearly that once the American spirit, and its productive capacity, was mobilized for the right cause, there was nothing in the world to stop it even if it meant great sacrifice by just about everybody. And, importantly, in the wars it had to engage in during the twentieth century it had consistently fought on the side of good, versus evil. It had taken up arms, reluctantly, to defeat fascism and it was prepared to do so again, if provoked, against communism. It had to do so in Korea and it chose to do so—but with much less conviction and success—in Vietnam. And it came awfully close a couple of times with the Berlin airlift in 1948, with the Hungarian uprising in 1956, the Cuban missile crisis in 1962, and the Prague Spring in 1968.

As I look back at the second half of the twentieth century, I still find it amazing that the world has so far escaped a major nuclear conflagration and that America is still the only nation that has used nuclear weapons in combat.

Ever since the start of the American Revolution, a sense of "American Exceptionalism" has been growing. While the notion of America being "a cut above" all other nations has many origins, the term "American Exceptionalism" probably stems from the French scholar Alexis de Tocqueville who wrote in his 1831 treatise *"Democracy in America"*: *"The position of the Americans is therefore quite exceptional, and it may be believed that no democratic people will ever be placed in a similar one."*

America is indeed an exceptional success story, starting with the birth of the nation in the struggle for independence, to the gradual conquering of the West, the Louisiana Purchase, and the purchase of Alaska from the Russians. It derives great strength from its strategic location with access to and protection from two oceans, from the vast expanse of its territory, and its water systems (rivers and lakes), from its abundant natural resources, and from its—largely immigrant—population.

John D. Gartner[10], who teaches at the Johns Hopkins University Medical School, addresses the character of the U.S. population in his book *"The Hypomanic Edge: The Link between (a little) Craziness and (a lot of) Success in America"*. He writes: *"We're a self-selected population. Immigrants have unusual ambition, energy, drive and risk tolerance, which lets them take a chance on moving for a better opportunity. These are biologically based temperament traits. If you seed an entire continent with them, you're going to get a nation of entrepreneurs."*

Blessed with these strengths, America has made exceptional contributions to world civilization, in war and peace, in exploration, in science and technology, in creating wealth, and in advancing human rights. But unlike thirty years ago, there is a sense of foreboding that we are witnessing the decline of an empire[11]. That the exceptionalism is fading. The one reason why I find myself to be a petulant immigrant to the USA is that, in most any respect, I feel America is underperforming against its capabilities and it should not be that way nor does it have to be that way.

There is no denying that in terms of its geography, natural resources, the size of its economy, and its relative youth as a nation, America is blessed unlike most any other nation on earth. Ever since the American Revolution, it has progressed on capitalizing on its unique advantages. But I believe that more recently it has not kept up the pace and—if I'm correct in that assessment—we need to have the courage to analyze in what respects the system is failing and why. I do not just want to be an armchair critic. In this chapter, I will offer my view of where America falls short of its potential (and my expectations) and in the next Section of this book, I will offer some solutions.

———

Some aspects of underperformance of American society were put forward in Section I of this book where it quoted IFITWEREMYHOME.com on comparative differences between the Netherlands and the USA. This source suggested, amongst others, that, if the Netherlands were your home instead of the United States, you would:

- Have 46.24 percent more chance to be employed
- Use 40.77 percent less electricity
- Experience 31.33 percent less of a class divide
- Have 27.6 percent more free time
- Have 24.1 percent less chance of dying in infancy
- Spend 48.19 percent less money on healthcare
- Consume 8.72 percent less oil
- Live 1.31 years longer
- Be 66.67 percent less likely to have HIV/AIDS

These findings hint at a number of flaws in the American system as it operates today:

- Inequality
- Unemployment
- Healthcare is more expensive and less effective than it can/should be
- Wasteful use of energy
- Work-Life imbalance

Not to dwell on the negatives, but I would add the following short-comings in America's performance to this list:

- Our political system is straining to keep up with the demands of our time
- We are not keeping our expenditures in balance with our revenue generation
- Great education is not universally available
- We are not winning the war on drugs
- We are not winning the war on terror
- We are not winning the war on poverty
- We don't have a forward looking immigration policy
- We have not kept up our infrastructure

Surveying the field today, the question keeps coming up: Are the best times behind us? Admittedly, this seems to be a question that gets pondered by each successive generation. What is different this time? Would a modern day Alexis de Tocqueville find anything exceptional in America?

We all see the tell-tale signs of trouble around us, from high unemployment, to increasing income inequality, lost or unfinished wars, a skyrocketing national debt, an ideologically divided voting public and—resulting from it—a dysfunctional political system. We see the unraveling of family structures and values, the proliferation of guns and drugs, the (relatively) poor academic performance, the prevalence of obesity in the population, and a crumbling infra-structure.

———

Was I blinded, thirty years ago, by my desire and ambition to become an immigrant to America, so that I did not see then what I see now? Am I making a mountain out of a mole hill for the purpose of writing a book? I don't think so. America had its dark spots in the early eighties as well. It had barely digested Vietnam and Watergate, but it was the undisputed sole super power in military and economic terms. Its national debt was manageable. Ronald Reagan could not only reach out to Mikhail Gorbachev and tell him "to tear down that wall" but also to Tip O'Neill, when a reset of the social security system was required. Inequality was not nearly the issue, it has become in our time. The drug problems were not as intransigent as they are today, our prisons held less than one-third of the prisoners they hold today and obesity was not the epidemic we experience now. It is hard to compare the standings of a country in different times, because the world does not stand still and the conditions today differ greatly from the ones in the early eighties. But we have other gauges of progress and regress. We now have the means to compare America's standing in the world with that of other developed nations.

According to an interesting new experiment, the Social Progress Index[12], the United States ranks sixteenth out of 132 nations when ranked by this index, which is designed to measure how well a country meets basic human needs, foundations of wellbeing and opportunity. This Social Progress Index ranks New Zealand number one, followed by Switzerland, Iceland, and the Netherlands. Canada ranks seventh and Germany (12th), Great Britain (13th), and Japan (14th) all rank ahead of the USA.

The Organization of Economic Co-operation and Development (OECD) gives us another useful gauge in its Better Life Index[13], which provides comparisons between its thirty-four member nations, all developed countries which compete with America:

- Our defense spending is exceptional. We are spending more on our military than the next seventeen countries (including China and Russia) combined (recognizing that a significant part of the budget is spent on assistance to allies).
- We rank first in death by violence among high income democracies at 6.47 deaths per 100,000 people. Finland ranks second in this category at 2.24 deaths per 100,000.

- Between 2007 and 2011 only China, Iran, Iraq and Saudi Arabia have executed more people than the USA. Do we want to be judged by the company we keep?
- In Gross Domestic Product (GDP) per capita we rank anywhere from sixth to ninth in the world depending on what source of intelligence you follow; Luxembourg, Qatar, Singapore, and Norway are ahead of the USA in all rankings of per capita GDP.
- We rank 22nd out of 27 developed countries in graduation rate from public high schools.
- We rank 15th out of 27 developed countries in tertiary education graduation rates.
- Our kids rank 18th in the world in reading, 29th in science and 35th in math.
- We rank below 16 other rich countries in health across our entire life span.
- We rank 49th in life expectancy at birth.
- Thirty-three countries have a lower child poverty rate than the USA.
- Forty-four countries have a lower infant mortality than the USA.
- We rank 15th among OECD Member nations in broadband penetration.
- Income inequality is higher in the USA than in 95 other countries in the world.
- The Heritage Foundation ranks the USA 13th amongst developed nations in business freedom.

In other words, we don't rank Number One in any of these measures of human wellbeing. And that raises the question: Do we have our priorities straight?

However, even if all of these ugly statistics are accurate, they are reflective only of this moment in time. In terms of resources, human and physical, America has plenty of capacity to become a leading nation once more in matters that constitute true measure of human progress. The question is if it can muster the political leadership and will to mobilize the population at large and get all of us pulling the cart in the right direction and back to the forefront. Somehow, it always seems to take a major outside force, like a war, a depression, a calamity, to get us to act decisively. Inertia causes us to be reactive more often than proactive, not just in politics, but equally so in business and in our families.

Part of the problem, as I see it, is that there is no clear national consensus that America has a problem, much less—if there is a problem—what it is. Just like a drug addict, or an alcoholic, cannot overcome the addiction until he/she accepts that there is a problem, the nation cannot recover its stride unless and until it recognizes where it is falling short and determines to do something about it. That is the rationale behind this book. It is not written out of righteousness but out of a conviction that the nation needs a candid discourse about what's ailing it, so that it can find the right prescription for a cure and become truly exceptional again.

Let's look a little closer at each of the shortcomings that I identify and that keep me searching for that elusive American Exceptionalism.

Inequality

Inequality may be at the heart of what is ailing the nation. You don't have to subscribe to every aspect of Charles Murray's book, "Coming Apart"[14], to recognize that a wide chasm has developed in American society between people who have every outlook on a productive, prosperous, and healthy life and people who have no such outlook. Let's call them, for neutrality's sake, the fortunate and the unfortunate (although I believe it to be dangerous and counterproductive to imply that it is just the luck of the draw that determines your fate). There is no doubt that modern society has always consisted of the privileged at the top, the underprivileged at the bottom, and a large group of people in between. Not much has changed in that respect but there is a growing unease that moving up in society has become more difficult than ever and, if that is correct, it would have to be characterized as very un-American.

Charles Murray illustrates that the fortunate have created their enclaves where they cluster together in high priced real estate, out of reach for the general population (Murray calls it, "Belmont"), and that the unfortunate get similarly bunched up in dilapidated, drug infested, and crime ridden neighborhoods (Murray calls it, "Fishtown").

Only the children of the fortunate can afford to go to the top prep schools, colleges, and universities. They get the better education, get to mingle with the right crowd, and end up getting the better jobs. Money is never an object. Because of the environment in which they live in Belmont, they get exposed to cultural influences that are out of reach for the inhabitants of Fishtown. They get to travel abroad and widen their horizons in a way that children from Fishtown can only imagine. If children from Belmont get in any kind of trouble, drugs, sex, or crime, there are abundant, but expensive, remedies available that can nip the problem in the bud before it gets out of hand. Social pressure and vigilance will further help staving off potential misdirection. Not so much for children growing up in Fishtown.

Before inequality becomes an intractable problem (if it is not already) it will have to be recognized and addressed with all the resolve, vitality, and inventiveness that has driven America forward through other crises. America will simply not succeed going forward if it does not find a way to run on all cylinders.

We blame the Islamic Arab world—and, in particular, the Kingdom of Saudi Arabia—for denying a good part of its population, the women, an equal role in building the future of their countries and we wonder how, in this day and age, a nation can prosper if it leaves a large percentage of its population on the sideline. The answer is, more likely than not, that it cannot prosper under those conditions. It can stay afloat for a while, particularly if the nation is a hydrocarbon rich country that can generate wealth by exploiting its natural resources. But it is unlikely that it can reach its full potential, if not the whole population is engaged in the nations building process.

Warren Buffet, in an essay published in *Fortune Magazine*[15], points to the same conclusion: "*The closer that America comes to fully employing the talents of its citizens, the greater its output of goods and services will be.*" He further states: "*No manager operates his or her plants at 80 percent efficiency when steps could be taken that would increase output.*" We point the finger at the Islamic Arab world for running their nations at less than 50 percent efficiency by denying women the right to participate. But we should not be blind to the fact that America runs at much less than 100 percent of its horse-power. If America wants to stay on top in the race of nations, it will have to find a way to run on all cylinders by getting a much larger percentage of its populus engaged in the productive process. And it will have to find a way to open up avenues that lead from Fishtown to Belmont through communities that are wide open for migration in either direction. America should be a place where participation, productivity, and learning get rewarded and lack thereof gets penalized.

Unemployment.

On the surface, the unemployment situation in America does not look overly concerning. At the time this book went to press, the Bureau of Labor Statistics pegged the national unemployment rate at 6.3 percent. Even through the severe recession of 2008-2011, the official unemployment number, for the nation as a whole, never rose above 10 percent. Considering that most economists will tell us that a number of around 4 percent effectively means full employment, the gap never looked unbridgeable. But is there more than meets the eye?

First of all, we need to realize that nobody counts the number of people employed in the USA. The federal government, through the Department of Labor, makes an effort (not very successfully) to measure the *unemployment* rate, but what would be really interesting to know is the number of people who are *employed* (and by deduction, the number of people who are left out of the labor process).

Isn't it somewhat befuddling that our government cannot tell us what percentage of the population is engaged in the labor process? And, therewith, the percentage of the population that is not? It seems to me that we don't want to know the truth.

The Bureau of Labor Statistics measures a metric that it calls the "Labor Participation Rate", which stood in April of 2014 at 62.8 percent. This statistic measures the number of people in the labor force that is either working or actively looking for a job as a percentage of the civilian population aged 16 and older. But actively looking for a job is not the same as being employed.

It also measures a metric that it calls the "Employment-Population Ratio", which stood In April of 2014 at 58.9 percent. This statistic measures the proportion of the civilian non-institutional population aged 16 years and over that is employed. It includes people who are under-employed in terms of the time for which they get paid or in terms of the level of work they are asked to perform. Thus it appears that in our country close to half of the population is left out of the labor process. Some percentage of this "unengaged" population is either below working age, retired with no intent to get re-engaged or studying full time.

The bottom-line is that the federal government cannot tell us with any degree of precision what percentage of the work-eligible and work-capable population is actually disengaged from the labor process and thus not participating in the growth of our economy and the strengthening of our nation.

But we can come at it from another angle:

We know from the census that the USA has a population of about 314 million; that about 74 million are below age 18 and about 42 million are over the age of 65. Since some unknown percentage of these age-groups are employed (let's assume 10 percent of this populus), it follows that our labor pool would be approximately 210 million. We also know that in April of 2013 we had:

- 11.7 million unemployed
- 14 million on disability (a staggering number!)
- 2.2 million in prison (a staggering number!)
- 7.6 million involuntary part time
- 2.3 million marginally attached

These five categories add up to 37.9 million people in the USA that would theoretically qualify for the workforce but were either unemployed or underemployed in 2013. That represents 18 percent of the labor pool of 210 million. Arguably, this number of 18 percent is a more accurate measurement of disengagement of the labor process than the unemployment rate of 6.3 percent that the U.S. Bureau of Labor Statistics put out in April of 2014. It certainly demonstrates that too many able bodies are disengaged from the labor process and that, also in this respect, America is not running on all cylinders. How much better off would America be, if it could mobilize the majority of these disengaged to re-engage and spur the nation's forward progress?

Health and Healthcare

Regardless of what you may think of the healthcare system in America and the merits of the Affordable Care Act of 2010 (ACA), better known as "Obamacare", no one will dispute the fact that healthcare in America requires lifesaving attention of its own.

The simple fact that President Obama pushed so hard for his healthcare initiative and was willing to spend much of his political capital in the process is, by itself, an indication that our current healthcare system is in trouble. In a nutshell, you can tally the deficiencies:

- It is too expensive
- It is unevenly distributed
- It is more curative than preventive
- The quality of healthcare is too locale dependent
- For most people it is not of world class quality
- It is failing in finding the right balance between prolonging life and quality of life

Our medical system is too much intervention-oriented (as opposed to outcome-oriented) and it is not hard to find the origins of that. On one hand there is a huge medical industry driving the use of equipment and technology regardless of whether it benefits the (quality of) life of the patient; and, on the other hand our physicians are all indoctrinated in the Hippocratic Oath to save life at the cost of just about anything else.

A comprehensive overhaul of the healthcare system should give special attention to the mental health segment. More than any other part of healthcare, the mental health service is in shambles, not because of competence and capabilities of the mental health providers, but mostly because of budget constraints and regulatory red tape. The result is that our prisons and streets have to substitute for mental health institutions.

Such overhaul should also include reconsideration of how much justification there is in prolonging life (at tremendous emotional and financial cost) in cases where the patient has no realistic prospect of recovery, as in the case of any form of dementia or a serious stroke or paralysis. As a nation we will have to develop the courage to have its citizens accept death as a logical and inevitable part of life and spend more energy and money on making death easier, comfortable, and embraceable for the patients and their loved ones and caregivers. The loneliest and most desolate place to die is the intensive care unit of a hospital where the patient is hooked up to machines rather than hooked up with the people who, with their presence, can ease the transition from life to death. A system that pays for medical intervention until the last breath, but does not cover much less expensive and more compassionate palliative and hospice care has both its objectives and its economics reversed.

We saw at the beginning of this chapter that, notwithstanding the emphasis on medical intervention in healthcare in America, the Dutch, on average, live sixteen months longer than Americans do. That may, however, have less to do with our healthcare system than with lifestyle issues developed over time in the United States. It appears that our life-expectancy, which has risen dramatically with the invention of modern medicine, may have peaked here, while it keeps rising in other parts of the Western world (it rises faster in the rest of the world where modern medicine and nutrition have only recently been introduced). The reason for this is evident all around us: It is in our automobile driven life-style, in drugs and obesity. It will be one of the first things that visitors from abroad will observe: The large percentage of grossly overweight people that dominate the street scene on Main Street, USA. Go to any public event, a football game or a mass concert, and you can't avert your gaze from people who have failed to keep their weight within acceptable and healthy limits. Safety belt extenders in airplanes are largely an American phenomenon. Obesity has become a full blown health crisis, in America more than anywhere else and particularly child obesity is a tragic example of failure to deal with the blessings of American prosperity in a responsible way.

Here the discrepancy between the Netherlands and America is glaring and in full view: Over there everyone, but especially children, is riding a bike and the street scene is dominated by bikes. Here kids get driven everywhere and you can't blame them or their parents because America has failed to build a safe network of bike paths to allow children to bike to school, the practice field, or gym. The use and abuse of drugs and pharmaceuticals is a little better hidden, but it shows up in alarming statistics about pre-mature death as a result of drug-violence and over-dose in emergency rooms all over the United States.

Waste.

America, much more than any other country in the world, has become a disposal society. It wastes more resources, food, water, and energy than most any other country consumes. And, unfortunately, it has become only moderately successful in turning its waste back into energy. As we saw before, the Dutch, who live a decent standard of living, consume forty-one percent less electricity and nine percent less oil per capita than Americans do. Part of the problem is that we don't price our energy right as long as we don't factor in the cost of cleaning up after use. The cost of dealing effectively and definitively with the nuclear waste we are creating in our nuclear power plants, and with the air- and water pollution we are creating by burning fossil fuels, is not, or at least not adequately, included in the price we pay at the pump and with our utility bills. Whatever we may think about the drivers of climate change and the steps to be taken to mitigate or eliminate the negative effects of climate change, we have a solemn obligation to manage our natural resources responsibly; cutting out waste and recycling will be a good place to start. America should get much better at that. It should set an example for the rest of the world.

Work/Life imbalance

It may be that, because we have so many people in America who have disengaged from the labor process for one reason or another, the rest of us has to work harder to compensate for time and output lost. Or it may be in our genetic make-up as John Gartner suggested[10], but the fact is that Americans have a hard time finding the right work/life balance. Apparently I am enough of an American that I have suffered from that same syndrome ever since I moved here. Why is it that in Europe everyone can take off six weeks out of a year without sacrificing productivity and why do managers in America feel guilty for taking off even a week to spend time with the family?

Aggravating factors are the concentration of higher paying jobs in the urban centers, necessitating long and stressful commutes to-and-from work. Compared to earlier, simpler, times in the U.S., the big difference is that households with two income earners are now the rule, rather than the exception, leaving less free time available. The result is stress, from having to fit ever more chores in the already short stretches of free time working Americans have available.

Education

Education in America is an almost perfect mirror image of American society at large. It is world class at the top and hopelessly inadequate at the bottom. In Charles Murray's parlance, the fortunate Belmont kids get a great education and the unfortunate Fishtown kids drop out of school. Between Belmont and Fishtown it is a checkered flag with pockets of excellence and large expanses of mediocrity. It is evident that American kids are falling behind their peers in other parts of the industrialized world in building the competencies they will need most in their professional lives: Science, arithmetic, mathematics, reading, and reasoning[16].

Here, too, immigrants show the way to success. How long ago is it that we saw a winner of the annual spelling bee competition who had a plain Anglo-American name? The answer is 2007 when Evan O'Dorney won. Since then, winners' names have been: Sameer Mishra, Kavya Shivashankar, Anamika Veeramani, Sukanya Roy, Snigdha Nandipati, Arvind Mahankali, and Kush Sharma. There were two winners in 2014, Sriram Hathwar and Ansun Sujoe, when the contest ran out of words with two candidates left. All these contestants were winners not so much because of excellent school support but because they were kids from immigrant parents who motivated them to reach for the top.

The nation's report card released just in May of 2014 shows that seventy-four percent of students scored below the grade-appropriate level in math and sixty-two percent in reading. In a globalized, interconnected, world our kids have to compete with the best from all other countries and we can't expect them to win that battle if we do not offer universally high quality education to every child willing to learn, whether the child lives in Belmont or in Fishtown.

Drugs

The Nixon administration coined the phrase "War on Drugs" with the intent to rid the country from the debilitating effects of illegal substance abuse. If anything, the problem has only grown since then. It is one of the biggest drivers of (organized) crime in the country. It is one of the main reasons why so many people are disengaged from the labor process and are doomed to live in Fishtown. And it is the reason why we have to keep building prisons, which are overcrowded the first day they are commissioned. A recently released report from the National Research Council states that U.S. state and federal prison populations have risen from 200,000 inmates in 1973 to 1.5 million in 2009. With the inclusion of local jails, the number of inmates totals 2.2 million adults, removed from the labor process. This increase is largely the result of criminalization of drug-related activity. The result is that while the U.S. has only five percent of the world's population, it has nearly one-quarter of the world's prisoners! As bad as this is in and of itself, there is a disturbing corollary to this high incarceration rate. Saskia Sassen, in her recently released book "*Expulsions*", reminds us that five million people in the United States are currently on probation or parole, which means that they are effectively marginalized and not easily incorporated in the labor market[17].

The drug problem rears its ugly head in so many forms and places in modern day America that it is literally mind boggling. We can think back with melancholy to the time, not very long ago, that "weed" was the problem. Now we have come to the realization that we have bigger fish to fry and we have become largely accepting of the legalization of marijuana. The larger problem is now with abuse of otherwise legally prescribed pharmaceuticals, specifically opiates, and with methamphetamines, cocaine and heroin as well as boutique drugs made with these ingredients.

It does not help—to say the least—that popular culture flaunts the use of illegal substances in front of our eyes and the eyes of our children.

I have not found any research confirming this, but I have to assume that drug abuse is behind the fact that America has fallen behind most other industrialized nations in terms of life expectancy and health across our life span. It is certainly behind the high dropout rate from high schools and colleges and thus it is a major contributing factor to the persistent inequality that has been building in American society.

Terrorism

By declaring the "War on Terror" after the 9/11/2001 tragedy, America has raised expectations that it would be capable to eradicate terrorism as a threat to stability and prosperity in the world. More than ten years into it, we find that the Bush Administration may have raised expectations that America is incapable of meeting. The danger in this is that it encourages our enemies and demoralizes our allies and our own population.

We have gradually come to understand that the threat against our national security is no longer coming from other nations but from transnational forces and ideologies that are connecting and conspiring against the American way of life in "out of the way" places and in cyberspace. They find safe havens in the growing number of nations where the governments have lost control of what happens on their territory like Libya, Somalia, Yemen, and Mali. The number of such safe havens keeps growing as Iraq, Afghanistan, Syria, and Egypt are all wrestling—with little success—to establish governments that have widespread popular support and have the capacity to control what happens inside their borders. America's military might resembles Goliath in this fight against pesky little Davids that pop up everywhere in our sphere of influence.

America's inability to win a war it declared with a lot of fanfare—like it did with the War on Terror, the War on Drugs and the War on Poverty—undermines its prestige and its self-confidence.

If you think about it, the Second World War is really the only and last conflict it has convincingly won in recent history. The fact that we have not had to suffer a second 9/11 type event and that—knock on wood—we have, thus far, avoided a devastating cyber war, does not mean that we have built adequate defenses against the most significant threats to our national security. America spends an inordinate amount of money for its national defense and security, but is it getting its money's worth?

Immigration

Maybe, by the time this book gets published, Congress has acted on immigration reform but I'm not holding my breath. Not having a growth-oriented, comprehensive, immigration policy hurts the American economy, its social cohesion, and its image and reputation abroad. The way I see it, immigration is good for America—even indispensable for its long term prosperity—and not overly complicated to channel properly:

- Immigration has served this nation well and there is nothing to suggest that, going forward, that will be no longer the case;
- Population growth is essential to economic prosperity and current birth rates are not sufficient to sustain the population of the USA in the long term;
- American citizens are no longer prepared to do many menial jobs that still need to be done;
- In a global economy we need to attract the best talent available to stay competitive as a nation;
- Modern information technology makes it possible to control immigration and keep undesirables out.

A problem with the current immigration policy in the USA is that we make illegal immigration too easy and legal immigration too hard!

The United States is often and rightly referred to as a "Nation of Immigrants". There is not another country in the world where immigration has as much contributed to population growth and economic success as it has in the USA. According to the U.S. Census Bureau about sixty million Americans—or one in every five people—are immigrants or the children of immigrants. These are the people that have propelled the USA to its superpower status. What is there to suggest that continuing immigration would suddenly become a negative rather than the positive it has been ever since the arrival on our shores of the Halve Maen and the Mayflower? As Paul Taylor[18] points out in his book *"The Next America"*, *"No nation has been better served than ours by immigration, and judging by the tens of millions of people from all over the world still clambering to come here, there's every reason to expect our long winning streak to continue."*

A fertility rate of 2.1 (2.1 births/woman) is required to sustain a population. The fertility rate in the USA is well below that number[19], which means that without immigration the country would regress in population, and the fertility rate would be substantially lower if it was not for a relatively high fertility rate of recent immigrants. In his book, *"The Next Hundred Million"*, subtitled *"America in 2050"*, Joel Kotkin[20] gives us a glimpse of the competitive advantage America is expected to have over other developed countries—including China and Japan—as a result of a much higher population growth. The next 100 Million Americans Joel Kotkin is writing about will not be there in 2050 without stepped up immigration.

Immigration by children and working age people will have to offset a graying indigenous population and provide a much needed improvement of the current growing imbalance between the working population and the army of retirees. Migrant labor has become (whether we like it or not) the backbone of the farm economy, which is in turn one of the most globally competitive sectors of business in the USA.

The book *"Immigrant, Inc."* by Richard T. Herman and Robert L. Smith[21] provides a complete, convincing account of the contributions made by immigrant entrepreneurs to the U.S. economy over the last decades. This account is so irrefutable that it does not need to be repeated here. Just consider that:

- Today's immigrants are nearly twice as likely as non-immigrants to launch a business.
- Immigrant founders are behind more than half of the high-tech start-ups in Silicon Valley.
- Some 40 percent of all Fortune 500 companies were started by immigrants or their children.

Unfortunately, in America we no longer raise the best and the brightest students in the world, but we are still blessed with a highly competitive elite university education system that is the envy of the world and attracts exceptional talent from other countries. We educate and stimulate these foreign students—in many instances at public expense—and then we practically force them to go back to where they came from because of our antiquated immigration laws and regulations. How smart is that? We train the best and the brightest in the world to compete with us!

It is a sign of hopeless dysfunction in Washington if, with all the good reasons to deal with the immigration issue in a constructive, forward looking way, we cannot get a comprehensive immigration bill through Congress. David Brooks wrote in a January 2013 column in the *New York Times*, titled *"The Easy Problem"* that, *"If we can't pass an (immigration) law this year (2013), given the overwhelming strength of evidence, then we really are a pathetic basket case of a nation."* As of the time of this writing, in the spring of 2014, there is still no realistic outlook for an immigration bill coming out of Congress. After all, it is (again) an election year!

Infrastructure

I simply cannot get over the fact that every time a major storm hits parts of the USA, millions of people and businesses lose power and—apparently—accept it as par for the course. For a social and economic disruption to be so predictable and yet not pre-emptively dealt with by government regulation borders on dereliction of duty. I would like to see realistic numbers on the damage done to the U.S. economy every year by the power outages caused by weather related disruptions of the power supply. The numbers are certainly astronomical and likely to increase as a result of climate change that seems to cause more severe weather extremes on the North American continent.

When I grew up in the Netherlands we never had a power outage. Already in the fifties and sixties of the last century, all power-lines had been moved underground. The lights simply never went out and that was not because they were generator backed. What is keeping America?

The regularly failing power grid is a metaphor for a generally underwhelming American infrastructure system. A country cannot be globally competitive without a competitive infrastructure and yet, there seems to be no willingness among our politicians, to do the planning for and create the funding of a national infrastructure strategy; and make it a high national priority. Maybe this is because of the opaqueness of who is responsible for taking the initiative; who is responsible for the funding and who is accountable for the outcome? Almost all U.S. infrastructure components are part of a national network, sometimes with transnational links into Canada or Mexico. And while the federal government exerts some authority over parts of our infrastructure, most of the physical plant is owned by the states, counties, municipalities, especially created public authorities like waterworks or port authorities, or by the private sector. With that much interdependence, who's going to take the lead and who will put up the money required to maintain and modernize the systems?

Debt and deficit

At the time Christie and I became immigrants to the United States, the National Debt stood at $1 trillion, which was a matter of concern to many in government and business. The National Debt stands at $17 trillion now, merely 30 years later. As a percentage of GDP it has grown from below thirty percent to over 100 percent over the same time period.

The young and unborn don't have an equivalent of the American Association of Retired Persons (AARP) to represent their interests and it shows (in Congress). For more than two decades, we have unabashedly been robbing the cradle by charging trillions of dollars of routine, operational expenses, to our national credit card, raising the National debt from $4 trillion in 1990 to in excess of $17 trillion at the end of 2013. The administrations responsible for the debt explosion were Republican and Democrat, so neither party can claim the moral high ground. Their actions and inactions, that have led us to the brink of a debt crisis, are both economically detrimental and morally decrepit.

We did not go into debt to invest in a better future for Americans, but simply because we allowed the expense of running the business of the country to exceed, year after year, the revenues we were collecting. We accepted year-after-year a budget deficit and for many years we abandoned the principle of budgeting our expenses altogether and just funded our runaway expenses with a series of continuing resolutions. To the point that our national debt, now, just about equals the size of our economy. There are all kinds of good reasons to leverage the size and dynamism of the U.S. economy by borrowing to cover calamities like wars, natural disasters, and cyclical downturns. Or to invest in the future in the form of infrastructure improvements, research and development, and investment in our human resources, but it is economically unwarranted to finance ongoing operations with debt. And that is what America has been doing.

We are deep in debt and we have not even put our existing entitlement programs on a path to long term solvency; much less have we created with the borrowed money a much tighter safety net. We are deep in debt without having addressed our decaying infrastructure or our education deficit compared to the rest of the developed world. We are deep in debt without having taken any steps to protect our people and property from the negative effects of global warming.

Admiral Mike Mullen, when he was Chairman of the Joint Chiefs of Staff, has repeatedly called the national debt the biggest threat to U.S. national security. It looks as if nobody in Congress or the administration listened. Only by default were some spending cuts enacted in 2013 when a mindless and indiscriminate sequestration—designed to be so unpalatable that it would never become law—took effect because the politicians could not agree on an intelligent way to bring continuing deficits under control.

The political system

If you look at this list of shortcomings that have crept up under the American system in place today, you have to come to the conclusion that there is something wrong with the political part of the system.

No one can, in good conscience, argue that a nation as rich and gifted as the United States, the largest and best functioning economy in the world and the nation that has won world wars, a Cold War and is leading the world in space exploration, might be under-resourced to solve the problems we have brought forward here. Maybe it cannot solve them all simultaneously, but it sure can address and solve them sequentially after first picking the low hanging fruit and then prioritizing the remaining challenges. All it will take is presidential leadership and congressional determination to get the job done. It is a political task to come up with a smart allocation of resources to the high priority challenges. But that seems to be the missing ingredient in the American system today; and, it explains why America appears powerless to solve its most apparent hurdles to future success.

As David Brooks of the Brookings Institute pointed out, all politicians love Social Security and they have effectively made it untouchable: The third rail of American political dogma. But the harsh reality is that Congress could not possibly pass a Social Security law today. That is how parochial and short-sighted our political apparatus has become.

I believe that America, as a nation, has become too complacent. It has come out of the Cold War as the undisputed world leader, the only real Super Power in economic and military terms. But it cannot afford to rest on its laurels. The job is never done. Rapid change is not reserved for the business environment, it rears its ugly head also in the geo-political realm and the status quo is constantly threatened. Will Rodgers saw this clearly when he so eloquently pointed out, *"Even if you are on the right track, you'll get run over if you just sit there."*

The nation is at serious risk of losing its dominance and vibrancy if the political constellation does not change. It has to find a way to break the logjam of inaction and deadlock in Congress and between Congress and the administration. The Constitution created a balance of power, but it was never intended to cause powerlessness because countervailing powers cancel each other out.

The Constitution presumes that, after a debate and weighing of alternatives, the legislative and executive branches of government find each other in measures and policies that advance the strength and the growth of the nation. That presumption is getting denied by the current dysfunction in the Beltway. Robert Gates, the former Secretary of Defense in both the Bush and Obama administrations, laments in his excellent memoir *"DUTY"*[22], which was published in early 2014, how hard it is to get anything done even for a well-liked, respected, and a-political Cabinet Secretary.

He writes: *"Why did I dislike being back in government and in Washington? It was because, despite everyone being "nice", getting anything of consequence done was so damnably difficult even in the midst of two wars. From the bureaucratic*

BIBLIOGRAPHY

Nicolas Berggruen and Nathan Gardels. *Intelligent Governance for the 21st Century, a middle way between West and East.* Published in 2013 by Polity Press

Sheila Bair. *Bull by the horns, fighting to save Main Street from Wall Street and Wall Street from itself.* Published in 2012 by Free Press

Katy Butler. *Knocking on Heaven's Door, the path to a better way of death.* Published in 2013 by Scribner

John Carver. *Board that make a Difference: A New Design for Leadership in Nonprofit and Public Organizations.* Published 1990 by Jossey-Bass

John Carver and Caroline Oliver. *Corporate Boards That Create Value: Governing Company Performance from the Boardroom.* Published 2002 by Jossey-Bass

Roger Connors and Tom Smith. *How Did That Happen? Holding people accountable for results the positive, principled way.* Published in 2009 by the Penguin Press

Tyler Cowen. *Average is Over, Powering America beyond the age of the great stagnation.* Published in 2014 by Dutton

John D. Gartner. *The Hypomanic Edge: The Link between (a little) Craziness and (a lot of) Success in America.* Published in 2005 by Simon and Schuster

Robert M. Gates. *Duty, Memoirs of a Secretary at War.* Published in 2014 by Alfred A. Knopf

Lisa Genova. *Still Alice.* Published in 2007 by Gallery Books

Richard T. Herman and Robert L. Smith. *Immigrant, Inc., why immigrant entrepreneurs are driving the new economy (and how they will save the American worker).* Published in 2010 by John Wiley and Sons

Michael Hirsh. *At War with Ourselves.* Published in 2004 by Oxford University Press

Jon Huntsman, Joe Manchin and others. *No Labels: A Shared Vision for a Stronger America.* Published in 2014 for No Labels by Diversion Books

Simon Johnson and James Kwak. *White House Burning, the Founding Fathers, our national debt, and why it matters to you.* Published in 2012 by Pantheon Books

Robert Kagan. *Of Paradise and Power. America and Europe in the New World Order.* Published in 2003 by Alfred A. Knopf

Robert G. Kaiser. *Act of Congress, how America's essential institution works, and how it doesn't.* Published in 2013 by Vintage Books

Joel Kotkin. *The Next Hundred Million, America in 2050.* Published in 2010 by the Penguin Press

Alvaro Vargas Llosa. *Global Crossings, Immigration, Civilization, and America.* Published in 2013 by the Independent Institute

Mike Marks, Tim Horan and Mike Emerson. *Working at Cross Purposes, How Distributors and Manufacturers can manage conflict successfully.* Published in 2006 by N.A.W. Institute for Distribution Excellence

Clayton L. Mathile and Echo M. Garrett. *Dream no Little Dreams.* Published in 2007 by DNLD Publishing

Dan Morgan. *Merchants of Grain.* Published in 1980 by Penguin Books.

Charles Murray. *Coming Apart, the State of White America, 1960-2010.* Published in 2012 by Crown Forum

Moises Naim. *The End of Power, from Boardrooms to battlefields and churches to states, why being in charge isn't what it used to be.* Published in 2013 by Basics Books

Timothy Noah. *The Great Divergence, America's growing inequality crisis and what we can do about it.* Published in 2012 by Bloomsbury Press

Sherwin B. Nuland, M.D. *How We Die*. Published in 1995 by Knopf Doubleday Publishing Group, Vintage Series

George Packer. *The Unwinding, an inner history of the new America*. Published in 2013 by Farrar, Straus and Giroux

R. Po-Chia Hsia and Henk van Nierop. *Calvinism and Religious Toleration in the Dutch Golden Age*. Published in 2010 by the Cambridge University Press

Amanda Ripley. *The Smartest Kids in the World, and how they got that way*. Published in 2013 by Simon and Schuster

Saskia Sassen. *Expulsions. Brutality and Complexity in the Global Economy*. Published in 2014 by the Belknap Press of the Harvard University Press.

Russell Shorto. *The Island at the Center of the World, the epic story of Dutch Manhattan and the forgotten colony that shaped America*. Published in 2004 by Vintage Books

Wallace Stegner. *Crossing to Safety*. Published in 2002 by Modern Library

John Paul Stevens. *Six Amendments: How and Why We Should Change the Constitution*. Published in 2014 by Little, Brown and Company.

Joseph E. Stiglitz. *The Price of Inequality, How today's Divided Society Endangers Our Future*. Published in 2013 by W.W. Norton & Company

Nassim Nicholas Taleb. *The Black Swan, the impact of the highly improbable*. Published in 2007 by Random House

Charles Taylor. *A Secular Age*. Published in 2007 by the Belknap Press of Harvard University Press

Paul Taylor. *The Next America, Boomers, Millenials and the Looming Generational Showdown*. Published in 2014 by Public Affairs

Richard S. Tedlow. *Denial: Why business leaders fail to look facts in the face – and what to do about it*. Published in 2011 by Portfolio Trade

Sean Wilentz. *The Rise of American Democracy, Jefferson to Lincoln*. Published 2005 by W.W. Norton and Company